# QUEEN

## THE DEFINITIVE
## BIOGRAPHY

# QUEEN

## THE DEFINITIVE
## BIOGRAPHY

### LAURA JACKSON

PIATKUS

## Visit the Piatkus website!

Piatkus publishes a wide range of bestselling fiction and non-fiction, including books on health, mind, body & spirit, sex, self-help, cookery, biography and the paranormal.

*If you want to:*

- read descriptions of our popular titles
- buy our books over the internet
- take advantage of our special offers
- enter our monthly competition
- learn more about your favourite Piatkus authors

**VISIT OUR WEBSITE AT: www.piatkus.co.uk**

First published in 1999 by
Judy Piatkus (Publishers) Ltd
5 Windmill Street
London W1T 2JA
email: info@piatkus.co.uk

Reprinted in paperback 2000

This paperback edition published in 2002

Reprinted 2006

ISBN 0-7499-2317-2

Text design by Paul Saunders

Data capture by Wyvern 21, Bristol
Printed and bound in Great Britain by
Mackays of Chatham Ltd, Chatham, Kent

*Picture credits:*
Pictures reproduced courtesy of:
Dave Dilloway
Bert Weedon
Rex Features (+44 20 7278 7294)
All Action (+44 20 7608 2988)
Pictorial Press (+44 20 7255 1468)

# CONTENTS

*This book is dedicated to David – my amazing and special husband*

# Acknowledgements

Grateful appreciation to everyone whom I interviewed about Queen. My thanks for all contributions to: Benny Andersson; Michael Appleton; Simon Bates; Mike Bersin; Tony Blackman; Tony Brainsby; Richard Branson; Pete Brown; Michael Buerk; Lady Chryssie Cobbold; Derek Deane; Bruce Dickinson; Dave Dilloway; Wayne Eagling; Spike Edney; Joe Elliott; David Essex; Kent Falb; Eric Faulkner; Fish; Dudley Fishburn; Trevor Francis; Gary Glitter; Scott Gorham; Mike Grose; Jo Gurnett; Bob Harris; Tom Hicks; Geoff Higgins; Tony Iommi; Mandla Langa; Gary Langhan; Jane L'Epine Smith; Hank Marvin; Malcolm McLaren; Barry Mitchell; Mike Moran; Chris O'Donnell; John Peel; Tony Pike; Nigel Planer; Andy Powell; Ken Reay; Noel Redding; Zandra Rhodes; Sir Tim Rice; Sir Cliff Richard; Professor Jim Ring; Paul Rodgers; Richie Sambora; Pino Sagliocco; Joe Satriani; Tim Staffell; Jackie Stewart; Peter Stringfellow; Ken Testi; Bjorn Ulvaeus; Barbara Valentin; Brian White; Terry Yeadon; Susannah York; Paul Young.

Also thanks for their help to: Sue Green; Gorel Hanser; Brian May; News International; Elgin Library staff. Special thanks to David for his invaluable help and support, and also thanks to my editor Rachel Winning and all at Piatkus Books.

'Queen ranks as one of the best bands of the century. Their principal strength was that all four members were great individual songwriters.'

**SIR TIM RICE, 1999**

# ONE

# COLLEGE CONNECTIONS

IN NOVEMBER 1995 Queen released their long-awaited album *Made in Heaven*. Utilising the very latest recording technology, Roger Taylor, John Deacon and Brian May had worked diligently at London's Metropolis Studios and May's home studio to add their live contributions to the best of a clutch of songs that a dying Freddie Mercury had, four years earlier, poignantly managed to leave behind as his final legacy to the band he had uniquely fronted for two decades.

Regarded as Queen's final work, *Made in Heaven* was the band's first new album release since *Innuendo* in 1991 and their lead singer's harrowing and untimely death, at the age of forty-five from AIDS, near the end of that same year. Details soon emerged of how, in his last working months, Mercury had courageously pushed his ravaged body to the limits of human endurance, sometimes having to numb his physical pain with liberal shots of vodka in order to be able to get up to the mike to sing. Brian May afterwards revealed, 'This is a man who can't really stand any more without incredible pain and is very weak. There's no flesh on his bones at all and yet you can hear the power, the will that he's still got.'

Anticipation had been steadily building among the supergroup's global army of staunch supporters, as well as in the music industry as a whole. And so, unsurprisingly, buoyed up by a very real and deeply felt wave of emotion, *Made in Heaven* rocketed straight in at the top of the UK album charts in its first week of release. It quickly went double platinum and would become undoubtedly Queen's most personal album ever.

Yet such success was quite natural for Queen. Their album sales by the end of 1995 would top 130 million worldwide and, by the end of the decade (measured by the number of weeks spent on the charts), Queen would rank in Britain second only to the Beatles in the UK's all-time most successful acts. From the psychedelic seventies to the chameleon eighties, Queen evolved from their earliest raw progressive roots, via glam rock, to become an adrenalin-driving stadium rock band *par excellence*. They had a threeway reputation as unbeatable live performers, superb studio craftsmen and – with the arrival in 1975 of the inimitable single 'Bohemian Rhapsody' – the true originators of the essential modern-day pop video.

Queen did not come from the generation of British bands like the Beatles and the Rolling Stones who began by endlessly travelling the countrywide gruelling 'buckets-of-blood' pub and club circuit. But neither were Queen an overnight success. They paid their dues, only in a smarter fashion; although the road to superstardom would never be smooth. The fact that each of the four band members had a distinctly different temperament made for a vigorous working relationship. Management difficulties and bouts of ill-health at crucial stages in their career also meant that theirs was a path strewn with its fair share of strife. Whereas Brian May admitted, 'We argue very badly sometimes', and John Deacon reasoned, 'We've been together so long, at times you do get on each other's nerves', the colourful Freddie Mercury inimitably declared that sometimes they had resembled 'Four cocks fighting'. But Roger Taylor, believing Queen to be a longer-lasting partnership than many marriages, best described what the band represented to them all when he said that at tough times in their personal lives they each knew that they could always come back to Queen. 'It was like coming home to mother,' he declared.

Over the years their relationship with the music press was largely a strained one. With the notable exception of reaction to *Made in Heaven*, critics were often scathing of Queen's work, and there were rumours that the group was on the verge of splitting up. But in a field notorious for band personnel upheavals, theirs ultimately remained a rock-solid arrangement with a line-up, once John Deacon joined in 1971, that stayed unchanged for twenty years; they were only forced into premature disbandment by the death of Freddie Mercury. The announcement that Queen was officially dissolving came days after the massive Easter Monday 1992 Freddie Mercury Tribute concert, staged before a 72,000-strong crowd packed into London's Wembley Stadium, and beamed by satellite around the world to more than 500 million viewers.

When the emotional back-slapping was over that day and the host of rock celebrity guest stars had dispersed, Taylor, Deacon and May experienced, in the immediate aftermath, a bewildering sense of having been ruthlessly beached. Roger Taylor had maintained, 'We've always been stronger together.' But those days were irrevocably gone. Brian May and Roger Taylor would go on to pursue solo careers but at first there was, understandably, a feeling of having been pitched into a forced and unwelcome early retirement. It was a period for reflection of all sorts, not least for nostalgically rewinding time back to when it had all begun.

Rock 'n' Roll may be the great revenge but none of the members of Queen had been down-at-heel kids from the back streets who, in gutsy rock music tradition, set out to kick over the traces of an unfortunate start in life. All four were educated at grammar or public schools, and all but Freddie Mercury would go on to attain academic degrees. It was at college that the pre-Queen band Smile had formed, teaming Taylor and May for the first time. But Queen's origins go back still further to a school band which, in the mid sixties, had the futuristic name of 1984, and which featured Brian May and Smile's third player, Tim Staffell.

Born on 19 July 1947 in the Gloucester House Nursing Home at Hampton in Middlesex, the only child of Ruth and Harold May (a senior draughtsman with the Ministry of Aviation), the lean and lanky Brian grew up in a comfortably middle-class semi-detached house in Feltham. Naturally inquisitive, he developed into an avid hoarder – perhaps an indication of a highly fastidious streak in his nature – and one of his favourite pastimes was collecting *Eagle* comics. He was good with his hands, enjoyed making model toys, and at the same time displayed an early flair for music.

By the age of five he had started taking piano lessons – he would eventually pass Grade IV – and a year later Harold taught him to play the ukulele, an instrument he was himself proficient on. Brian found a real aptitude for the ukulele but very swiftly set his sights on a guitar. His first was an acoustic steel-stringed Egmond that he and his father immediately set about customising; in particular, equipping it with crude but effective home-made pick-ups to electrify the sound once it was plugged into the back of the family radio.

May derived his musical inspiration from the prevalent influences of the day – Buddy Holly, Lonnie Donegan, et al. But his highly analytical approach meant that, instead of being content just to play along as he repeatedly listened to these records, he quickly progressed to systematically dissecting, and working out for himself, their underlying musical structure.

It was no surprise therefore that, whilst attending Hampton Grammar School, he should set about forming a band. Guitar-playing was not encouraged there, which meant that any practice had to be conducted during clandestine lunchtime jam sessions. One of May's classmates, Dave Dilloway, recalls, 'One day someone told me that there was a guy playing a guitar in the geography room. So, out of interest, I went to see. When I looked in, Brian was sitting on a stool surrounded by schoolkids playing and singing Guy Mitchell's hit "I Never Felt More Like Singing the Blues" and although it was just a simple three-chord song, I was very impressed.'

Dilloway and May started hanging out together, mainly visiting each other's house to dabble in recording their own musical efforts. Dilloway explains: 'We mainly played instrumental material from artistes like Les Paul, Chet Atkins and the Spotniks. Brian had his Spanish acoustic with its pick-up and I had a home-made six-string electric guitar as well as a home-made bass. At this point I used to tackle the lead guitar and Brian played rhythm. We'd record these two parts together on to a tape and then, while this pre-recorded track was played back, we would record on it again. This time Brian would be playing my home-made bass and I played drums – by which I mean anything percussive that we could find. Even Meccano strips doubled for cymbals.'

Brian May had tapped in to the shifting emphasis in music as the fifties fizzled out and moved towards a guitar-based sound – a vital development from which would spring a new generation of talent. His list of heroes was expanding all the time – the latest to catch his attention was the UK group the Shadows who, in July 1960, topped the singles chart with the instrumental number 'Apache'. May was intrigued by the skill and distinctive playing style of the band's lead guitarist Hank Marvin (a musician May would work with later in life). And Marvin has no trouble in understanding the attraction of the popular new trend for the budding guitarist.

'Putting it simply, it was a more accessible form of music,' explains Hank. 'The big band music of the forties and fifties wasn't the sort that you could recreate with your mates. But, with the advent of rock and roll, electric guitars came into their own. All you needed was a bass, drums, two guitars and a singer and you had a band. Because the guitar was portable you could also perform anywhere, any time. And not to be forgotten, of course, was the cool image! Just think of Elvis Presley. The guitar was very synonymous with rock and roll. There is no instrument like it.'

Come 1963, along with May's desire to be part of a band, was a yet stronger yen to own a proper electric guitar. Family funds did not stretch to the new, wildly expensive Gibsons and Stratocasters, so Brian and his father decided to build one themselves.

With meticulous planning and immense patience, over eighteen months at a cost of around £17, they constructed a guitar from an antique solid mahogany fireplace, a piece of oak, some blockboard and a few odds and ends, including two valve springs from a 1928 Panther motorcycle. Because of the deep reddish-brown of the mahogany, Brian christened it the 'Red Special' and it went on to play a huge part in giving May his own highly distinctive guitar sound, as well as becoming probably the world's most famous custom-built guitar.

May is quite open about the special bond he has with the instrument. 'It's quite an emotional thing, playing the guitar,' he maintains. 'You need to be in contact with your strings, because that's all you've got.' His then hero Hank Marvin concurs. 'It's like another person you're embracing – an extension of your body. Some guitarists abuse the instrument and act out a lot of violence. I don't know that it's erotic love. You'd have to be pretty warped to feel like that about a bit of wood. But there's certainly a relationship between you and your guitar.'

At this point May was spoiled for choice when it came to the bands he and his friends could see locally. The best known 'hall' in the area was at Eel Pie Island in the River Thames at Twickenham where a plethora of future famous names performed, including the then fast-rising Rolling Stones, as well as Cream and Fleetwood Mac. All this only intensified Brian's urge to get into music.

May's first band – 1984 – started out as a four-piece, initially with no name. He played lead guitar, Dave Dilloway handled bass, a schoolfriend called Malcolm provided the rhythm guitar until he was swiftly replaced by local boy John Garnham, and another classmate John Sanger briefly drifted in to play piano. Not knowing anyone who could drum, at first they made do without. The band was also bereft of the all-important singer, but not for long.

One night Brian attended a local dance and during the course of the evening he noticed another guy from school standing at the back of the building. He was unobtrusively playing harmonica and singing along. His name was Tim Staffell. The two got talking and discovered a shared interest in music; in Staffell's case because it provided a welcome distraction from the drudgery of school life. 'School was a total drag as far as I was concerned,' states Tim. 'That was in part down to the fact that I lost a lot of ground after I had been involved in a serious road accident which had kept me off school. Being part of a group, for me, was a way to escape.'

With Staffell on board, the band set about rehearsing seriously, mainly at Chase Bridge Primary School in Whitton, next to the Twickenham rugby ground, and the discipline imposed at these sessions sharpened everyone's playing. Ideas flowed fast and they forged strong friendships. After advertising in a local music shop window, they also acquired a drummer, Richard Thompson from Hounslow. It was at this point, as the group swelled to being a six-piece, that they gave themselves a name. 1984, after George Orwell's novel, was not the only suggestion but the best that they could come up with and so it was adopted. They liked the futuristic sound. What's more, they'd just landed their first fee-paying booking.

Years later Brian May would remember, '1984 was purely an amateur band formed at school. Although perhaps at the end we once got fifteen quid or something.' In fact, 1984's debut public performance at St Mary's church hall in Twickenham on 28 October 1964 produced the princely going-rate fee of £10, to be split between the six of them. Within a month, 1984 secured their second gig, this time at Richmond Girls' School, after which John Sanger left to study at Manchester University. The band was never going to be a long-term arrangement – the boys were at the wrong age and academic stage for that. But they were happy to cram their rudimentary equipment and as many of themselves as would fit into a tiny Heinkel bubble car whenever they could get bookings, which tended to come feast or famine fashion.

According to Tim Staffell, 'We had a sort of regular gig at the Thames Boat Club on the riverfront at Putney, in the same building, in fact, in which Michael Winner's remake of Raymond Chandler's *The Big Sleep* was shot. We played mainly on a Saturday night for only a few pounds and for considerably longer than was average for bands – often as long as three hours.' Reflecting on these early appearances, Staffell recalls that they tended to inject a fair amount of juvenile humour into their performances but that it seemed to go down well at the time.

Despite using cheap under-powered equipment and having little or no reliable transport, 1984 managed to survive, even when the band members inevitably dispersed to pursue higher education. Dave Dilloway went to read electronics at Southampton University, while Tim Staffell headed off to Ealing College of Art in London to study graphics. May, whilst enjoying his music, had also knuckled down at school, attaining ten O-levels as well as four A-levels in physics, pure maths, applied maths and additional maths. In February 1965 he had been awarded an open scholarship in physics at London's Imperial College of Science and Technology and that summer, aged eighteen, he arrived to study physics and infra-red astronomy; he intended to become an astrophysicist.

But music, though perhaps not a priority, remained important to him, and although he and Tim Staffell were now both in London, Dave Dilloway was not. Still, they were collectively determined to overcome this obstacle. Dilloway tells how, 'I was only an hour or so away and had a motorbike, so I'd make it home at the weekends. We would listen to material, decide what to learn and go away and practise. Then, if new ideas came to us while we were apart, we'd write.' It was an arrangement that lasted for just a few months, as, after failing his exams at the end of 1965, Dilloway left Southampton and took up an HND electronics course at Twickenham College of Technology. This brought the three mainstays of 1984 once again within easy reach of each other.

Rehearsing harder than ever, they pursued more regular gigs, as their experience (and their repertoire) grew. For years Brian had tinkered with writing songs but now he and Tim Staffell were seriously attempting to pen their own collaborative material. In addition, May would devote hours to figuring out different song variations, experimenting with his own arrangements. May remarked, when talking about this time, 'We never really played anything significant though in the way of original material. It was a strange mix of cover versions – all the things people wanted to hear then, like Stones and Yardbirds things.'

Beatles numbers also featured, with May taking part in the three-part harmony sections of songs like 'Help'. As 1984's singer, Tim Staffell is gracious about May's contributions. 'Sometimes Brian would sing lead on "Yesterday" and the audience loved it – they would scream and bring the house down with their applause.' Tim adds jokingly, 'It left me dead jealous, the rat!' Healthy competition also arose whenever they challenged each other to see who could hit the highest note; an accolade May lays firmly at his 'rival's' door. 'No competition,' he says. 'Tim always won.'

In fact, May showed little appetite for the limelight. A reed-like figure, over 6 foot tall, with a profusion of frizzy curls, not unlike the Afro style associated with the American blues guitar maestro Jimi Hendrix, he was content to stand left of centre playing lead electric guitar with such disciplined dexterity that audiences were often left stunned. Dilloway concurs: 'Really because of his skills we were able to play almost anything. His unique talent was obvious, even then. I have no idea how many other bands ever tried to steal him from us, but I imagine that he had quite a few offers.'

May might have begun to suspect that 1984 was going nowhere fast but for the moment the gigs continued. Most were stimulating, others were fun and the rest were downright dangerous. (When playing in some of the rougher places brawls and fist fights were known to spontaneously break out among the punters.) His spirits had been temporarily lifted in early 1967 when the band won the first heat in a prestigious annual national talent search competition held at the Top Rank Club in Croydon, only to be dashed when they lost out in the final.

But this disappointment was forgotten when, months later, on 13 May they played a memorable support gig at Imperial College – topping the bill was Jimi Hendrix who was then right on the edge of his big breakthrough. 1984 were booked to play first for dancing downstairs but made sure that their set ended in time for them to hurry up some back stairs to see Hendrix in the main hall. According to Brian May though, it was the American who first took a peek at the amateurs at work. He states, 'That night we played Jimi's "Purple Haze" and rumour has it that Jimi looked in, smiled and moved on!'

As the year moved on, 1984's last hurrah was about to take place at what was, for them, their most prestigious venue yet. Chance had brought the band to the attention of two pop promoters during a gig at the London School of Medicine, and this had resulted in them being offered a support slot at a star-studded marathon event to be held on 23 December 1967 at Olympia. Billed as *Christmas on Earth*, the night's line-up included Hendrix, Pink Floyd, the Herd, Traffic and Tyrannosaurus Rex. Even though 1984 were fifteenth on the bill this did not dampen their enthusiasm; indeed May and Staffell decided to include in the list of cover versions that they planned to perform, a number called 'Step On Me', which they had co-written.

It turned out to be a memorable occasion in more ways than one. They had been kitted out at the promoters' expense with new stage clothes bought in London's trendy Carnaby Street. (On the night they were told they could keep these outfits.) They felt suitably honoured at being part of such an illustrious bill, would be playing through the kind of expensive Marshall equipment they could usually only dream of, and to their largest crowd by far. But snags were quick to surface.

As is the nature of these marathon affairs, the performances over-ran and 1984 did not get to play their half-hour set until dawn on Christmas Eve. Dave Dilloway explains, 'By this time we were quite tired. And when the moment came we didn't get a sound check or anything fancy like that. We were just pushed straight on and expected to play.' But worse was to come as soon as they came off stage. Not only had their dressing room been burgled and their wallets stolen but when they emerged – blinking into the daylight – to start loading up their gear, they discovered that all their cars had been towed off to the Hammersmith pound.

Dilloway recalls, 'We had to walk, still in our stage gear and make-up, to the pound to scrape up whatever it cost then to retrieve our cars.' The long trudge, of course, was accompanied by some weird stares from passers-by; stares which were duplicated on arrival at their destination. Dave adds, 'My hair was piled up in a backcombed style and my eyes had been heavily made up to give me a mean, moody look. At 7 a.m. in the police pound, it didn't go down very well!'

The new year, 1968, was not very old when May decided to pack in 1984. His college studies had always taken up a lot of his time, and with finals approaching at the end of his three-year course this burden would only increase. But his decision was not solely due to academic pressure. Referring later to his first band and his departure from it, he said, 'We did a few things, but I was never happy about it. I left because I wanted to do something where we wrote our own material.'

To May's tutors at Imperial College, Brian was certainly a young man going places . . . but as a scientist. One of those tutors, Professor Jim Ring, recalls, 'Brian was an excellent student. At that time, at least in my mind, there was no suggestion of him becoming a rock star. To me, he was first and foremost a very bright physicist.' Very likely, but May *was* feeling the loss of a musical outlet. It felt strange not being involved in a band and Tim Staffell, with whom he remained in touch, felt the same way once he too had quit 1984.

It was only a matter of time, therefore, before May and Staffell would set about forming a new band. To this end, they advertised on the Imperial College student union noticeboard for a 'Mitch Mitchell/Ginger Baker-type drummer'. Brian explained the reasoning behind the style specification: 'By this time Cream and Hendrix were around and I wanted a drummer who could handle that sort of stuff.' Among the many students drawn to this advertisement was Les Brown. Not for himself, but for Roger Taylor, a dental student at the London Hospital Medical School with whom he shared a flat in Shepherd's Bush. Taylor played drums and, as Brown knew only too well, he was lusting to join a good band.

Born Roger Meddows Taylor on 26 July 1949 in the West Norfolk and King's Lynn Hospital in Norfolk, by the mid-fifties Roger had moved (with his younger sister Clare and their parents, Winifred and Michael Taylor, a Potato Marketing Board employee) to Truro in Cornwall. A lively boy with an infectious sense of fun, his first musical leanings emerged when he was not much more than eight years old.

He had had his eye on mastering the guitar but, like Brian May, Roger's first musical instrument turned out to be the ukulele, on which he taught himself to play the basic chords. After practising in the family garage, Taylor, along with some friends, formed a skiffle group they called the Bubblingover Boys. This was an odd quartet that involved two guitarists, himself on ukulele and a fourth member playing a tea-chest bass. It was a short-lived venture though. They played before an audience on less than a handful of occasions – their largest crowd being at a dance held at the local Bosvigo School which Roger attended. Taylor was later brutally frank about why the ensemble folded. He revealed that none of them could actually play. 'We just stood and twanged tuneless chords. It was dreadful!' he said.

By the age of eleven, whilst at Truro School (a public school which he attended as a day boy), he had joined the cathedral choir. The pressure of singing at three services every Sunday quickly put him off, although the voice training he received later proved invaluable, as he went on to play a vital role in the strongly harmonic style that would become the bedrock of so much of Queen's music. But in 1960 Taylor was more interested in mastering the cheap but cheerful acoustic guitar that he had managed to save up for.

Treading the time-honoured path of so many youngsters at this time, he spent hours glued to the radio, taping his favourite songs and teaching himself to sing and play along with the artistes. By now, he was already convinced that his future lay in music. And his mother clearly recognised her son's striking combination of ambition and self-confidence for she later reflected that he had always known that he would one day make a name for himself.

That may have been true, but Taylor also realised that it would not be as a guitarist. His interest in this instrument waned quite quickly, the more obvious it became that his sharpest talent was in percussion. His early equipment was a ragbag of mismatched items. He started out by acquiring a snare drum and a hi-hat cymbal, and augmented these when, for Christmas 1961, his parents gave him a reconditioned bass drum, plus a tom-tom. Delighted, Roger soon managed to buy another tom-tom and a brand new Zildjian crash cymbal. His long-term sights would soon be set on getting to London where it was all happening, but, for now, he had to bide his time.

Growing up in a part of the country that took life at a leisurely pace, he was one of those fortunate students who was bright enough not to find school work particularly taxing. He sailed along with, at times, the minimum of effort – only cramming almost on the eve of exams and still passing them with flying colours. Taylor himself declared, 'I was a lazy scholar. I hated studying.' Yet he was sufficiently sharp to realise that – leaving aside his musical ambitions – having a good education under his belt would be useful, just in case his pursuit of fame did not work out. Slender, with blond hair and developing good looks, he was also popular with the local girls; and his popularity was later enhanced by the 'prestige' of playing in a locally successful band.

In his early teens, again with friends, Taylor had formed his first semi-serious group – called a variety of names, including Beat Unlimited, Cousin Jacks and possibly, at one stage, the Falcons – but it disbanded after about a year. Then in 1965 he joined local outfit Johnny Quale and the Reactions, with whom he had his first taste of success – in mid-March at Truro City Hall the band, against stiff competition from fifteen other West Country groups, came fourth in the annual Rock and Rhythm Championships of Cornwall. Keen to capitalise on this achievement, they promptly set off on the regional circuit of municipal halls that took in Newquay, St Just, Falmouth and Penzance.

When lead singer Quale quit later that year he was replaced by Roger Brokenshaw, who used the stage name Sandy, and the band's name was immediately concertinaed to, the Reactions. They played soul and rock music. In the latter case, Taylor shared the vocals, eagerly overcoming the difficulties inherent in simultaneously singing and drumming.

The Reactions had a pretty fluid line-up, as members came and went. To back Roger Taylor's vocal and drum skills, other musicians would, over time, include guitarists Mike Dudley, Graham Hankins and Geoff Daniel; bassists Jim Craven and Richard Penrose; John Snell on tenor saxophone; and Mike Dudley who shifted from guitar to keyboards. This was the most popular band with which Taylor had yet been involved and they quickly built up a local and regional following as they gigged about the clubs, including one in Truro called PJ's.

Very much in his element, Roger started to show his particular musical leanings – Mike Dudley later recalled that Taylor was 'quite orientated towards pop'. The sixteen-year-old Taylor had a school-boy's short-back-and-sides haircut, but his dominant features were his large almond-shaped bright eyes and an attractive smile; and his increasing popularity with the girls impressed his mates.

The band's reputation swelled still more when, a year later in mid-March 1966, they returned to, and this time won first place at, the Rock and Rhythm Championships. Part of the prize for the band – which that same month shortened its name yet further to simply Reaction – was to open for Gerry and the Pacemakers when these Merseyside hitmakers came to play at the Flamingo Ballroom in Redruth.

The Blue Lagoon Club in Newquay was also one of Reaction's favourite haunts. Here Taylor enjoyed rubbing shoulders with several London bands who came down to perform at this venue. During 1966 his band also backed groups such as the Kinks, T Rex, Slade and the musician Ritchie Blackmore in his pre-Deep Purple days. Taylor lapped it up but, with his taste already running to Otis Redding, come 1967 he had been turned on to Jimi Hendrix. By the time he left Cornwall for London he had gone totally psychedelic.

Academically, Roger had a particular aptitude for the sciences and, having left Truro School that summer armed with seven O-levels, complemented by three A-levels in biology, chemistry and physics, he had been accepted for a degree course, starting in October, at the London Hospital Medical School to study dentistry. When he got to

London he rented a flat in Shepherd's Bush with a friend, Les Brown, who was studying at Imperial College.

Although he knuckled down to his studies, Taylor still liked to return occasionally to Truro during vacations when earning some money was the number one priority; a necessity that uncovered in him an enterprising streak, especially when he teamed up with a Cornish friend who owned a marquee company. In 1968 during the summer holidays Roger's friend arranged for a marquee to be erected on various beaches along the coastline for Reaction to stage pay-at-the-door gigs. Taylor rushed around in a mini van plastering up fly posters for the event, now dubbed the 'Summer Coast Sound Experience'. Imaginatively, they also set up and operated a crude psychedelic light show and, despite difficulties like sand getting into their equipment and having to run lengthy cables to the nearest electricity supply, their popularity grew. The crowds had risen to a couple of hundred before the local authorities twigged that they had no official sanction to be holding these events and shut them down.

Taylor's desire to be in a band had only been whetted by all this. Dentistry was a skilled profession, but seriously mundane when measured against a career as a glamorous pop star. So he leapt at the chance when Les Brown returned one night to their London flat with the news that two students, Brian May and Tim Staffell, were seeking a drummer to start a new band. He duly responded to the telephone number on the card.

On getting Taylor's call, May and Staffell immediately headed over to Shepherd's Bush. Years later, Roger would recall how auditions were normally depressing affairs with dozens of drum kits in a line, but this audition was decidedly informal. The visitors arrived at the flat to discover what Taylor could do. His drums had remained in Cornwall and so Roger had to rely on a set of bongos with which to impress the pair.

Because both Brian and Tim had brought along acoustic guitars they knocked out a few tunes together and found that they clearly jelled.

Says Tim Staffell, 'I wouldn't actually say we auditioned Roger as such. It wasn't like that. It just became obvious that he was dead right for us.' This certainty did not prevent Staffell and May from wanting to see how it would sound when everything was properly plugged in, so Brian organised the use of the Jazz Club room at Imperial College for a second try-out. It was an even bigger success.

May would later state, 'We thought he was the best drummer we had ever seen. I watched him tuning a snare – something I'd never seen done before – and I remember thinking how professional he looked.' Staffell recalls, 'Brian and I were tickled pink by Roger's style of drumming; it was flamboyant, confident, loud and disciplined. He was a showman-drummer. The chemistry too was spot on and it was immediately obvious that the three of us would effortlessly evolve into a unit as equal partners. We had the same musical tastes and fundamentally the same aspirations.'

Roger's crisp, assertive drumming would go on to articulate future Queen songs and play a key role in creating the band's distinctive sound. Personality-wise, there was also a tireless, buoyant energy about Taylor, to which the other two naturally responded. Says Tim, 'Roger always struck me as being comfortable with himself, with not much trace of the kind of personal angst that many people at the time exuded daily. He had a sharp sense of humour and was capable of easy self-parody. I also think he appreciated, more than myself or Brian, the role that entertainment should play in the construction of a successful band.'

Between the three of them they knew very little about the music business, but collectively they felt empowered and were determined that they stood a good chance of succeeding. Inflated by such optimism, it was hardly surprising that they decided to call their new band Smile.

# T W O

# PERSIAN
# POPINJAY

I N  T H E  S U M M E R  of 1968 the British music scene was
changing again. Flower power and the previous year's so-called
'Summer of Love' had fragmented, to be replaced by a harder-
edged, much heavier sound. Whilst steeped in their own rehearsals,
all three members of Smile were keeping tabs on these emerging
influences. They paid particular heed to those bands playing what
was then dubbed progressive rock – bands that included Deep
Purple, Free, Pink Floyd and, arguably the best exponent of all in this
field, Wishbone Ash. Progressive rock had an intricacy and depth to
it that strongly appealed to true musicians.

Andy Powell, lead guitarist with Wishbone Ash, explains, 'After
the watershed album *Sgt Pepper* the floodgates had opened and, post-
1967, everything was up for grabs. There was no corporate rock.
There was a great innocence and ignorance in us. We would
draw on fifties jazz, folk music, Celtic music, R & B – anything that
got the juices flowing. We had no embarrassment about delving
down alleys in search of inspiration and it got very eclectic, never
mainstream.'

This new music certainly had some impact on Tim Staffell and Brian May. May has clear memories of attending the first-ever large-scale free open-air rock gig in London's Hyde Park on 29 June in which another progressive rock band, Jethro Tull, took part. He remembers being mesmerised by the experience. He says, 'I was absolutely knocked out by Mick Abraham's guitar playing – wonderful tone!' And, as Staffell revealed, Smile were also much impressed with the work of Yes. He says of their own band's inspirations, 'We wanted to be heavy rock and to make music which was more arranged than you might expect from a trio. We also wanted to be intelligent. This was our criteria.'

Both 1984 and Reaction had relied heavily on performing cover versions of existing songs and so, almost entirely, did Smile at first. But, as they worked at building up a stage act, the urge to write their own material grew stronger. Brian May was approaching his finals but eagerly made time to collaborate with Staffell. Tim states, 'From my point of view this was the beginning of taking myself seriously with music. I wrote my first songs with Smile, some with Brian, some on my own.'

With the bit between their teeth, they also set about other aspects of turning Smile into a real band. According to Staffell, a fellow dental student of Roger Taylor's, called Peter Abbey, acted as their manager for a time but strictly on a casual basis.

Peter Abbey and Smile simply drifted apart. More importantly, a close schoolmate of Staffell's and May's, Pete Edmunds, after trading in his MG sports car for a little green Ford Thames van, provided Smile with their transport and became the group's first official roadie. Unusually, the band decided to adopt a logo and Staffell put his design skills to good use, coming up with a widely grinning mouth, scarlet lips and gleaming white teeth. But they really began to feel that things were falling into place when they landed their first gig.

Two days after Brian May had graduated with a BSc (Hons) degree, on 26 October 1968, Smile made their public debut at Imperial College, playing support to Pink Floyd, whose latest album *Saucerful of Secrets* had reached number nine in the UK charts. While it cannot be said that Smile made any dazzling impact on this first stage appearance, their performance did not actually bomb, despite them being nervous and unknown. They played mostly cover versions of familiar hit songs but in a somewhat wild fashion. Tim Staffell maintains, 'This was probably as a result of my bass playing. I wasn't as disciplined as I should have been and initially we were quite a loose trio.'

Still it was invigorating, and, with their debut out of the way, they actively pursued as much regular work as their studies would permit. It was now that Roger Taylor's West Country music connections came into their own and, through these, Smile's engagements diary steadily filled up. 'We travelled around the country a fair bit, as far as Cornwall, and we did well in some places,' remembered Brian May.

In fact, such was their confidence that they began to bill themselves around the Cornish clubs rather grandly as 'The Tremendous London Band Smile'. Their hype, however, was justified by the size of the crowds that they began to pull and the considerable following they attracted. Tim Staffell possessed a distinctive style of singing that was just right for the era, May's guitar skills were reaching dazzling proportions, and this combination was amply anchored by the speed, strength and power of Roger Taylor's drumming. They were also now benefiting from the skills of the latest addition to their crew, in the shape of John Harris. Initially recruited to help their roadie Pete Edmunds, Harris' valuable electronics expertise was put to good use in getting the best possible sound out of their equipment.

These were heady times as Tim Staffell recalls. 'We would set off in the van and head west with anticipation. It's sometimes necessary to remind people that these were semi-pro days so the social nature of the activity was at least as important as the music. Many people, myself included, regarded membership of a band as a particularly effective social device, especially where attracting females was concerned. Weekends in Devon consisted of alcohol, music and sex, usually in that order. We were all footloose bachelors. Roger was a strongly heterosexual adolescent and he was the one who was most popular with the ladies. There's a simple explanation for this – he was the best-looking member of Smile and had a more accessible personality. I used to think it had something to do with him being a provincial lad.' He adds, 'We would regularly play at PJ's club in Truro, a smoky upstairs UV sweat box, at beach parties, Fowey Carnival, St Ives and the Flamingo Ballroom in Redruth. It was all exciting stuff.'

Spending so much time playing gigs all over the countryside was fun but all three far preferred the college circuit. Times had moved on from the beginning of the decade when bands had been prepared to tough it out in roughhouse pubs, usually for minuscule fees. Come 1968, a more civilised circuit had evolved – these college gigs paid more, as the student unions were only too willing to throw out the lure of decent money to attract quality bands. More specifically, concentrating on the London college circuit suited Smile best – in particular, the Kensington area (for years already *the* in-place to hang out).

For Brian it also meant more opportunity to see a girl he had met, Christine Mullen – known as Chrissy – who was a student at the Maria Assumpta Teacher Training College in Kensington. Chrissy's friend Josephine Morris was dating Roger Taylor and it was through Jo that she and Brian had been introduced to each other at one of Smile's Imperial College gigs. Chrissy would become May's future wife and at this point they were growing closer all the time.

Says Tim Staffell, 'Jo and Roger were also a serious item and lived together for a time. I was never quite sure why they split up.' Taylor, whose sights had long been set on living and working in London, now had an added impetus. By the end of 1968, he had dropped out of his course at the London Medical School. Having achieved the first part of his dental degree in August, he had opted to take a year off to concentrate all his energies on becoming a rock star. To him, that meant being at the centre of things. His veering away from academia did not appear to his friend Tim Staffell as a reckless move. 'Roger was never feckless,' states Tim. 'He was much too self-assured to make questionable decisions of that nature.'

Everyone in Smile knew that they needed to gain more visibility.

They were popular at Imperial College where they regularly played, as well as in Cornwall, but they were still big fish in a little pond and that could be frustrating. May later reflected, 'We never felt we were getting anywhere because if you don't have a record out people tend to forget who you are very quickly – even if they liked you on the night.'

But if making a record right then seemed like pie-in-the-sky, landing another major gig, they felt, ought not to have been within their reach. In the period since they had opened for Pink Floyd, although they had supported Family and Tyrannosaurus Rex nothing else seemed to be happening – at least until after the new year in early 1969, when matters took a significant turn.

Firstly, they secured an important support gig to the popular band Yes at the Richmond Athletic Club. Then they managed to hitch themselves onto the bill of a concert to be held in support of the National Council for the Unmarried Mother and Her Child. This was an Imperial College-organised event due to take place at one of London's most prestigious venues, the Royal Albert Hall, on 27 February. The night's line-up included Joe Cocker, the Bonzo Dog Doo Dah Band and Free. To their amazement, instead of being tacked onto the end of the bill, Smile had been placed above the gutsy band Free, featuring the gravelly vocalist Paul Rodgers. Compère for the night was to be the influential DJ John Peel, famous for using his late-night radio shows to provide a platform for underground bands that were denied airplay elsewhere.

Brian May described Smile's determination to be part of this event as getting themselves invited 'By hook or by crook'. But their delight at landing the gig was tempered by a problem. The Albert Hall was not a venue to turn up to with below-par equipment but money was short, as always. Tim Staffell, though, came to the rescue by pulling off an unexpected coup.

He recalls, 'Down the Ealing Road a new music shop had opened up. We'd go in occasionally, strum on the guitars and generally pester the owner with questions about gear that we couldn't possibly afford to buy. Just before the Albert Hall gig I said to the guy, semi-jokingly, wouldn't it be a good idea if he lent us some of his stuff and that way it could get prominent display at a prestigious venue? To my amazement he agreed! So we were able to use a quality Simms-Watt PA system on the night.'

The big moment when Smile were announced on the Albert Hall's huge stage suddenly took a dive when, seconds after Tim ran on before the audience, he quickly discovered that he was several feet short of guitar lead. He had had no idea anything was wrong until he went for the first chord, only to realise that his jack plug had been sprung from its socket, leaving him with an embarrassing deafening silence. To add injury to embarrassment, he had for some reason opted to play this gig shoeless and ended up getting his feet stabbed by splinters from the stage.

There was ample compensation, though, in their subsequent delight at their performance. It was a short set which, though not recorded, had been filmed from the wings by Douglas Pudifoot, a friend of Roger Taylor's, as a black and white 8mm home movie. It was silent and visually of rather grainy quality but it still stands as the first film footage of the two original Queen members in performance together. Smile were happy too to have attracted their very first review when a journalist wrote – according to May it appeared in the *Times* – that they were 'the loudest group in the western world'. Unfortunately the guy omitted to give them a name check.

Tim Staffell later defended Smile's tendency to belt out the decibels. 'We had disciplined loudness. We didn't just rely on power to punch a song through. We made songs dynamic in the proper sense of the word.' That night was such a big event in their lives that they often enjoyed reliving it in detail with their mates down the pub in Kensington, among whom, recently introduced into their circle by Tim Staffell, was a 22-year-old art student called Freddie Bulsara.

Farookh Bulsara had been born on 5 September 1946 in the Government Hospital on the exotic island of Zanzibar in the Indian Ocean, the first child of Jer and Bomi Bulsara, an accountant in the British civil service. Zanzibar, with its beautiful sultans' palaces, had a culture made up of a cosmopolitan mix of Arabic, Indian and African influences. Farookh's earliest years were thus an idyllic mixture of days spent on miles of golden beaches bathed in glorious sunshine, followed by nights getting lost in the never-ending fairytales told to him vividly by his father. His fertile imagination fed avidly upon these fantasies of Arabian princes and heroic deeds done in far-flung lands.

From the age of five he attended the local missionary school, run by British nuns, until Bomi's work required the Bulsara family – newly swelled by the arrival of a baby sister called Kashmira – to relocate to Bombay in India. It was a major upheaval for the family but a welcome one. His parents being devout Parsees – today's descendants of ancient Zoroastrianism – were happy that there was a large concentration of Parsees in and around Bombay. As was customary, at the age of eight the boy's formal induction into the ancient religion took place by way of an old and solemn Navjote ceremony conducted by a Magi priest.

By now Farookh, known to his friends as Freddie, attended the St Peter's School, a type of British public school in Panchgani, Maharashtra. In Bombay the Bulsaras lived in a substantial house, staffed with servants, but because there was some unpredictability about Bomi's job, Freddie's parents chose to send him to boarding school. In addition to traditional academic subjects, St Peter's placed a strong emphasis on sports. Freddie took to boxing, was a fiend at table tennis and, with a skinny frame built for speed, usually left his schoolfriends in the dust at athletics. But, for all that, sport was not Freddie's natural element.

The place that drew him like a lode star was Bombay harbour. He loved watching the chaos that surrounded merchant ships preparing to put out to sea and adored wandering the rabbit warren of narrow streets crammed with stalls, where snake charmers piped eerily hypnotic tunes and fakirs stretched out on gruesome-looking beds of nails. This exoticism, coupled with the city's fabulously opulent architecture, gave Freddie a powerful sense of colour, flamboyance and grandeur. Years later, as Mercury, the rock star millionaire, he would boast that, just like the Queen of England, he never deigned to carry money, instead leaving one of his personal assistants, on his many staggering shopping sprees, to make the necessary financial arrangements. But back then, the waif-like black-haired boy, with noticeably buck teeth and only a few rupees in his hand, was as streetwise as the next when it came to haggling with the wily Arab street traders.

His other developing interest was music. Bombay's hugely cosmopolitan society offered a smorgasbord of genres to choose from, almost all of which influenced the young Freddie Bulsara. From his parents he absorbed a passion for opera, which contrasted with the ever-present local influence of traditional mystical rhythms. Then, by the late fifties, came traces of an exciting new craze called rock 'n' roll.

For years Freddie had been taking piano lessons and by the time he attained Grade IV he was mad about music. In particular, he was enthusiastic about singing. He was a member of the school choir and participated in several amateur productions but this did not quite serve his burgeoning need to express himself. To this end, he formed his own band, called the Hectics, only to be stifled when the school forbade them from performing publicly. The band was, however, permitted to play at school fêtes and parties and on such occasions Bulsara's combination of choirboy training and his exaggerated sense of theatrics proved to be the first pointers to the flamboyant career that lay ahead.

For all his over-the-top outward tendencies, though, the young Bulsara already hid a lot about his inner self. Boarding-school life was partly responsible for this, as Freddie later confessed. He said, 'One thing boarding schools teach you is how to fend for yourself, and I did that from a very early age. It taught me to be independent and not to have to rely on anybody else.' He was very often lonely and over time cocooned himself within a protective outer shell. He kept himself very much to himself, even when it came to the most significant developments in his life.

In his last two years at St Peter's he experienced at first hand two phenomena that are synonymous with English public school life – bullying and homosexuality. With his experience in the boxing ring, Freddie easily handled any bully that came his way. Homosexuality he viewed differently. As the celebrity rock star, he revealed precious little about his personal background and, despite projecting himself as an outrageously camp performer, never to his dying day did he publicly admit to being gay. But he later privately admitted to his first homosexual encounter having taken place at school.

By the turn of the decade the Bulsaras were on the move again, this time spurred by the fierce political unrest in India to emigrate to Britain. On their arrival, they settled in Feltham, Middlesex, initially living with relatives until they found themselves a small semi-detached house near Feltham Park. These years as a teenager were difficult for Freddie. Everything about him – his looks, his manner-isms, his accent – made him stand out and he became the butt of much bigoted humour. His answer to the relentless ridicule was to turn the tables on his tormentors by playing the Persian popinjay to the hilt, thereby parodying himself. It became an effective front, but it took its toll. All through his life Freddie was very emotional by nature and, at this point, he went through a period of real unhappi-ness and insecurity.

These negative feelings resulted in his school grades slipping and he passed only three GCE O-levels, in English, history and art. This did not unduly bother him; he already knew that he was not destined to go to university. Music and art were what mattered to him and at Isleworth Polytechnic one A-level in art was all he needed to get into art college. In September 1966, armed with the requisite qualifica-tion, he enrolled on a graphic art and design course at Ealing College of Technology in West London. 'Art schools,' declared Freddie, 'teach you to be more fashion-conscious; to be always one step ahead.'

For a larger-than-life personality who would make such an indel-ible imprint on the music world, the twenty-year-old Freddie was fairly timid and reserved. He would later be dubbed 'unremarkable' by former tutors – apart from an annoying tendency to giggle – and denigrated by an ex fellow student as having been 'a talentless drip'. But summer 1967 saw him make some progress. Inspired, like so many others, by the colour and style of Jimi Hendrix, Freddie Bulsara, his hair worn fashionably long, now strutted about in fashionable velvet jackets, tight trousers and chunky-heeled platform shoes, weighed down by tons of shiny junk jewellery.

Musically obsessed with Hendrix, it was not uncommon – emboldened by lunchtime drinking sessions in the pub – for Freddie to mount his desk at Ealing College and cavort about giving a wild impersonation of his idol. He would howl the lyrics while pretending that his twelve-inch wooden ruler, dug suggestively into his groin, was a guitar. These displays naturally drew attention from other students, among then a guy called Niger Foster and also Tim Staffell.

Staffell recalls, 'My first impressions of Freddie were that he was quite straight culturally. That's to say, conservative – I didn't ever think about his sexuality. You wouldn't have described him as being at all "in your face". He had a fair degree of humility. Freddie didn't particularly shine. Having said that, though, he was intuitively a performer and his persona was, even then, rapidly developing. As far as being a star was concerned, I personally think he was already in the ascendant. People responded to him.'

Tim, Freddie and Nigel Foster were among the Ealing students who liked to make music when they could but Staffell insists, 'Tales of us regularly singing three-part harmonies in the echoing gents lav at college are greatly exaggerated, since it might have happened a time or two, but not enough to imply consistency.' Desperate to join a band, Freddie quickly learned that Tim played in a group; Tim was soon to discover that Freddie wanted an introduction to Smile.

When, in early 1969, Staffell introduced his young college friend to his band mates – the extrovert Roger Taylor and the studious Brian May – the singer at first remained reserved. But not for long. Giving vent to his natural verve and vitality, he quickly made it clear that he was eager to turn Smile's trio into a foursome and was soon showing up at their rehearsals. Brian May said he and Roger Taylor initially thought 'he was just a theatrical rock musician'.

While Freddie's infectious enthusiasm certainly helped to invigorate Smile's already strong determination to launch themselves properly, his relentless intensity made him the bane of their lives at practice sessions. He loved their music but had opinions on everything, especially their presentation, and he didn't only express these in private. When attending their gigs, he would cup his mouth with his hands and yell from the audience, 'If I was your singer, I would show you how it was done!'

Tim Staffell recalls, 'We didn't take Freddie that seriously as a singer at first, as it took a few years for him to develop the quality and assurance he showed when he was into his stride.' Bulsara, therefore, had to be content with considering himself as Smile's unofficial fourth member.

On 19 April 1969, after a gig at the Revolution Club in London, Smile were approached by an impressed Lou Reizner. Reizner, who went on to produce Rod Stewart, was involved with Mercury Records and he asked Smile if they would like to sign with the American label which was planning to branch into the British market. Their immediate reply was a resounding yes! Tim Staffell recalls, 'Lou was a very laid-back individual charged with spotting London talent for Mercury America, whose offices were at the Marble Arch end of Knightsbridge. He was the first serious music biz guy I'd ever had anything to do with. I was too young to evaluate people the way I do now, but I don't recall us being made any worthless promises.'

With a contract under their belt, Smile soon found themselves in Trident Studios, Soho, ready to record a single with producer John Anthony. The A-side was 'Earth', written by Tim Staffell, and backed by 'Step On Me'. According to Tim, 'Earth' had been selected because it was the strongest of his original compositions. 'There were no musical influences on that song at all,' he explained. 'I wrote it because I was a bit of a sci-fi buff.' Anticipation among the trio was, understandably, high when its release date was set for August.

Now that Smile had cut a single as a trio, Freddie Bulsara probably thought his hopes of joining them professionally were pretty ground-less but come the hot summer that year things took an unexpected turn with the arrival in their midst of a Liverpool group called Ibex. This three-piece band comprised lead guitarist Mike Bersin, bassist John 'Tupp' Taylor and drummer Mick 'Miffer' Smith. With them was their manager Ken Testi, a man who would give valuable assistance to Queen.

Ken Testi's girlfriend was Helen McConnell whose sister, Pat, was a fellow student of Brian May's girlfriend, Chrissy Mullen. The McConnells shared a flat in Earls Court which gave Testi and Ibex a place to crash. Says Ken, 'Not long after we arrived it was Pat's birthday and we decided to take her out for a drink. She insisted that we went to "The Kensington". She'd been going regularly to see a band called Smile and, since she fancied Roger Taylor like mad, she dragged us down there and promptly introduced us to them. They had a friend with them who wasn't in the band, although he clearly felt that he ought to be, and this was Freddie.'

Ibex were impressed with Roger, Brian, Tim and Freddie. Says Testi, 'They were all good-lookin' dudes, which made us feel like northern hicks. And Smile had actually just cut their first single! Freddie, for his part, looked the business in a short fur jacket and his long perfectly groomed hair. I suppose to him we must have seemed very unsophisticated, but you'd never have guessed it. On first acquaintance, Freddie would be very reserved with you.'

At closing time they all trooped back to Pat's flat. Ibex guitarist Mike Bersin recalls, 'For me, it was Brian May who made an instant impression. He's a gentle giant, soft-spoken and kind. He's also the sort of guy who, if you ask him how he's doing, will give you a detailed reply!' He goes on, 'I was dead keen to hear him play though, and the big surprise was to discover that he used a sixpence coin instead of the usual plectrum.' This idiosyncrasy would fascinate guitarists for years, although to May there is a simple explanation for it. 'I could never find a stiff enough plectrum,' he stated. 'The coin is totally rigid, so you feel the movement from the strings in your fingers.'

Ken Testi adds, 'Suddenly Brian, Roger and Tim began to play us their songs, and Fred kept throwing in harmonies as if he couldn't help himself. I noticed that Freddie was clearly extremely comfortable in that company, and when they began to talk about what they were looking for, I knew immediately that I was in the presence of something extraordinary. It was a seminal Queen and they were special. Everyone listening to and watching them in the flat that night knew it.

Both bands often socialised after that and Freddie was quick to spot an opening. Says Mike Bersin, 'One evening we were all outside the pub discussing music as usual and Freddie pipes up, "What you guys need is a singer." We looked at each other, wondering how he could possibly have known that because he hadn't heard Ibex play. Anyway, he promptly offered to front us. We asked him along to a couple of our rehearsals in a basement flat but, far from doing much singing, he really just talked his way in.' Nobody was fooled however. Ken Testi declares, 'It was obvious to us all that Freddie's heart was still set on joining Smile but that wasn't going to happen, so that's why he turned his sights on Ibex.'

But Bulsara did manage to maintain a link with Smile – apart from that of friendship – by suggesting to the medical school drop-out Roger Taylor that, to make some much-needed money, they rent a stall together at Kensington Market. For £10 a week they set up business in an avenue that traders depressingly dubbed 'Death Row'. Ken Testi remembers, 'I had to laugh when I saw it referred to, years later, in Queen's publicity blurb, as "a gentleman's outfitters". Their stall was about the size of a telephone box.'

Even so, they stocked it with paintings and drawings, courtesy of Freddie and Tim's art college friends. This did not bring in sufficient cash so they switched to selling clothes which began to turn a small profit. Tim Staffell briefly had a stall of his own there and he recalls, 'At Freddie and Roger's stall there was a strong emphasis on personal adornment. There was also an air of narcissistic coquettishness that I loathed. I suppose it was influential in creating the outrageousness that Freddie cultivated but I, personally, found it a little too deliberate.'

This period established a particular bond between Mercury and Taylor, as Tim Staffell confirms, 'Roger and Freddie developed a close friendship during the time of the Kensington market stall. As I say, to a stronger extent than did myself or Brian, Roger appreciated the role entertainment ought to play in the construction of a successful band and I imagine that the key to his relationship with Freddie lay in that simple fact.'

Tim adds that, up to a point, Taylor also shared Mercury's lust for stardom. He says, 'Yes, Roger was driven towards fame, but I don't think he was as passionate about it as Freddie. I used to think that Freddie *would* become famous, because whatever forces there were in the world that would try to deny him, they were just not strong enough. If fame had been denied Roger, I think he would have eventuallly shrugged it off and got on with something else.'

With ambitions intact and everything to aim for, it was a free-spirited time. Brian May was dating Chrissy Mullen, while Roger Taylor (who always had an eye for the ladies) kept his options open. And, as for Freddie, he was seeing a girl who would play a major role in his life. Her name was Mary Austin. She worked in the trendy boutique Biba and their feelings for each other had steadily grown, Freddie presumably having chosen to suppress his homosexual tendencies. The presence of a girlfriend in Freddie's life had certainly cast doubt among his friends as to his true sexual orientation. As Mike Bersin recalls, 'I guess it threw us off the scent, because in his behaviour in every other respect he was wonderfully camp. In many ways, Freddie almost wasn't real.'

There was also an air of unreality about the arrival of Smile's debut single 'Earth'/'Step On Me'. It was released in August, but only in America and so was nowhere to be seen in Britain. Staffell later took a pragmatic view of it, saying that, as Mercury Records was an American label, there had been no contract to release it in Britain – and he understood that, as far as the record company was concerned, Smile had not achieved anything which warranted the company putting any high-profile push behind the single. Staffell later declared, 'I don't recall the single being much of a big deal. None of us were over the moon because there was no money in it.'

This did not prevent Smile from accepting Mercury Records' invitation to return to the studio to cut a few more tracks for an album with producer Fritz Freyer. Tim says, 'We cut several tracks, including "April Lady" on which Brian is vocalist, "Polar Bear", "Blag" as well as "Earth" and "Step On Me". We were happy with the results but the record company chose not to release the album. It ended up being released years later in Japan.' This time disappointment set in.

Smile's solution was to throw themselves into playing as many gigs as they could – in addition to their regular work at Imperial College. To help secure these gigs, they had enlisted the help of the Rondo booking agency in Kensington Church Court, which already represented the band Genesis, and for whom Staffell had carried out some graphic design work. As for Freddie, Ibex manager Ken Testi was proving to be a man with many contacts, particularly in the north of England, and so a great deal of time was spent travelling between London and the north. Ken also arranged gigs for Smile whenever he could, and they often tagged along to return Freddie's moral support of them.

These were hectic and happy, if tiring, times and a good learning curve. Some memories of these days remain vivid. Mike Bersin particularly recalls getting ready for an Ibex gig at the Bolton Octagon Theatre one Saturday lunchtime. He says, 'Freddie stood out a mile. All he had to his name was one pair of boots, one pair of trousers – admittedly white satin – one granny vest, one belt and one furry jacket. At the theatre he stood for ages twitching at himself in the mirror. Eventually I'd had enough and shouted, "For God's sake Freddie, stop messin' with your hair!" To which he gaily tossed back, "But I'm a star, dear boy." He meant it. But he was also right. Freddie never copied another performer. Freddie was always Freddie, very angular, very showbizzy about everything he did and was entirely his own creation. As a front man, he was, to say the least, a culture shock but there wasn't a lot of difference between then and when he became famous with Queen. All the poses were already there.'

For another friend whom they met around this time, Geoff Higgins (who for a while also played bass for Ibex), the abiding memory was of a night when Ibex were due to play a gig at the Sink in Hardman Street, a basement club below the Rumbling Tum in Liverpool. As Smile were appearing elsewhere in the city they had also travelled up in the cramped van. Along with a few of their friends, both bands had decided (since the Sink was not licensed to sell alcohol) to visit a nearby pub. On the way they encountered a gang of skinheads. To these bovver boys, with their heavy boots and aggressive-looking shaven heads, hippies made excellent Saturday night punching material.

Says Geoff Higgins, 'It was outside the Liverpool Art College. Round the corner came this gang of skinheads and I thought "Aw Naw!" There was about nine of us and a whole lot more of them. We were dressed in velvet trousers and frilly shirts and you didn't dress like that in Liverpool then. We looked a right bunch of poofs. I was just wondering how long we'd survive when suddenly Roger bluffs it out. He told them that he was a black belt in judo and that by law he had to warn them first and if they chose to ignore him and got hurt, it was their own fault. I had my head well in my hands by now. I thought, Bastard Taylor! He'll get us all killed! I hissed in his ear, "You don't try it on with scouse skins, you idiot!" But it worked. I've no idea if they believed Roger or admired his hard neck, but they left us alone and walked on. We were all shivering with fear.'

Having returned safely to the Sink, Higgins recalls something special about the Ibex gig that night, 'The Sink was so small and clammy, it made the Cavern look like the Empire State building. Freddie was poncing about as usual and being really uncool, as we thought. We told him he was embarrassing us, but he didn't take any notice.' Geoff taped the performance and states that, during a Beatles number, Freddie was singing way off tune. However, he adds, 'Smile had been playing at a ball at the Liverpool Art College that night and later crashed in on our gig. Practically as soon as they arrived they came on stage, which meant that that gig, on 9 September 1969, was the first time that Freddie, Roger and Brian all performed together on stage.'

Once back in London, by late 1969 life became ever more meshed for Ibex and Smile when they all moved into a flat in Ferry Road, Barnes, with a shifting assortment of friends, some of whom would turn up on spec, lugging a mattress and looking for somewhere to kip. Mike Bersin reveals, 'It was only supposed to house three people so when the landlady came for the rent, we'd all hide in the bedroom.' It was a tatty place furnished with odd pieces of old furniture, often torn, with discoloured stuffing hanging out. Still, it was here that Brian, Freddie and Roger began regularly rehearsing harmonies together. May too would sit writing songs at the kitchen table.

Says Geoff Higgins, 'At Kensington Market we'd get marijuana mixed with jasmine tea and at home take it in turns to separate the grass from the tea. Freddie in those days wouldn't go near dope. One day, whoever took it home hadn't had time to separate it so Freddie made himself what he thought was a pot of jasmine tea and ended up smashed out of his head! When we got home he was wheeling around the room, flapping his arms to Frank Zappa music.' Having come down from his high and learned what had happened, Freddie soon afterwards pulled a mischievous trick on policemen who one night arrived to tell them to turn their music down. Freddie placated the officers with tea and cakes which had been marijuana-laced. The cops left feeling remarkably good about how they had handled the situation, not realising what lay ahead once the effects set in.

News from the music front, however, was more sobering. At the end of the year, Smile played a showcase gig organised by Mercury Records, at the famous Marquee Club in London's Wardour Street. They were there as support to the group Kippington Lodge but the half-hour slot bombed. They failed to connect with the crowd and left the stage feeling thoroughly dejected, it seemed to sum up their whole relationship with Mercury Records, from whom they would soon part company.

Freddie, too, was in the doldrums. Ibex had long since changed their name to Wreckage, at Bulsara's suggestion, but the cosmetic alteration made scant difference and in early 1970 he would quit. Before doing so, he briefly tangled with a band calling themselves Sour Milk Sea. Taking Roger Taylor with him for moral support, Freddie had successfully auditioned in Leatherhead to join Paul Milne, Rob Tyrell, Jeremy Gallop and Chris Chesney but the band had folded within weeks.

By February Smile was entering its death throes. Tim Staffell reflects, 'Just as most student bands did at that time, Smile suffered from a lack of finance. We'd played some notable gigs though, and supported some big names and we'd had a good time doing it. I'd say that at our worst we may have been a little shaky, but at our best I'm sure we were quite worth the admission fee.'

When Staffell called it a day he moved on to join Colin Peterson's band. Peterson had been a drummer with the Bee Gees and Tim felt, on balance, that his quieter style might suit him better right then. He admits, 'I wasn't a hundred per cent convinced that I was doing the right thing. But I had grown tired of rock played loud so I left Smile for my own reasons.' He goes on, 'Was Smile a genuine precursor to Queen? I honestly don't know. But in one sense I was moving out of the way and the birth and evolution of Queen was a natural and inevitable outcome.'

Soon after Staffell left, Mercury Records dropped Smile. It was, as Tim said, natural then that Brian May, Roger Taylor and Freddie Bulsara, already friends, should come together to form a new band, and Brian singles Freddie out as having been the main force that pulled them together. Individually, though, they'd all felt a burning ambition to make it in the glitzy world of rock music. And so it was, in April 1970, that these three first set themselves up as Queen.

# THREE

# THE QUEEN SCENE

'WE HAD INCREDIBLE belief in ourselves – quite blind and ridiculous belief in some ways,' Brian May later admitted. And indeed, a powerful self-confidence would prove to be Queen's hallmark from their earliest beginnings. But right then, having decided to form a new band together, their most pressing need was to find a bass player. Roger Taylor immediately came up with a solution by inviting Mike Grose, a one-time member of his former band, Reaction, to join them. A fine bassist, Grose was also the co-owner of PJ's in Moresk Road in Truro.

Says Mike, 'When Smile used to play at PJ's, sometimes there was friction between Roger Taylor and Tim Staffell – just squabbles, nothing serious. But anyway, one night they turned up for their gig and Tim had left so I stepped in and played. A few weeks later, Roger rang and asked me to join the band. They didn't have a name for it, but it was Freddie, Brian and Roger. The timing was spot on as far as I was concerned because the club was under a demolition order, so I said yes to Roger's offer and went to London to stay with them in their Earls Court flat.' Besides his musical expertise, Grose also took with him a good-quality amplifier and a Volkswagen van.

With a full line-up now, the band's next problem was finding somewhere to rehearse. Brian May had rejected a prestigious post at Professor Sir Bernard Lovell's research laboratory at Jodrell Bank in Cheshire, in favour of doing his PhD as part of a research team studying zodiacal light headed by Imperial College's Professor Jim Ring. And so May's links with IC remained strong (he also gave tutorials there two half-days a week) and, through his tutor Ken Reay, Brian managed to obtain the use of a room at the college in which to practise. Ken confirms, 'I used to book lecture theatres in the physics block for them to use free. Brian would just bring along a steady flow of forms for me to sign.'

In the rest of their free time the four sat about in the flat or its garden tossing around ideas. In the cramped conditions, however, patience sometimes snapped and, according to Mike Grose, Roger and Freddie were frequently at odds. Says Mike, 'Roger has a quick temper and a feisty personality but Freddie was also a live wire and those two used to squabble a lot. If it got too much for Brian he baled out and went home to his parents for a spell. But it was extremely claustrophobic.' The hothouse atmosphere, however, more often produced positive results.

Mike maintains, 'Brian and Freddie spent a lot of time writing songs. Almost all the songs which later turned up on Queen's debut album got their first airing in that Earls Court flat. And all three of them could sing. Roger has a tremendously high voice. A lot of Roger later went into 'Bohemian Rhapsody' – the operatic high-pitched 'Galileos' were his. And the band's direction was endlessly debated. Roger and Brian always had plenty to say about this – even I had some input. But Freddie, I must say, was the ideas man. He had great plans. The name Queen, for instance, came up for the very first time one day as they were jamming outside in the garden.'

Freddie later explained the thinking behind the choice, saying that it was very grand, very pompous, which entirely matched his grandiose outlook. The fact that it also gave off gay overtones, although recognised by the others, was in the end disregarded as being generally unimportant.

What *was* important was playing their first live gig together. That event took place at Truro City Hall on 27 June 1970; a charity performance organised by the British Red Cross in Cornwall. It was actually a long-standing Smile booking and because no one had bothered to inform them that a different band was coming, Queen made their public debut billed as Smile. Only a couple of hundred people turned up, which for bassist Mike Grose was a decided blessing.

He admits, 'We'd practised hard, but doing the real thing is very different. We also had complicated arrangements worked into our repertoire and when you write original music, those constantly change as you perfect it. The danger though is that one person will remember a song being one way, while someone else remembers it another way. We tried hard to hide the gaffes but, to be brutally frank, we were rough. I certainly didn't expect us to be asked back – put it that way.'

Still, as unknowns they collected a tidy £50 fee for their pains and also had the satisfaction of knowing that they had at least made an impact on their audience with their visual presentation. Rock was then an ultra-macho world, with the dressed-down look of bands like Black Sabbath being the order of the day. But Queen, contrarily, opted for stylish black silky costumes, set off by gaudy junk jewellery. It was a statement that they were different, and Freddie Bulsara was about to make another.

It was just after this first gig that he decided to change his name. It was no disrespect to his family, but it was also true that, in interviews, Freddie would always carefully skirt around his Asian background. From the time he had left home for a life in London he had deliberately distanced himself from his parents' religion and culture. Now, pursuing a career in rock music, he preferred to adopt a glamorous name to match the stylish lifestyle he was convinced would be his. Dipping into Roman mythology he came up with Mercury, the messenger of the gods; and from July 1970 Queen's lead singer became known as Freddie Mercury.

Furthering their band's image was one thing but – although they'd only formed four months earlier – Queen were frustrated at their lack of progress. Brian May later revealed their obsession with figuring out the fastest route to get to the point of making a record. Not put off by Smile's experience, he explained that they had decided that the key was playing and doing down well in places like London's Marquee, getting known, becoming popular.

Coming to the notice of the right people, however, was not easy – Mercury's habit of haunting Kensington High Street every Saturday in the hope that he might accidentally-on-purpose bump into some influential figure in the record industry was not paying off. Nor did they reap any record contracts from a showcase gig they staged in Lecture Theatre A at Imperial College on 18 July. A few of the music business executives that they had invited turned up but none had been sufficiently impressed. It was just a case of plugging on.

Exactly one week later, they played their first gig billed as Queen. The date at PJ's, though, turned out to be the last for Mike Grose, who was fed up with living in squalor on very little money. 'I didn't want to be a part of it any more,' he says. 'I knew I'd regret leaving. I knew in my bones that they were going to make it. But I thought, to hell with this.'

The amicable parting left a gap to fill and, into the breach, Roger Taylor drafted a friend of a friend, again from Cornwall, called Barry Mitchell. Barry recalls, 'I was given a telephone number to ring Roger Taylor and he invited me to meet Queen. I went to their flat, just around the corner from Imperial College, and from there we walked to a lecture theatre for my audition.' After running through a couple of bluesy numbers and settling down to a chat that carried on afterwards back at the flat, Mitchell was in.

The first gig with their latest line-up was on 23 August 1970 at Imperial College. High hopes were once more pinned on this performance – again music executives were among the invited guests – and a special effort was made to further improve their overall look and presentation; they even laid on food and soft drinks free of charge for the audience. In the hope that this was the night that Queen would crack it, Freddie wore what he called his 'Mercury suit'. Based upon his own design and made by a dressmaker friend, this was a black one-piece costume so skin-tight that it left little to the imagination. Designed to expose his hairy chest and with a quilted wing effect at the wrists, he had also had a replica made in white.

This kind of flamboyance was not what Barry Mitchell had been used to. Barry recalls, 'Earlier on that night I had walked into the flat and stopped dead to see Freddie not only dressed in this slinky outfit, but with huge curlers in his hair! I thought, "Wait a minute – what's goin' on 'ere then?" I wasn't getting into any of this lark for a start!' Mitchell could only stare, as Mercury set about deftly styling his long hair with a set of heated curling tongs.

When, for a second time, nothing came of this showcase performance Queen returned to playing as many gigs as they could land. In this they were fortunate to still have the help of their friend Ken Testi. He was now living and working up north in St Helens but he kept in touch with Queen by calling Taylor or Mercury at the public call box at the end of the row where the two had their market stall. Says Ken, 'I'd phone to let them know when and where I'd fixed them up with a gig. Sometimes it took forever to get an answer. Then whoever picked up the receiver had to run like hell to get Freddie or Roger to come quick before my money ran out.'

Testi booked enough gigs for Queen in the north of England to make it worthwhile travelling regularly to Liverpool; although these constant nights on the road exposed them to some hair-raising moments. Ken reveals, 'I nearly killed Queen once. I'd been driving virtually non-stop for forty-eight hours and it wasn't all motorway in those days. One misty night on an elevated stretch of the M1, with fields falling away either side, it was like driving across clouds. Anyway I was so tired I dozed off just for a second. Next, there was a piercing scream from Pat McConnell and I snapped awake to find that I was halfway across the hard shoulder. I'm not being dramatic but Pat's scream saved us all from certain death that night.'

At the start of 1971 Barry Mitchell called it quits with Queen. To some extent, he had never felt that he really fitted in. Even though

Brian May later admitted that himself, Taylor and Mercury had undoubtedly formed themselves into an 'efficient little machine' which was resistant to outsiders, Mitchell lays the blame for his departure squarely at his own door. 'It wasn't them,' he stresses. 'It was me. Maybe it was because they were all so well educated that I felt out of it, which is my own fault, but to a certain degree I always felt like an outsider.'

Mitchell had found all three of them friendly, although he had recognised a particular deep quality in Freddie that had made it less easy to relate much to the singer. But there were other, more practical reasons, as he explains, 'Really I had had it with never having enough money in my pocket. At that point I didn't feel either that they were going anywhere, and not just because Freddie often sung off key. Plus Queen were more or less performing all of their own compositions by now, which weren't to my personal taste. Queen's first two albums contained what I felt was a lot of pretentious stuff, although they found their hard-rock base eventually.'

Barry's last two gigs with Queen were in early January 1971: one on the 8th, marking Queen's debut at the Marquee; followed the next night by one at Ewell Technical College in Surrey. There they were one of two bands supporting the Kevin Ayres and the Whole World Band, the other support group being Genesis. 'Peter Gabriel fronted Genesis in those days,' recalls Barry. 'And, in the classroom that we were using as a dressing room, Gabriel was trying hard to talk Roger into quitting Queen and joining Genesis. Roger though wouldn't hear of it.'

Reduced once again to a threesome, Taylor, Mercury and May pondered over their inability so far to hold on to their bassists. Although both Mike Grose and Barry Mitchell individually pinpointed lack of earnings as partial reasons for leaving Queen, Brian May's viewpoint on why they went through bass players was that 'Either the personality or the musical ability didn't fit.'

One guy, called Doug, temporarily filled in but it quickly became clear that the excitable bassist's stage style was not going to be compatible with Queen and he was not invited back after their gig on 20 February at Kingston Polytechnic. This had been in support of Yes and Wishbone Ash, who shared top billing, and Wishbone's lead guitarist, Andy Powell, can confirm that Queen's music at this stage was still anchored in progressive rock. He states, 'What they were playing then was, I would say, similar to us, although you could detect an edge to them that was a shade more mainstream. I think you could tell they wouldn't stay playing progressive rock and, of course, it wasn't long before they became a glam band.'

Tony Blackman, an ex-Kingston Polytechnic student, was struck not only by how Queen looked that night, but also by their expertise. He says, 'Really nobody knew Queen at this time and yet, quite amazingly I thought, they didn't come over as in any way inferior to either Yes or Wishbone Ash. And the other thing was that they stood out. They were all dressed in very tight-fitting thin black costumes. There's no doubt that they were deliberately projecting – especially the singer – a very effeminate image. That wasn't the thing in those days, yet here was these guys going out of their way to flaunt it.'

Brian, Roger and Freddie were unquestionably growing in confidence about their abilities. They were beginning to carve out a style and becoming stronger musically all the time, but frustration ran high at not finding a fourth member that was right. To seek out potential candidates, they attended as many other bands' gigs as possible. It was one night, during a dance at the Maria Assumpta Teacher Training College, that Taylor and May met a bass player called John Deacon who had specifically asked to be introduced to them.

John Richard Deacon had been born on 19 August 1951 in the St Francis Private Hospital, London Road, Leicester, to Lillian and Arthur Deacon, an insurance company worker. By 1960 he had moved house with his parents and four-year-old sister Julie to Oadby, on the outskirts of the city, where he was enrolled at the town's Langmoor Junior school. An intelligent boy, his main hobbies from a young age were music and especially electronics. His father shared the latter interest which meant that John and he spent many happy hours together operating Arthur's ham radio and adapting an old reel-to-reel tape recorder so that John could tape music off the Sunday night weekly rundown of the hit parade charts on BBC Radio 1.

His first guitar, given to him when he was seven, had been a toy plastic one. But, with the dynamic explosion of music in Britain in the sixties stimulating legions of boys to form bands, the young Deacon (a big Beatles fan) had saved up his pocket money to buy himself a proper acoustic guitar. He taught himself to play on this, and by autumn 1965 he had formed his first band with some friends.

It was called the Opposition and comprised guitarist/vocalist Richard Young, who later shifted to keyboards, bassist Clive Castledine and drummer Nigel Bullen, with John initially taking on the role of rhythm guitarist. They practised in various friends' garages, experimenting with all the latest musical styles, including Tamla Motown and soul, and made their public debut in October at the Gartree High School in Leicester – where John was a pupil. Two months later, on 4 December 1965, the band, along with an extra vocalist, Richard Frew, played their first decent gig in support of a local band called Rapids Rave at Enderby's Coop Hall for the princely fee of £2.

It was when Clive Castledine left the band the following spring that John Deacon crossed over on to playing bass, acquiring his first EKO guitar. His band mates were quick to notice that Deacon had a, then, unconventional style of playing bass. Instead of using the traditional plectrum, he plucked the strings with his fingers and in an upward action.

Just as the line-up would alter from time to time, so too did the band's name – mutating around April 1966 to New Opposition. Although not a particularly ambitious band, that October they entered and won their heat at the Midland Beat Championships, getting into the semi-finals held at the end of the following January, which they also won. The finals, however, due to be staged in March 1967 at Leicester's De Montfort Hall, were unfortunately abandoned. By now they called themselves simply Opposition. Then a year later, in March 1968, it changed again to Art. By 1968 psychedelia had belatedly penetrated the provinces and, as Art, they experimented with a crude but exciting light-show using projectors and medicine bottles containing water and globules of oil.

At seventeen, though active on the local band circuit, John still devoted plenty of time to his studies at Beauchamp Grammar School in Leicester. His friends remember Deacon at this time as being shy and reserved, yet at the same time quietly competent and capable – a classic dark horse. He was also a very bright student, with a very logical mind, and by the time he left school in June 1969 he had attained eight O-levels and three A-levels in maths, further maths and physics – all A passes. These good grades secured him a place at Chelsea College of Technology, part of the University of London, where he would begin a degree course in electronics in October of that year.

By 1969, musically John had been turned on to Deep Purple and, maturing from the round-faced, clean-cut schoolboy, he had finally begun to grow his hair longish. Art had made a three-track acetate at a local recording studio but, as Deacon left school, their days were numbered. He played his final gig with the band on 29 August 1969 before heading off to London to take up his college placement.

During his first year Deacon concentrated almost exclusively on his studies and, whilst retaining his love of music, he had temporarily shelved any idea of being in a band. But he found that he missed that part of his life and began attending a variety of gigs. One of these had been at the College of Estate Management, Kensington, one October night in 1970 when the band playing had been called Queen. They struck no particular chord with him, other than the fact that on the poorly lit stage the four members clad in black appeared more like spectral figures.

Deacon shared a flat in Queensgate with a fellow student and musician, Peter Stoddart, and along with a couple of other friends often enjoyed playing jam sessions. This casual quartet did play once in public – a support slot at Chelsea College on 21 November 1970 – and for this they called themselves Deacon. But it was only a one-off and after that John was on the lookout to join a new band. Early in 1971 he learned on the grapevine that Queen had an opening. As

John Deacon later revealed, 'I heard from a friend that they were looking for a bass guitarist and so I got myself introduced to them.'

That night at the Maria Assumpta Teacher Training College disco John, through Peter Stoddart's friend Christine Farnell, first met Roger Taylor and Brian May. Wasting no time, they asked John to an audition for Queen, which they set up in a matter of days. Imperial College was the venue and Deacon arrived at the lecture theatre to find Brian with the AC30 amps he favoured set up and his Red Special guitar, Roger at his drum kit, and the third member, Freddie Mercury, armed with an amp and a quality microphone. Along with his bass guitar John Deacon carried in his own small amplifier (that would later become known in Queen circles as the Deacy Amp).

As seemed to be the norm, the audition was more like an informal lengthy blues jam session but some serious weighing up was going on, despite the apparently relaxed atmosphere. Deacon's obvious musical skills deeply impressed the other three, as did his electronics wizardry. Roger Taylor later declared, 'We thought he was great and a great bass player too,' whilst Brian May confirmed that they each knew instantly that Deacon was the right one. They were also much taken with his placid, unflappable nature. As May remembered, 'He was so quiet. He hardly spoke to us at all.'

After the audition ended, Freddie, Brian and Roger got down to serious discussion but there was never any question of them rejecting John Deacon. He was the final piece of the jigsaw. Over the next twenty years it would become clear that there were no passengers in Queen – each individual was extremely talented in his own right. And when it came to the blend of personalities, there too they had the perfect mix.

Freddie Mercury once said, 'Not two of us are the same.' And he was right. From early on in their career the blond-haired Roger Taylor – always considered the looker in the band – projected a corresponding free-spirited high energy. He liked the classic extravagant bachelor rock-star life of beautiful women, fine wine and fast cars. The steady, studious, fine-featured Brian May, by contrast, exuded a quiet strength and sensitivity. By his own admission, he preferred familiarity to change and, considered by some as the worrier in the band, his was clearly an intense nature.

Then there was Freddie Mercury whose invigorating flamboyance and infectious sense of fun effortlessly magnetised audiences. His dark-eyed, dark-haired, arrogant exoticism on stage could have made him a huge sex symbol in the straight sense, but, by sending out mixed messages about his ambiguous sexuality, he created a mysteriously alluring aura that held a spicy hint of danger. John Deacon, on the other hand, was a total enigma. A very self-contained, controlled man, he would become the business brain in Queen, studying the stock market and scrutinising the contracts. He was also capable of bringing the sometimes warring factions back together after a creative clash of wills. As he rarely gave interviews, he revealed very little about himself. His still, deep waters completed the unique balance of the band.

In late February 1971, knowing that the search was over and their line-up was finally complete, the four embarked on several months of intensive rehearsal – often three or four nights a week. To capture and keep the audience's attention, Freddie firmly believed that Queen had to develop a well-crafted stage act and they concentrated their efforts accordingly.

Vocally, Roger could be husky, where Brian was melodic, so they worked on blending their voices to provide a complementary harmonised back-up to Freddie's distinctive clear tones. Although John joined in, he never considered himself a singer. Their attitude at the outset was to get on, sock it to 'em, and get off; it was an energised display intended to create a lasting impression. As yet, Queen had everything to prove, but they certainly felt up to the challenge.

# FOUR

# TRIALS AND
# TRIBULATIONS

A S THE NEW Queen line-up set about polishing up their
act, they were frequently missing one member. Brian May's
astronomy work often required him to study zodiacal light
at an observatory he had helped set up on the slopes near the
dormant volcano Mount Teide in Tenerife. Fellow research student
Tom Hicks vividly remembers that when their day's work ended
May frequently produced a small acoustic guitar. 'He would thrash
out all these wild chords on it,' says Hicks. 'It was weird hearing
hard rock on a Spanish guitar. Brian wasn't around a lot with Queen
when they first started up because he was out in Tenerife so much.
Yet I would swear that what he was playing ended up on their first
album.'

The complete Queen's first appearance was at a Surrey college on
2 July 1971. Then, nine days later, they played a gig at Imperial
College. To the IC crowd, John's was the only unfamiliar face.
Deacon had wondered what reaction he would get but it was a good
night. And it became a potentially interesting one when it transpired
that record producer John Anthony – with whom Smile had worked

in 1969 – was in the audience. On his way out at the end though Anthony only casually said that he'd be in touch. So, wisely, no one was holding their breath.

What preoccupied all four right then was making ends meet. Tim Staffell had cited perennial shortage of money as a factor in Smile having foundered and Queen were determined to avoid this pitfall. John Deacon was a full-time student and Roger Taylor now returned to college by registering for a biology degree course at North London Polytechnic. He would be studying plant and animal biology, and he was eligible for a handy grant. Since graduating from Ealing Art College with a diploma in graphic art and design, Freddie Mercury augmented his sparse takings at the market stall by carrying out freelance work for the Austin Knight commercial agency whenever he could get a commission. And Brian May, having stopped giving his tutorials at Imperial College, later – in 1971 – took up a full-time teaching post at Stockwell Manor School in north Brixton. Music, however, remained their main motivation. And when Taylor managed to organise an eleven-date tour of Cornwall, they hit the proverbial two birds with one stone by clawing in cash and gaining valuable experience.

After kicking off on 17 July at the Garden in Penzance, Queen played such diverse venues as the Young Farmers' Club in Wadebridge and the NCO's Mess at RAF Culdrose. The servicemen there were not the only people to find Queen's long-haired looks and unconventional stage image hugely provocative. Mercury's ambiguous body language, in particular, often led to tensions, sometimes necessitating a swift undignified exit for fear of having their heads kicked in; once a bunch of locals in an ugly mood even gave chase after the band had driven off. Rows with landlords over the loud volume at which Queen insisted on performing also punctuated the tour. All in all, it proved an eventful trip.

Two months later, on 6 October, after they returned to London, Queen staged what they once again hoped would be a showcase gig for an invited audience at Imperial College. This time it included representatives from several agencies responsible for booking bands into major London venues. But, yet again, nothing tangible came from it. It was disappointing but they remained optimistic. As Roger Taylor later reflected, 'For the first two years progress was nil. We had great ideas though and somehow I think we all felt we'd get through.'

In the meantime though, the first step towards Queen's breakthrough had come courtesy of Terry Yeadon who, in autumn 1971, was part of a small team setting up a new recording studio in Wembley called De Lane Lea. Says Terry, 'A couple of years before, I'd caught one of Smile's gigs at Imperial College and thought that they were pretty good. I was working as a maintenance engineer at Pye Recording Studios at Marble Arch at the time and when I got talking to Roger and Brian they asked me if there was any way they could get some recording done. It was all informal but, along with a disc-cutting engineer, Geoff Calvar, I recorded two tracks of Smile – "Step On Me" and "Polar Bear" – and Geoff did acetates.'

He goes on, 'By 1971 I had moved to De Lane Lea and, with Geoff Calvar, I was putting this new complex together. We needed the noise of a rock band playing at full blast in order to test for possible problems with isolation between the studios and coincidentally Brian May chose that moment to track me down again. He and Roger had teamed up with a new bass player and a new singer and were now called Queen. They wanted to hear what they sounded like in a good recording studio. We needed that sound – so it was heaven-sent as far as I was concerned – and we came to an arrangement.'

That arrangement put Queen into the biggest of the three studios. 'De Lane Lea hired a load of Marshall amps to give us the power we needed and Queen played as we tested,' says Yeadon. 'It meant too, of course, that they had a few demos cut during this time. We did these on four-track in studio three, which is the smallest and was always going to be the rock and roll studio.'

Queen had been put to work with producer/engineer Louie Austin and were entirely in their element. Their enthusiasm even helped them to overlook the customary teething troubles associated with working in brand new studios. It had not escaped their notice either that they were perfectly placed to meet the very people whom they'd been dying to get the chance to cultivate an acquaintance with for so long. Their delight increased when, despite many technical hitches, they were eventually able to listen to the first professional demo of four of their own compositions: 'Liar', 'Keep Yourself Alive', 'The Night Comes Down' and 'Jesus'.

For Terry Yeadon these sessions with Queen were memorable. 'They were a little rough at the edges, which was only to be expected, yet Queen was very much there and had already been there before Freddie joined them, with Brian's guitar playing and Roger's drumming being to a large degree responsible for the sound. But Freddie, unquestionably, put the cream on it.'

He goes on, 'They were four completely different types. Brian was very laid back when I first met him as part of Smile, whereas Roger was the exuberant one. What stuck out most for me about Roger was trying to slow him down. Like any young guy in a band in a studio for the first time he was trying to do too much. It's a well known fact that what a musician *doesn't* play is as important as what he *does* play but on "Step On Me" Roger was really frantic and wanted to drum the whole way through – right to the bitter end, having to smash the cymbal as if this was him getting the last word on record, if you like. It was hard keeping him back, calming him down.

'There was a difference when I later met Queen. They were all more subdued than Smile had been. John Deacon, I'm afraid to say was just the bass player but I don't mean any disrespect by that. You must remember that although the Beatles had been very much four individuals, a lot of bands tended to be known as the lead singer and the band, and Queen at this point were a little bit like that. It was later that it became obvious that they were four talented individuals who happened to play in the same band. As for Freddie? He was just larger than life, and with such a personality that he kind of instantly bowled you over. Even in the almost sterile environment of a studio Freddie was very much a showman. It was almost as if he literally couldn't sing a song, if he didn't also do all the actions to go with it. They weren't so young either, compared to other bands that is, and that was bound to factor into it, but Queen were *so* sure that it was going to happen for them. And really although a lot of bands came through De Lane Lea, I have to say that there was always that certain something about Queen.'

Someone else who had this degree of faith was Ken Testi, now living back in London. Ken had been a loyal friend to the whole band for some time already, and he stayed at Roger Taylor's flat in Wimbledon whilst looking for a place of his own. Personally, he says his fondest memories are of Freddie, whilst Brian and John were more reserved. 'Roger,' says Ken, 'tends to appear callous, but he's not. He swapped from dentistry to biology because he couldn't stand all the blood.' Professionally, Ken's belief in Queen had never wavered and he was still trying to bring the band to the attention of the people who mattered.

Says Ken, 'I knew two bookers who worked for separate agencies and I used to pester them to death to book Queen. One was Lindsay Brown and the other was Paul Conroy who I shared a flat with for a time. Principally they worked for their agency but when the occasional support slot became available they did indulge me a few times, which meant a lot to Queen.'

He goes on, 'One day I took a Queen demo tape to let Paul and Lindsay listen to it. Afterwards they went off to a bedroom for ten minutes to discuss it privately. When they returned I said, "What do you think then? Great huh?" For the life of me I couldn't imagine anyone thinking anything else but Paul's reply was, "The last thing the music world needs right now, is another Led Zeppelin." He added, as he handed me back the tape, "I don't think they're going anywhere. Sorry." ' Paul Conroy later became managing director of Virgin Records. When given an opportunity to comment on this early opinion of Queen, he declined to take it.

Ken believed they were wrong. 'It wasn't going to deter me from taking the demo round the record companies,' he said, and, in addition to the band's work at De Lane Lea, Testi encouraged Queen to tape other material. 'I was very frustrated that they seemed to be going nowhere fast right then. One of Roger's friends had a reel-to-reel facility and, as he was going away for a while, he told Roger that they could use his flat to record themselves.' It was this tape that Ken Testi took around the various record companies. Ken remembers that much of Queen's first album release was on that tape, although clearly later re-recorded. When Testi went knocking on doors, usually one or other of the band members went with him.

For what already seemed a long time, Queen's only impetus was their collective self-belief that they were good enough to make it. Now, with the experience being garnered at De Lane Lea, their vision burned even brighter until virtually the only thing that mattered to them was breaking into the rock world. Roger Taylor gave up the market stall at this point, leaving Freddie to team up temporarily with Alan Mair, who ran a boot stall nearby. Brian May was fast fading from the academic scene, preferring what was going on with Queen. Together, the four of them endlessly debated the way forward.

Both Taylor and Deacon would go on to attain their respective BSc (Hons) degrees but in their hearts these qualifications were really for a 'plan B life' that they hoped would not be theirs. To justify turning their backs on their academic careers, however, they really had to put their all into succeeding. As May put it, 'We all had quite a bit to lose really.' This was a sentiment firmly endorsed by Mercury, who echoed, 'If we were going to abandon all the qualifi-cations we had got in other fields to take the plunge into rock, we weren't prepared to settle for second best.' It was a laudable attitude with which to start out, but they still needed to get off the starting blocks and that meant making that first vital contact.

As 1971 drew to a close, Queen were still being given the run of De Lane Lea studios, and a variety of producers and engineers regularly came to look over the recording facilities. Nothing came of this until one December day when two men walked in: John Anthony, the producer who, months earlier, had casually said he would ring

Queen; and Roy Thomas Baker, a staff engineer with the then influential Trident Studios. The two visitors liked what they heard, and,
after talking with the band, agreed to take a demo tape to play to
their boss, Norman Sheffield. With his brother, Barry, Norman
Sheffield co-owned Trident but Queen's excitement at this development was shortlived when Sheffield would say no more than that he
found it interesting. Brian May recalls Queen's deflation: 'Once
again we heard only a deafening silence.'

Nevertheless Queen and Ken Testi continued to trail round the
A&R departments of several record companies – those that were
even prepared to see them, that was. 'It was a thankless task,' admits
Ken. 'I've a list of the names of those people who told me that
Queen were no good.'

But that negativity changed early in the new year when Tony
Stratton-Smith, head of Charisma Records, liked Queen and quickly
offered to sign them. Not many bands would have had the guts to
turn down the first deal to come their way, not knowing whether it
might be the last; but Queen did. They had two reasons. Firstly,
there was not a great deal of money on offer – and they desperately
needed to update their equipment. And secondly, Charisma was not
one of the giant labels and Queen believed it essential to have the
weight of big muscle in the recording industry behind them.
According to Ken Testi, there was also another factor: 'Stratton-
Smith had a big involvement with the band Genesis and Queen
suspected that they might always be relegated to second fiddle.' That
incredible, almost blind belief in themselves, that Brian May later
owned up to, was certainly in evidence right then.

This decision meant, of course, that they were back on the circuit
hoping to be noticed, and on 10 March 1972 Queen played a one-
hour support gig at King's College Hospital Medical School in
Denmark Hill, South London. Arranged by Ken Testi with the Red
Bus Company in Wardour Street, Paul Conroy had also had a hand
in securing this gig. Testi states, 'I've never forgotten that. Although
Paul had said he had no confidence in Queen, he and Lindsay still
put work their way when they could. Paul helped me get Queen this

King's College gig – the one that ended up showing Queen off properly to record company executives.'

Queen's fee for the night was £25, for which they performed eleven numbers: 'Son & Daughter', 'Great King Rat', 'Jesus', 'Night Comes Down', 'Liar', 'Keep Yourself Alive', 'See What a Fool I've Been', 'Stone Cold Crazy', 'Hangman', 'Jailhouse Rock' and 'Bamalama'. The first six songs on Queen's playlist that night would end up on their debut album more than a year later. Quite a few record representatives watched from the audience and that night there seemed to be a more tangible buzz about. Although Trident had not snapped them up, Queen were aware that the Sheffield brothers were still interested in them. It looked hopeful therefore when, after this, they said they wanted to see one of Queen's live performances. Queen had just one booking in their diary for two weeks' time at London's Forest Hill Hospital and Roy Thomas Baker persuaded Barry to attend.

Acutely conscious of what hinged on this performance, Queen were understandably nervous but the gods smiled on them and everything went smoothly; moreover they brought the house down and altogether it was enough to impress Barry Sheffield. That night he offered Queen a contract with Trident Audio Productions. Two months later, nothing had been signed.

Remembering their experience with Mercury Records, Brian May and Roger Taylor felt that they ought to seek a bigger say in matters; Freddie Mercury and John Deacon saw the wisdom of this too. After discussion among themselves Queen therefore came to Trident's negotiating table with specific stipulations about the terms of any agreement. They wanted three separate contracts, individually covering recording, publishing rights and management. Trident had probably never experienced such a reaction from an unknown group before, and it is perhaps indicative of their strong desire to sign Queen that they eventually agreed to draw up documents to encompass this new deal structure. Even so, a seven-month delay stretched between Trident's offer to sign Queen and the contracts being finalised.

In the meantime Trident kitted Queen out with brand new equipment. The company was a major player in the recording industry with a sound financial base; to advance their new band's career they also brought in a full-time manager to handle Queen's daily affairs. His name was Jack Nelson and the American's priority task was to secure Queen a recording contract with a major record label.

When Nelson began knocking on doors he had with him a 24-track Queen demo, and photographs of the band, together with mini biographical details of each member and specimen lyrics. Encouragingly, the giant company EMI were quick to respond favourably. They were on the brink of setting up a new heavy rock label and Queen appealed to them. But then a snag emerged. Jack Nelson had instructions from Trident to sell Queen as part of a package deal, along with artistes Mark Ashton and Eugene Wallace. At this stage EMI only wanted Queen. A stalemate set in, which resulted in EMI reluctantly backing off.

It must have been hard to recover from a blow like EMI slipping through their fingers but Queen launched themselves into working on their debut album. Trident Studios accommodated stars like the Rolling Stones, Elton John and David Bowie. Queen, no one had heard of and so they were allocated what was termed down-time, which basically meant that they were permitted the use of the studio facilities only when no other artiste required them. At times it was demoralising to be so far down the pecking order as to have to wait till all hours of the day to be able to snatch some recording time, but such was their lot at this point.

There were occasional moments of light relief such as the day when, killing time, they were approached by producer Robin Cable who was busy re-recording the 1969 Beach Boys' Top Ten hit, 'I Can Hear Music'. Cable first roped in Mercury; he was quickly followed by May and Taylor – and the result was interesting. Cable's aim was to emulate the legendary Phil Spector's famous 'wall of sound'. Roger's power drumming and heavy tambourine presence took him halfway there; whilst Mercury rose to the occasion and, by pitching his distinctive vocals higher than normal, formed the crystal-clear centrepiece; Brian May's normally distinctive guitar work was largely lost because of the song's style. But the result stood up well. The producer promised that, if and when he ever did anything with the recording, he would let them know.

By late summer, Queen had still not been signed to Trident. After sustained pressure from all four band members Trident had agreed, however, to pay each of them a weekly wage of £20. It was not a vast sum, to be sure, especially living in London, but they had to settle for it.

On 1 November 1972 Queen finally signed with Trident Audio Productions. The deal was that they would record for Trident – and they, in turn, would secure a good recording and distribution deal with a major record label. Trident were taking a chance here. No other independent production company had yet assumed complete responsibility for a rock band.

Five days later, Queen appeared at the Pheasantry Club in Chelsea's King's Road with the express intention for the umpteenth time, it now seemed, of impressing those invited A&R representatives who bothered to turn up. This time, problems with the PA threw their diligently rehearsed act into a spin, even though John Deacon came to the rescue with his electronics expertise, the damage had been done.

Problems seemed to follow them off stage too when they listened to the results of their studio recording work – when their first album was completed at the end of November they quickly discovered that one track had been overdubbed on to the wrong backing tape and, in general, they were not happy with the mixes. Engineer Roy Thomas Baker supported Queen's insistence that they be given more time to deal with these problems; the band also fought for more control over the sound.

The next stumbling block arose in January 1973, when Queen's debut album was finally ready, but they were at a dead end – having no record company set to press and distribute it for sale. All eyes fell on Jack Nelson to nail this elusive record company deal for Queen.

But ultimately it was an executive of Feldman Music Company, called Ronnie Beck, who proved crucial in bringing the band to the notice of Roy Featherstone, one of EMI's top executives.

At the annual Midem festival in Cannes in the South of France, Featherstone was working his way through a mountain of demos from aspiring bands when Ronnie Beck drew his attention specifically to the Queen tape. Roy liked what he heard, which made him susceptible to Beck's bluff that if EMI hoped to snap up Queen they would need to act fast, as a couple of other labels were circling. Featherstone telexed Trident at once. Queen, he urged, should not sign to any other label until he had had a chance to talk to them.

The timing was spot on. Queen had just landed their first recording session with the Radio 1 programme, *Sounds of the Seventies*, recorded at the BBC's Maida Vale studios under the aegis of producer Bernie Andrews. Ten days later, on 15 February, the show was transmitted to an enthusiastic audience response. It was enough to consolidate EMI's interest. But Trident could still have cost Queen dear at this juncture. Again, they made it a condition that EMI take Queen as part of a package. The record company's position remained unchanged from before and frustration ran high. 'I remember bus journeys with Freddie to Trident's offices,' recalls Brian May; presumably they hoped to convey to Trident that this was the big break they had been yearning for. Weeks of worry ensued for Queen. Then in March 1973 they formally signed their first recording contract with EMI.

With Britain and Europe thus covered, attention turned to the large and lucrative American market. The next month, whilst Queen played a gig at London's Marquee Club, Jack Holtzman, managing director of Elektra Records in New York, was in the audience. Holtzman's interest in Queen had already been aroused and seeing them in live performance was sufficient to make up his mind. Banishing their anxiety about impressing the American, Queen did the business that night. When a convinced Holtzman left the country, Queen's US contract was assured.

None of the members of Queen ever lacked confidence in themselves – and having signed with a major record label only increased this solid self-awareness. Mercury now set about designing a distinctive regal crest that would become an integral part of the band's image. Their stage image also developed, as they started using dramatic face make-up to help accentuate a style already established by the tight-fitting black or white slinky clothes they wore. In their teenage bands Roger Taylor and John Deacon had toyed with crude light-shows, and, although Queen would later become famous for their elaborate stage effects, the young Queen did what they could with ultraviolet lighting. May recalled, 'In the beginning when we couldn't afford a light-show, we used projector lamps. We just got through somehow.'

By late spring 1973 Queen enjoyed a near cult following. They were ultimately determined to plough their own furrow but naturally kept abreast of the rapidly changing British music scene. Progressive and hard rock had first given way to gentle folk rock and teen heart-throbs like David Cassidy. This trend was itself now being replaced by glam rock – a movement that spawned a plethora of exponents. And it was at this time that Robin Cable chose to release 'I Can Hear Music'.

EMI was releasing the single but, as the launch of Queen's debut album was imminent, it was deemed best not to highlight Taylor, May and Mercury's involvement with this lightweight cover version. It was decided, therefore, to release the record under the name of Larry Lurex – a send-up of the chart-topping Gary Glitter who, famous for his extravagant silver stage wear, was widely considered to be the king of glam rock. This decision was not Queen's, as Brian May confirms: 'We had no control. We all had a small session fee and Robin, along with Trident, owned the record. It was they who decided to put it out. By then it was already more or less unimportant to us. All we were concerned about was our album.'

Unfortunately, the joke completely backfired. Seen as a satirical dig at a hugely popular performer, disc jockeys boycotted it and record buyers shunned it. Mercury's vocals in no way aped Glitter's and no malice was intended towards 'The Leader', as he was nick-named, and none was taken by the star himself. Says Gary Glitter, 'I thought it was great! It was only meant in fun and anyway, what does it matter? After Elvis Presley, let's be honest, it's all parody.'

For Queen it was easy to turn a blind eye to any perceived offence – they were too wrapped up in the work going into the design of their first album cover. Their friend Doug Pudifoot, who had filmed Smile from the wings at the Albert Hall in 1969, arrived at Freddie Mercury's Holland Park flat to take some group photographs. The ideas flowed fast and furious, but they narrowed it down eventually to a Victorian look with sepia tinting, against a maroon oval background, for the front cover. Then May suggested stretching coloured plastic over the camera lens and having the band's photo taken through this, to produce a uniquely distorted look. The collage idea for the back cover ran aground because Freddie endlessly vetoed any snapshot of himself that wasn't sufficiently flattering. When they submitted their ideas to EMI for consideration, the band's opinion was invited as to which track should become their debut single.

EMI ultimately decided upon two Brian May compositions: 'Keep Yourself Alive', backed by 'Son and Daughter'. It was released in Britain on 6 July 1973 – to mixed reviews. Queen could have no idea what lay ahead with the rock critics, but they did know that if radio ignored a record then it was as good as dead. The single was despatched to all local and regional stations but only Radio Luxembourg included it on its playlists. Licensed commercial radio was just around the corner but this left the BBC still enjoying a virtual monopoly of the pop airwaves, and so the fact that Radio 1 rejected Queen's debut single five consecutive times meant that 'Keep Yourself Alive' was rendered effectively stillborn.

This poor showing made the success of the band's forthcoming eponymous debut album all the more vital. It was unfortunate then that an inadvertent mishap with the album's publicity material could also have sent it slipping into oblivion.

# FIVE

# SWEET SUCCESS

QUEEN WAS RELEASED on 13 July 1973. White labels — early pressings of an album which bear no brand name or record label because labels and sleeves are still being printed — are circulated by record companies for promotional use, but to be of any value they must be accompanied by the appropriate publicity bumph. The hippest rock programme on UK TV at this time was the BBC's late-night show *The Old Grey Whistle Test*, presented by Bob Harris, and EMI sent out a white label to them. Unfortunately, due to a mix-up, it arrived without a shred of PR material. The show was snowed under with white labels and it was sheer luck that the producer, Michael Appleton, happened to pick up Queen's album and be curious enough, despite its anonymity, to play it.

He recalls, 'I listened to it and liked it so much that myself and Bob Harris decided to use it on that night's show. In those days we played tracks accompanied by our own visualisations. We chose "Keep Yourself Alive" and played it along with a cartoon of the President Roosevelt Whistle Stop tour.'

Bob Harris likewise remembers his initial reaction to *Queen*. 'From the moment I heard the white label I absolutely loved it and I thought the track "Keep Yourself Alive" was wonderful,' he states. '*Whistle Test* often used old black and white cartoon footage and in this case we used one from the thirties of an overcrowded train hurtling out of control down a steep hill, with loads of people clinging desperately on to the sides. The frantic imagery, I thought, matched the raw excitement of Queen's music.'

Queen would go on to forge an important link with *OGWT* which provided them with essential exposure, especially throughout the vital early years of their career. 'We put quality sound before vision,' says Michael Appleton. 'That was peculiar to us in broadcasting then, and I think Queen appreciated that and reciprocated by being very professional to work with.' Bob Harris, with whom the band would form a strong association, adds, 'Personally, I was very enthusiastic about Queen.' Alas, the same was not true of the general public, and the album's initial sales were disappointingly slow.

Other disappointments had also been felt within Queen. John Deacon had been unhappy to discover that his name had been printed on the album sleeve as 'Deacon John' – this being what the rest of the band initially called the bass player. Brian May admitted, 'He objected to it and said he wanted to be called John Deacon.' The other cause of dismay, felt by all four, was the album's material. Because trends were shifting so swiftly, six months could be an age in music. For Queen a lot longer than that had elapsed between having written the songs that went on to the album, and the album's eventual release, and they worried that the material would seem old-fashioned. They were so concerned about this that they had included in the sleeve notes an explanation that this was the result of three years' work.

What also bugged them – according to Brian May – was that because other bands like Roxy Music, who had emerged at the same time as Queen, had already achieved success ahead of them with similar material, it might look as if Queen were jumping on to the bandwagon. Queen found this prospect appalling, particularly because, as May pointed out, 'We'd actually had all that stuff in the can from a very long time before. It was extremely frustrating.'

Roger Taylor later acknowledged that *Queen* was interesting, vibrant and varied, but that he did not like the drum sound on the album. However, at the same time, certain tracks, such as 'My Fairy King', had laid down significant markers. As the original Queen-style epic number, with its many overdubs and harmonies, it would one day be recognised – with hindsight – as the beginnings of what eventually led to 'Bohemian Rhapsody'.

Whether or not they were aware of Queen's feelings about the album, Trident now sent the band to Shepperton Studios, Middlesex, to make their first promotional film, optimistically intended for worldwide distribution. To handle Queen's PR they also called in the services of one of Britain's top freelance publicists, Tony Brainsby, whose clients have included Paul McCartney and Chris de Burgh.

Says Tony, 'Our first meeting was in my office and they made a deep impression. Of all the bands I've looked after, only two had a particular effect on me. One was Thin Lizzy, and Queen was the other. They not only knew precisely what they wanted, they also knew that they would be big. It's that kind of conviction that makes stars, and makes my kind of job a lot easier.' Following that meeting Brainsby was further convinced when he saw one of their live performances at a London polytechnic: 'There was no stage and so Queen were at the same level as the audience, which can be quite a disadvantage, but they were remarkable that night. I knew I was seeing *real* talent.'

Tony was also swift to get an understanding of the personalities of his latest clients. He reveals, 'Obviously Freddie stuck out the most. He was such a raving poofter, I couldn't believe my eyes at our first meeting. He was dressed in red velvet skin-tight trousers, had black varnish on his fingernails, long hair and of course all those teeth – he was extremely touch about his teeth. He was strong-willed, nakedly ambitious but also very charming. In those days, though, Freddie was an inwardly very aggressive and angry man in the sense that he knew he should be a star and wasn't, yet. It's not a side of him that he allowed too many people to see, but it was definitely all the way through him. He felt that stardom was his by rights and he was extremely frustrated at the time it seemed to be taking for him to reach it. In my view, he was very much the fight in the band.'

That said, Tony Brainsby is clear that it was never a case of the band being Freddie Mercury and Queen. He states, 'It was always a group and from the start we were all made very conscious of the importance of treating them absolutely equally, which was quite right. Brian May was always very quiet and modest but, with the combination of his incredible guitar sound, Roger Taylor's amazing drum skills and high falsetto voice, and John Deacon's extremely strong bass lines, each one had a particular sound to add to Queen's identity.'

As Tony set out to gain Queen as much exposure as he could, the band began work on their follow-up album, this time under more favourable circumstances. Their music may not yet have been setting anyone alight, but at least they were no longer relegated to recording on down-time. *Queen* was released in America on the Elektra label on 4 September and, after attracting reasonable radio play, managed to notch up the achievement for an unknown British band of entering Billboard's Top 100 chart, albeit at number 83. Just as in Britain, however, 'Keep Yourself Alive' failed to chart in the States.

It was at this point that Jack Nelson decided Queen's most pressing need was to be seen on tour. As they were clearly not yet headlining material, securing them a good support slot came top of his agenda and he approached an acquaintance, Bob Hirschman, who managed the then popular group Mott the Hoople to broach the subject of Hoople making Queen the opening act of their forthcoming UK tour. It wasn't an easy sell, not least because Hirschman had never heard Queen play. A £3,000 contribution to sound and lights helped to ease his qualms and give Queen the job.

The buzz this gave the band spiced up their energy for the half dozen dates which Jack Nelson quickly fixed up as a kind of pre-tour warm up. Commencing on 13 September at Golders Green Hippodrome, they travelled weeks later to their first foreign dates at the Bagodesberg in Frankfurt, followed the next night with a gig at Le Blow Up in Luxembourg before they returned home for three London performances. The final one was on 2 November at Imperial College and Brian May's college friend, Tom Hicks, vividly recalls this gig. He says, 'It was a free concert for the physics students and I was knocked out by the difference in Queen's playing. It was absolutely deafening too. I'm not joking, you heard it through your chest that night!' A journalist, Rosemary Horide, also there later prophesied in her glowing review – aware of their place in the upcoming Hoople tour – 'Queen could turn out to be a bit more than just a support band.'

That was Queen's ultimate intention, but ten days later, when they opened for Mott the Hoople at the Town Hall in Leeds, they were entirely geared up to give the support role their best. It was their first taste of playing practically every night in a different city and all four found it an invigorating experience. From the first night, Mercury, in particular, was determined to live it up; with adrenalin still pumping, he headed straight off after the performance to a local nightspot which is where he first met nightclub owner Peter Stringfellow.

Says Stringfellow, 'He came into my Cinderella Rockerfella club in Leeds and I thought he was a really nice bloke. He obviously wasn't a mega star yet and had no entourage with him so he sat at my table and we had a laugh and a few drinks. I asked if I could take his photo with my Polaroid camera but what a performance it turned out to be! I used up two packs of film before Freddie decided that one shot was okay to keep, then he promptly destroyed the rest. His vanity was out of all proportion but, with hindsight, it was a lesson in professionalism. I remember thinking to myself, "This guy is certainly different!"' He adds, 'I had absolutely no idea that Freddie was gay then. There was nothing in his behaviour to remotely suggest it. I'd say that was the first and last time that I had a truly enjoyable evening with him though. Later on he was always completely mobbed.'

The mob that turned out nightly on that 23-date tour came primarily to see the headliners but Queen knew that with each gig they were gaining in confidence and popularity. These were still early days for Queen – the tight musical bedrock against which Freddie Mercury's flamboyance could shine would be perfected over time – but they were already beginning to draw their own reaction. Tony Brainsby, who also handled Mott the Hoople, confirms, 'That tour was one helluva experience. You came out of gigs just breathless with it all.'

This claim was borne out at the last date, on 14 December at London's Hammersmith Odeon. Having played two shows, Queen received a rapturous response from the thousands of young people who were excitedly making the theatre jump. The successful pairing of Hoople and Queen and the easy rapport established between the bands meant that Mott had already asked them to be their support band for an upcoming American tour. And this was not the only reason for joy. As a result of being seen and appreciated around the country, sales of their album had enjoyed a revival. But where Queen fell down was in failing to impress the music press, most of whom either panned them or, perhaps worse still, ignored their existence.

Tony Brainsby is blunt about this: 'Queen were accused of being a hype band but in reality the press resented the fact that their management put a lot of money behind them and that I was successful in getting them lots of exposure. Of course, Freddie, with his wild antics and being the way he was, was an easy target for any journalist out to make a name for himself. In those days it was considered essential to have the music press on-side, so naturally the criticism hurt the band. They were all extremely anxious about their press image and what was being said about them.'

TV presenter Bob Harris has his own theory as to why, over the years, press hostility towards Queen grew. He says, 'It possibly stemmed from their inability to label Queen and they took their own inadequacy out on the band. When Queen were huge and they still attacked them, it was the same old thing. The British press love to build them up and knock them down. You sometimes get the feeling that they feel duty-bound to smash holes in people.'

It was not all bad, however. Tony Brainsby recalls Queen's excitement the first time they saw a poster of themselves in *Jackie*, one of Britain's most popular teenage magazines, and they enjoyed recording sessions for Radio 1 with their DJ friend Bob Harris. Giving an example of Queen's total dedication from the outset, Harris reveals of these sessions: 'I was watching from the control room and there was a pin spotlight on Freddie. He was giving so much to his performance that the veins were literally standing out on his temples and neck. I thought, How much more can you give?'

Their gigging was not yet over for the year – they had four more dates of their own to play in Leicester, Taunton, Peterborough and finally Liverpool. This last appearance at the Top Rank Club on 28 December was in support of 10cc and was a long-standing booking arranged by Ken Testi (one of the last things that Ken had done for Queen before they parted company).

After signing to EMI, in some recognition of the invaluable help Testi had been to them in the past, Queen invited Ken to become their personal manager – a salaried member of the team. Testi was thrilled but unable to take up the offer. He explains, 'At this point Queen were getting £30 a week each and I was offered £25 which I thought was good but on that money I couldn't have made the payments on my house and I also had to look after my mother and sister who needed me more. You can't live on what-might-have-beens, but I've regretted it to this day. It was a tough break for me.'

As Queen ended 1973, dubbed 'Britain's Biggest Unknowns', they faced a few tough breaks of their own, starting straight away in the new year. They were booked to headline at the Sunbury Music Festival in Melbourne at the beginning of February, but Brian May had suddenly fallen ill after the band underwent the required inoculations to go to Australia. His arm had become gangrenous and it was touch and go for a while whether he would lose his arm. Apart from the personal concern, this also disrupted rehearsals for their first headlining foreign gig. And that was only the start of their troubles.

When they arrived at the open-air site for the festival there was palpable tension in the atmosphere. Queen had had a specially designed lighting rig transported over, along with the rest of their equipment. The complicated apparatus needed the band's own crew to ensure it operated properly, which unfortunately stepped on the toes of the local site technicians who were thus deprived of their fee. This grievance fuelled a more general sense of resentment that an unknown British group was taking top billing over the Aussie groups.

On top of all this, half the band was feeling unwell; Brian was in considerable pain with his arm and Freddie had an ear infection for which he was taking antibiotics. The medication was making him drowsy and he felt disoriented because he could not hear himself sing. It seemed par for the course when, due to having to wait for darkness to fall for the lights to be effective, Queen's delay in coming on stage produced a barrage of slow handclapping from the disgruntled audience. Then, when they were mid-performance, the controversial lighting system failed.

Queen may not have been around long enough yet to have earned the term 'troopers" but, remarkably, they refused to buckle under these cumulative strains. Furthermore, they set out all the more determinedly to overcome the compère's unfortunate introduction when he referred to them as 'stuck-up Pommies'; through their music, they proceeded to win over a large enough section of the audience to have them actually shout for an encore at the end. The compère saw to it, however, that this enthusiastic swell was quelled in favour of the crowd calling instead for one of their own home-grown bands.

Although they could take comfort from their professionalism, the humiliation continued the next day when the Australian press mirrored their British counterparts and slated Queen. Recognising that health problems and bad publicity were stacking up against them, the band pulled out of the intended second night's performance. This inevitably gave their detractors more ammunition and angered the promoters. Nevertheless, Queen boarded a flight back to Britain. All in all, they had gone halfway around the world to be left out of pocket (they had had to pay their own return air fares) and demoralised. Even so, Brian May declares, 'None of us thought it was disastrous. We just thought, one day we'll be back. And we were.'

It was true that the sun did not take long to shine for Queen. In February, Elektra Records released a second single in America from *Queen* called 'Liar', which failed to chart. But in Britain an *NME* readers' poll voted the band Second Most Promising New Name (Leo Sayer had come out on top), and within a couple of weeks they would make their debut on BBC TV's prestigious music show *Top of the Pops*.

It was every artiste's dream to appear on this programme and the person instrumental in landing Queen this coveted television debut was Ronnie Fowler, head of EMI's PR department, who was already wildly enthusiastic about their music. Learning from the show's producer, Robin Nash, that a last-minute vacancy had arisen because David Bowie's promo clip for 'The Jean Genie' had not arrived in time, Fowler had pressed Nash to give Queen a try. Nash agreed to hear a demo but it alone was insufficient because performers normally mimed to specially recorded backing tracks of their songs. With the clock ticking, Fowler asked a favour of Who guitarist Pete Townshend – could Queen borrow some of his studio time to record the necessary backing tape? He agreed and, the day before the show went out, Queen, armed with this tape, excitedly assembled at the BBC studios to pre-record their appearance.

On 21 February 1974 Queen made their *Top of the Pops* debut, performing 'Seven Seas of Rhye'. That Thursday evening, Roger, Freddie, John and Brian all grouped around an electrical goods shop window to watch themselves through the glass on the display TVs inside. Although there was no sound, it was still one of those memorable moments and 'Seven Seas of Rhye' would certainly come through for Queen, in a way that 'Keep Yourself Alive' had not.

The Freddie Mercury composition, which indulged his penchant for grand crescendos and fantasy lyrics, had not yet been officially released. But, to capitalise on Queen's *Top of the Pops* debut, Ronnie

Fowler and Jack Nelson saturated the radio stations next day with white label copies of the single. The day after that, on 23 February, EMI rush-released 'Seven Seas of Rhye'/'See What a Fool I've Been'. By the second week of March it was nestling in the singles charts at number 10.

This chart success added welcome impetus to the prospect of embarking on their first UK headlining tour. Mercury would soon declare, 'I've always thought of us as a top group'. In keeping with this, they now focused more closely on their proposed stage image: specifically, on what they would wear. It no longer seemed appropriate to have their Kensington seamstress friends run up their outfits, and they turned to top fashion designer Zandra Rhodes.

Says Zandra, 'Queen had liked some outfits I had designed for Marc Bolan. Also, I was seen then as a very colourful bird of paradise with my bold make-up, freaky hair and long scarves and I think it was an imagery that drew them.' Zandra's Paddington workshop in those days was, what she herself terms 'a deathtrap', reached by a rickety winding staircase with a low ceiling. The two band members she particularly remembers coming to see her there were Mercury and May. She designed truly sumptuous outfits for the whole band but the most eyecatching was reserved for Freddie – naturally, as he was the one doing all the dashing about on stage. In time, Mercury's Zandra Rhodes' creation in white satin, with an extravagant pleated-wing effect, would become world-famous. Says Rhodes, 'Queen's look was very much part of their success and has always been important to their whole make-up, in conjunction with the music. They only really toned it down years later when Freddie became ill and started trying to look straight.'

While Queen's image was certainly integral to their success, in other ways their showy bombastic style could also create a degree of misunderstanding, in that some people confused the stage persona with the real person, as Roger Taylor once eloquently revealed: 'Quite a lot of people who are close to me now originally thought I was a complete prat. I had to get over this "Queen barrier" which I had never realised existed.'

Raring to go, however, and ready to knock their audience dead with their new glitzy image and tightly rehearsed sound, Queen kicked off this first headlining tour on 1 March 1974 at Blackpool's Winter Gardens. For the first two gigs they played without a support band but it was tough going, as Brian May's arm had not fully recovered, and for their third gig, at the Guildhall in Plymouth, they were joined by a Liverpool group called Nutz who stayed on as support for the whole tour. Years later Queen would close each show by playing their version of the national anthem – an extension of the audience's curious habit, which started during this tour, of singing 'God Save the Queen' while awaiting the band's arrival on stage.

On 8 March, the same day as Queen were due to appear at the Locarno in Sunderland, their second album *Queen II* was released. The title might have been unimaginative but the material was original – as was their innovative use of white and black sides to replace the standard A and B. Encouragingly, as they gigged around the country, it became clear that an increasing proportion of the audience were familiar with the lyrics of the new songs; accordingly, *Queen II* was rocketing to number seven in the album charts before the tour's end.

It was well-deserved recompense for all the work Queen had put into making this album, which they categorised as their first foray into pure studio music. Queen's guiding principle was that a record ought to have several layers built into it to be discovered, something they said they had learned from listening to the Beatles and Jimi Hendrix. However, this time they did so many overdubs that the tape was literally in danger of disintegrating. Having had to record their debut album on down-time, they had never had the chance for such an indulgence before. But, in striving for this layered depth, Queen felt that they had produced the kind of emotive, adventurous material that they were capable of, even if some of it ended up being a little too complicated to be replicated live on stage. 'We thought of it as almost baroque,' stated Brian May and indeed the album had almost been called *Over The Top*.

Once again, however, Queen's efforts failed to find favour with the rock critics. Since one reviewer had slaughtered their debut album as 'a bucket of stale urine', it was reasonable to assume that anything would be an improvement on that. The new work, though, was attacked for lacking depth and feeling and one writer savagely denounced Queen as 'the dregs of glam rock'. Even buttressed by their unshakable self-belief, this kind of ruthless criticism – potentially crushing for a young band – must have found a few chinks in their armour. But Queen chose to focus on the proof of their own eyes, for, at the crucial point of live contact between band and audience, they were unmistakably thriving.

In no small part this came down to the immense energy and imagination they put into each performance. During this tour, the driving authority of Taylor's drums and the mesmeric bass work from Deacon enhanced May's powerful lead guitar, thereby providing scope for the band's captivating dynamo, Mercury, to parade, preen and pirouette to electrifying effect.

On a couple of occasions that electricity actually ignited. It might be argued that any self-respecting rock band had to spark a riot or two along the way, but it was not a reputation Queen cared to court. Nevertheless, midway through the tour, a skirmish broke out in the hall at Stirling University in Scotland after Queen's third encore. This resulted in four people being hospitalised – two with stab wounds, one with cuts and the other suffering concussion. The band themselves had to be locked in a kitchen for their own safety while police tackled the rioters.

The lurid press headlines that followed had hardly died away when, in the tour's final week, after a gig at the Douglas Palace Lido on the Isle of Man, a party thrown in their hotel spun clean out of control and attracted yet more controversy. The negative coverage, although unwelcome, had the side-effect of highlighting the band's name even more and by the tour's end they were playing to sell-out crowds.

The adulation, it seemed, was temporarily going to Freddie's head for, by their penultimate gig at the Rainbow Theatre on 31 March 1974 (the first time Queen headlined at a prestigious London concert venue), Mercury's prima donna antics had got out of hand. During the sound check earlier in the day a row erupted in the band when the normally patient Brian May felt sufficiently goaded by the singer to tell him that he was behaving like an old tart. Freddie flounced off and stayed away a worryingly long time. May had a hunch that Mercury was not actually that far away, despite everyone's concerns, and he began taunting loudly over the mike, 'Freddiepoos? Where are you?' It worked when a livid Mercury burst back into the theatre and – with a glare – got back to work. With fatigue, egos and tour pressures, this would not be the last time tensions erupted in Queen; although Freddie turned out to be the peacemaker more often than not.

Life was at last beginning to feel satisfyingly hectic for Queen. Two weeks after ending their first UK headlining tour, they would play their first American date, as support band on Mott the Hoople's spring US tour. To the Americans, Queen were total non-entities. Although Elektra tried to rectify this by releasing *Queen II* there on 9 April, it peaked at number 49; 'Seven Seas of Rhye' was their third single to completely fail to chart in the US. But this did not dampen their spirits. Roger Taylor later reminisced, 'When we first went to America it was all big, new and very exciting.'

Viewing this trip as a great opportunity to make their mark, Queen opened for Hoople at Denver's Regis College on 16 April, breaking through the initial neutral response and warming the audience to them by the end of their set. And that established the pattern thereafter. It was tougher than they had anticipated – even the long distances to be travelled between gigs verged on the arduous – but experience-wise it was invaluable. They, halfway through the six-week tour their assault on America was utterly derailed by an unexpected development.

Starting on 7 May, they had played six consecutive nights at the Uris Theater in New York, during which time Brian had begun to feel unwell. After the final gig he collapsed and, assuming that it was fatigue, he was simply advised to rest before their next scheduled gig in Boston. Next morning, however, when he awoke in Boston's Parker House Hotel it became clear that something was seriously wrong. After an anxious wait, the doctor's diagnosis was that Brian had hepatitis. The contagious, potentially dangerous, illness sealed the band's fate; for them the tour was over. It was a bad blow but, once back in Britain, as May was hospitalised for six weeks, Mercury spoke for the others when he said, 'Sure, a whole tour would have helped us more, but we did what we had to do and there's no such thing as "We lost our chance".'

Instead, they channelled their energies into starting work on their third album, which by early June took them off to Rockfield Studios in Monmouth, South Wales. Convincing himself that he had recovered, Brian joined them there to rehearse, write new songs and lay down backing tracks. He was obviously still in a weak condition, however, and when recording itself began at four separate studios the next month, he once more collapsed and was rushed to King's College Hospital, where this time he underwent emergency surgery for a duodenal ulcer. This latest health scare put the lid on Queen's planned return to the States and, conscious that Brian might start to worry about being replaced in the band, Mercury visited him once again to speak for his friends in allaying any such fears.

They were wrapping up work on their new album at London's Sarm Studios when they learned that *Queen II*, by selling more than 100,000 units, had earned them a silver disc. This brought with it an increase in media interest in the band, but one that they greeted with caution in the light of their treatment thus far. They preferred to concentrate on selecting which one of the new album's thirteen tracks should be their next single.

As on their first two albums, Roger Taylor had contributed a number. In addition, John Deacon made his songwriting debut with 'Misfire', and the track 'Stone Cold Crazy' marked the first song to be credited collectively to Queen. Brian May made four contributions and the rest were Freddie Mercury compositions. In the end they opted for one of Mercury's; and on 11 October 1974 'Killer

Queen' was released, backed by 'Flick of the Wrist'. According to Freddie it was about a high-class call girl. Mercury rarely had patience to explain the meaning of his compositions but of 'Killer Queen' he stated, 'I'm trying to say that classy people can be whores as well.' The single stormed up the charts, only to be held off the top slot by the David Essex hit 'Gonna Make You a Star'.

Essex considers Queen to be the best British band to have come out of the seventies. Says David, 'Everyone knows now that they were a highly innovative band, but it was obvious even then. Image quickly took over from music but their musical ability had the staying power where others vanished. With their stacked-up voices and guitar work, 'Killer Queen' (which is, funnily enough, my favourite Queen record) was extremely well produced and very clever.'

It was indeed several cuts above the average glam rock number, as Oscar-winning lyricist Sir Tim Rice, who years later became personal friends with Freddie Mercury, attests. He says, 'I hadn't particularly liked "Seven Seas of Rhye" at first, although I got to like it better once I knew the band. But it was "Killer Queen" which really turned me on to Queen. The composition of its lyrics was quite sophisticated, especially for its time. I have absolutely no doubt about Freddie's immense talent as a songwriter.'

Brian May has maintained that no Queen song was ever penned with *only* chart success in mind, whereas John Deacon offers a more pragmatic view, stating bluntly that they coveted big success and went flat out to achieve it.

'Killer Queen's' success took Queen back to *Top of the Pops*. By now all four wore their hair long and Mercury's stage act had evolved from the homosexual aura he had exuded on the college circuit, to a more polished ambiguity. At the height of the glam era other bands, such as Sweet, perpetuated a bisexual image as a joke. Mercury's intentions were less certain as he caressed the sawn-off shiny shaft of his microphone stand that had become as much his trademark as would his scoop-necked revealing leotards.

That 'Killer Queen' was no chuck-away cheery tune was proved when it earned Mercury his first Ivor Novello songwriter award.

Whether or not Queen were a glam band at this point was a tricky question, for 'Killer Queen' was entirely different from such numbers as the popular, brash 'Cum On Feel the Noize' by Slade or Mud's chirpy 'Tiger Feet'. For Gary Langhan, tape operator and assistant at Sarm Studios, there is no doubt. 'No way for me were Queen glam rock,' he states. 'For a start there was a far greater content to their records. I spent *days* working on the harmony structures, the guitar solos and so on for "Killer Queen". It was so meticulous.'

Having reached a decided turning point in their career, Queen, with this number two hit under their belt, went on the road again for a two-month UK and European tour, starting in late October in Manchester and ending on 10 December in Barcelona. It had partly been arranged to compensate for their aborted return to the US, and they pulled out all the stops – including an impressive light show, coupled with an experimental fireworks display. The press, perhaps predictably by now, hated the showy theatrics but the fans felt thoroughly entertained.

The fans' delirium, in fact, could occasionally verge on the dangerous. For instance, whilst performing at Glasgow's Apollo Centre on 8 November, Mercury was dragged completely off the stage into the grasping clutches of a seething, near hysterical mob. Fights immediately broke out, resulting in damage to property and personal injury to some people; overall, it was rather frightening for Freddie. That same day the album *Sheer Heart Attack* was released in Britain, and in America four days after that.

With such audience reaction, and their third album release, they felt that they were finally on their way. For John Deacon this was certainly a milestone. In a rare interview he later revealed, 'I was possibly the one person in the group who could look at it from the outside because I came in as the fourth person in the band. I knew there was something there, but I wasn't convinced of it until the *Sheer Heart Attack* album.' This was an album he felt would have broader appeal than the first two. Further proof of Queen's rising popularity came when a second night at the Rainbow Theatre in

London had to be hastily organised to cope with demand to see them. Recording these gigs on 19 and 20 November made a live album release possible; they were also filmed, as the idea of making a feature film of the band had taken root.

Their busy twelve months gigging around the world paid off when, in December, Queen were voted Britain's Best Live Act of 1974 by *Sun* readers. But they had still made no headway with the press. Increased media interest in them had been met by a decided wariness on the part of the band. This had left them in a no-win situation, as their unwillingness to open up to journalists was read as further proof of Queen's conceit.

Within Queen there was also discontent over the wages they received from Trident, with whom each member had had long and often frustrating meetings to discuss the position. Their salaries had more then trebled by now but, with rocketing album sales (*Sheer Heart Attack*'s highest positions in Britain and America would be numbers two and twelve respectively) and chart success, they felt this was still nowhere near enough. Trident and Queen would end up parting company, but everyone knew it was not going to be easy.

# SIX

# HYSTERIA

A T THE START of 1975 Queen found themselves in the unwelcome situation of being – despite their increasing public popularity – privately strapped for cash and concerned about mounting debts for lighting and sound services. That this was a common enough plight among recording artistes was cold comfort for the four of them living respectively in cramped or decrepit lodgings. Their disagreements, too, with Trident had been getting nowhere and so the band had by now enlisted the services of a music business lawyer called Jim Beach to look into ways in which they could sever their links with the Sheffield brothers; there followed lengthy negotiations before the situation could be resolved.

On 17 January the fourth single from *Sheer Heart Attack*, 'Now I'm Here'/'Lily of the Valley' was released in Britain. Very different from the stylish 'Killer Queen', this heavier number, written by Brian May during one of his hospital stays, displayed the band's diversity and it would stall at a still healthy number eleven. The next day John Deacon became the first band member to marry, when he and long-time girlfriend Veronica Tetzlaff wed at the Carmelite Church in London's Kensington Church Street. Queen's next milestone came just over two weeks later when they embarked on their first headlining tour of America and Canada.

The two-month stint opened at the Agora Theater in Columbus, Ohio, on 5 February; mingled with the intense anticipation and excitement, was a nagging apprehension. Their publicist understood why. Says Tony Brainsby, 'As happened with most bands, Queen's effect on America had been slow. It was a throwback to the sixties when American bands couldn't get arrested in their own country. Then the only bands that counted were British. And it's my opinion that, by the seventies, there was a backlash. In other words, the Yanks got their own back by being deliberately reticent about any English band trying to crack their market.' Queen's image created another possible stumbling block, as Mercury's foppish posturing was anathema to the hard-rock machismo favoured over there.

On the other side of the coin though, 'Killer Queen' was their first single to chart in America, reaching number twelve, which they decided must augur well. They were proved right in one respect – from early in the tour, the high demand for tickets at each scheduled gig resulted in several extra dates having to be squeezed in. But from American critics they got a mixed reaction. Brian May remembers that what he calls 'the Anglophile element and the new A&R generation' had already made Queen heroes and he maintains that, on the whole, it was the only place where the band got good reviews. However, it is also true that many US rock writers compared Queen unfavourably to Led Zeppelin.

Once again, where it truly mattered – at ground level – Queen were gaining in popularity, which delighted them, as did the demand for extra gigs. In practical terms, however, it was making the pace crazy – in the space of just over two weeks in February at the Music Hall in Cleveland, Boston's Orpheum Theater, the Avery Fisher Hall in New York and the Erlinger Theater in Philadelphia they were playing two gigs in the same day. It was double work for them all, but it took the greatest toll on Mercury who developed problems with his voice.

The first sign of real trouble arose after the end of the second performance in Philadelphia on 23 February when Freddie found it hard to speak and a throat specialist from the University City Hospital had to be called in. The doctor suspected that the singer might be developing nodules on his vocal cords, but he certainly had voice strain and he warned Mercury against singing for a while. Freddie, fond of making flamboyant pronouncements, once declared, 'I'll sing until my throat is like a vulture's crotch!', and so, with a show-must-go-on mentality, Mercury ignored this medical advice.

His bravado did him little good. The next night, Queen had no sooner taken the stage at Washington's Kennedy Center than Mercury knew that he was struggling; by the gig's end he was in agony and another local specialist had to be summoned. As Roger, Brian and John awaited the outcome of the doctor's examination, it must have seemed as if America was just not made for them. Health problems had axed their first US tour as support to Hoople, then prevented a second from taking place at all. Now, this attempt to woo Americans to their music was also hanging in the balance.

It turned out that Mercury had severe laryngitis – painful certainly, but not enough to send them packing back to Britain. Instead they were forced to cancel the next six gigs to allow Freddie, with medication and rest, to recuperate. Reluctantly they cooled their heels as ordered, but were considerably cheered to learn in the interim that, back home, Queen had newly been voted Band of the Year by *Melody Maker*. Keener than ever to restart the tour, the band slipped back into harness on 5 March at the Mary E. Sawyer Auditorium in La Crosse, only to discover that the rest had been too short when Mercury suffered a relapse.

The remainder of the tour, as they gigged from Madison to Miami, New Orleans to Calgary, operated on this staggered on/off pattern, always determined by the condition of Mercury's voice. Then, after their gig on 6 April in Seattle, the intended final date, the next night in Portland, had to be cancelled at the last moment. This was not the note upon which they had hoped to end their first head-lining US tour and, although they had completed thirty-eight gigs in two months, because of its erratic nature it was difficult to gauge whether they had made any significant impression in the States; less than a fortnight later they were to make the kind of impact that they had so far only dreamed of.

From Seattle, Queen had left for a brief holiday in Hawaii to unwind and recharge their batteries, ready for the next challenge – their forthcoming tour of Japan. It was alien territory to them but they hoped to meet with a friendly reception. As they emerged from their Japanese Airlines jumbo jet, they walked into blind hysteria. Thousands of delirious teenagers swarmed all over the airport, screaming and shouting themselves hoarse from the rooftops and creating sheer bedlam inside the terminal building by surging forward against barely adequate security barriers as soon as the four stepped into the arrivals hall.

As airport security tried to steer Queen through, they were impeded every step of the way by fans straining to offer Roger, Brian, John and Freddie single red roses, and by autograph-hunters fanatically thrusting record sleeves and glossy publicity shots into their hands. The band gazed with delight at the seething mass, thrilled at the sight of all the welcoming banners, and the sound of the rhythmic chanting of their name, but they were also thoroughly bemused. Speaking on the band's behalf, Brian admits, 'We couldn't take it all in. It was like another world.'

It was a world they would soon become accustomed to, but right then it was a heady experience. It was more teen idol hysteria than the rock band adulation Queen craved, but it was fun. It could also be frightening. Kicking off on the best high yet, they played the first of their eight Japanese dates to a sell-out crowd at the Budokan Martial Arts Hall in Tokyo on 19 April 1975, only to find that the frantic airport scenes had been a pale forerunner of the real thing.

Brian May recalls the promoters' pre-gig warning, 'They said, "The audience will be very quiet, but don't worry!" ' In fact, they had worked themselves into a frenzy before Queen played a note and from the first number, although their amps were up full blast, the only sounds discernible in the hall were the audience's screams. As the gig progressed, the electric atmosphere began overheating alarmingly until the crazed crowd finally lost control and rushed the stage.

In the first split second, the sight of the frenzied human beings stampeding towards them was an exhilarating one but it was also shocking and potentially very dangerous to themselves and to the fans. When seats began to buckle and collapse under the weight of hysterical teenagers Queen sensed that they had a possible disaster on their hands. Suddenly Freddie stopped singing to appeal over the mike for calm. His urgings took a while to register in the mêlée, but eventually the band managed to calm the crowd down.

Queen's respect for their worldwide legions of fans meant that they were always mindful of crowd safety, but there can be no legislating for band mania. What's more, the hysterical scenes accompanied Queen to their next gig in Nagoya and beyond, through Kobe, Fukuoka, Okayama, Shizuoka, Yokohama and to their return visit to the Budokan which ended their tour on 1 May. The entire trip was unforgettable. Off-stage, too, they were treated as a major force in music, with their hosts showing them great deference and spoiling them with expensive gifts. Queen's best way of returning the compliment was by playing the very last encore of their final gig dressed in traditional Japanese kimonos, thereby sending the audience berserk.

The only other band currently enjoying this level of adulation in Britain, as well as in Japan, was the Bay City Rollers. The five tartan-clad Scots lads – Britain's original boy band – were at their commercial peak with their long-running number one hit 'Bye Bye Baby' and were creating the kind of chaos and public disorder not witnessed since the days of Beatlemania. Their guitarist Eric Faulkner can easily understand Japan's overwhelming impact on Queen. 'It is like a separate planet for bands there,' he says. 'They go absolutely mad for Western rock. In fact, their own bands don't get a look in unless they are lookalikes of Western bands. At one time there was a

Japanese lookalike Queen, Bay City Rollers and Status Quo. The press hype you before you arrive and by the time you get there, they're ready to swallow you whole!'

As for the kind of turn-on such adulation provides, Eric adds, 'Of course you enjoy it and you definitely get a sense of power from it. But idolisation is weird, and if you believe it you'll go clean off your head. When you're at the mania pitch, it's a strange world – you end up looking out at it from behind a wall of bodyguards.'

Publicist Tony Brainsby also noted the effect that this Far East tour had had on Queen. He recalls, 'They were all smitten by the country's culture. They couldn't wait to buy all things Japanese, although Freddie was the most affected in the long run. But why not? It had been a thrilling time for them and they had made it big in Japan before they made it big in Britain, so naturally it made a huge impression on them.'

When the band landed back on British soil, they were very unimpressed to find that there had been no shift in the deadlock over the business of breaking loose from Trident. However, they were determined not to let this stalemate stem their creative juices, which were flowing faster and stronger than ever, and they immediately started work on their fourth album. The experience accumulated on their foreign tours, topped by this recent taste of hero-worship, fuelled their already plentiful store of self-confidence. And this was reflected in their increased productivity throughout the summer, as they beavered away in six different studios.

Meanwhile, behind the scenes, their lawyer had also been hard at work, and in August the severance agreements were finally ready for signature. The upshot was that EMI would assume more direct control of recording and publishing, and the band were free to hire new management. The bad news was that they had to pay Trident £100,000 in severance fees, together with the rights to 1 per cent of album royalties. Says Brian May, 'We effectively had to trade the first three albums' sales up to that point for our future.' And later, reflecting on Queen's early career, Roger Taylor recalled, 'For so many

years you seem to be in debt. You see all these telephone numbers –
fortunes you have to pay back. You never seem to have any money
of your own.' On top of this a planned American tour had had to be
called off because of the upheavals, which meant a further substantial
loss for all concerned. The plain truth of the matter, therefore, was
that, after headlining in America and Japan and being on the verge of
releasing their fourth album, Queen were broke again.

To cap it all, because of the discord surrounding them, rumours
swiftly surfaced that Queen were on the brink of disbanding. And
certainly, in the summer of 1975, May was approached by brothers
Ron and Russell Mael who fronted the pop group Sparks – they
hoped to lure the already respected talents of the guitarist to their
line-up. But May declined, not least because the rumours of Queen's
break-up had no foundation. But that was not to say that the band
did not have their concerns – management for one.

In spring, whilst in America, they had been headhunted by the
showbusinesses manager Don Arden. He had talked of highly lucrative deals if Queen could be free to take him on as their manager.
Prior to the tour's end, Arden had got all four members to sign a
letter of authorisation which would allow him to act on their behalf
and deal directly with the Sheffield brothers. Ultimately, though, this
had come to nothing and Queen had to look at their options.

They concentrated on three potential managers. One was 10cc's
manager but he proved too elusive to even make contact with.
Another was Peter Grant who handled Led Zeppelin, but his condition that Queen sign to Swan Song, Zeppelin's own production and
record company, ruled him out. And so it narrowed down to the third
– John Reid, who managed the very successful solo star Elton John. As
Reid metaphorically had 'better fish to fry', the prospect of Queen at
this juncture was not one to make him sit up and grab his pen.

Setting aside Queen's conviction that they were destined for
superstardom, in the cold light of day at this stage they were merely
an impressive live act which had notched up a couple of hits and
scored healthy album sales. In other words, they were better than
many bands around at the time and not as successful as others. Even

so, Reid clearly spotted something, for by the end of September 1975 he had become Queen's new manager.

John Reid immediately assigned a new personal manager to his latest signing, a former colleague called Pete Brown who would remain with Queen for the next seven years. Says Pete, 'I went everywhere with them, to recording studios, gigs, on tour – the lot.' He jokes, 'I vividly remember Freddie saying, "I decided John Reid was the right man for the job of our manager the moment he fluttered his eyelashes at me!" Freddie was always kidding around like that. But seriously Queen were in dire need of help right then – their finances were in a total mess.'

To help Queen out of this mire, Reid, together with lawyer Jim Beach, focused on where to find the colossal sum the band owed Trident. Realistically, it hinged on nailing a music publishing deal, and before the November deadline ran out EMI came up trumps by providing £100,000 as an advance against future royalties. With this secured, Reid threw a glitzy party at the London Coliseum where Queen, attended by much publicity, were presented with a variety of gold and silver discs for the sales of 'Killer Queen' and their three albums to date.

The next step was to choose their next single release. By October, Roger, Brian, Freddie and John had agreed that, of all the tracks they had been working on throughout the summer, the one they wanted to extract first was a Mercury composition called 'Bohemian Rhapsody'. John Reid was speechless. In its original state it was a herculean seven minutes long and in three distinctly different sections – the middle one of which was operatic. For any other rock band it might have been commercial suicide.

Pete Brown reveals, 'A lot of us thought Queen were quite mad considering this as their single. I thought it was far too long and tried to dissuade them, and privately John Deacon initially agreed with me. But Freddie, Brian and Roger felt very strongly that they needed to establish their credibility and they completely dug in their heels over it.'

Record producer Gary Langhan can vouch for Queen's emphatic attitude about their choice. He says, 'I guess you could call it arrogance, but only in the sense that it came from a total belief in the number. And I can understand it. I vividly recall being at the back of the control room at Sarm Studios when "Bohemian Rhapsody" was nearing completion and I just knew that I was hearing the greatest piece of music I was ever likely to. I felt it in my gut and Queen did too.' He adds, 'Their attitude to it being twice the usual time slot given to each record on radio was – if that's so, then DJs will just have to have one less record on their playlists.'

What concerned John Reid – quite rightly, as their manager looking out for their interests – was that DJs might instead leave 'Bohemian Rhapsody' off their lists altogether (Queen had already experienced the unhappy results of radio ignoring a single). He admired the band's courage, but felt it his duty to remonstrate with them over the potential consequences of their decision. When he found them implacable, however, he wholeheartedly joined the fight to keep the single at its original length. Freddie Mercury declared that cutting up a song was one compromise that Queen would never make. But in the end 'Bohemian Rhapsody's seven minutes was edited down to a, still lengthy, five minutes and 52 seconds.

It is never admitted that Mercury ever suffered any doubts as to whether they had made the right decision in releasing 'Bohemian Rhapsody' as a single but it is very possible that he did. At this point, in autumn 1975, Queen were not in any position to expect special treatment – they needed the oxygen of radio airplay just like any other band. And perhaps this is why Freddie quietly slipped along to see his friend DJ Kenny Everett with an advance copy of the single.

On learning the record's length, Everett privately doubted that radio stations would welcome it but, once he heard the single, he went into a rapturous spin, uttering the words that would go down in Queen folklore – 'Forget it! It could be half an hour long. It's going to be number one for centuries!' A typically enthusiastic Everett exaggeration perhaps, but the colourful and flamboyant disc jockey threw his professional weight behind the unreleased single by playing it repeatedly on his show over the next two days, despite the fact that Capital Radio hadn't yet officially accepted it.

Pete Brown recalls, 'Kenny would yabber about this record he had, but couldn't play, yet, then say, "Oops, my finger must've slipped." and on it would come again and again.' Everett's agent, Jo Gurnett confirms, 'Kenny was hugely instrumental in getting Queen airplay for "Bohemian Rhapsody". He was incredibly enthusiastic about the record and played it all the time at home too.' And Tony Brainsby remembers, 'It was the kind of record that would either go to number one and make Queen, or it'd die a death and be their epitaph. I liked it, but I also thought, Who the hell is going to play it? It was a risky move but they were all astute enough to take a chance with it.' Judging by the fact that Capital Radio's switchboard was jammed with calls from stunned listeners eager to find out when the single would be released, the gamble was about to pay off.

'Bohemian Rhapsody'/'I'm in Love with my Car', in a picture cover sleeve, was officially released on 31 October 1975 and the bizarre melding of rock and opera knocked the music industry sideways. The mid-seventies was already a kaleidoscope of musical styles but this defied any definition. The song had three distinct parts to it. Starting with a melodic ballad, it then segued into complicated multi-tracking harmonic operatics which had involved nearly 200 vocal overdubs, before exploding into foot-stomping, head-bending hard rock. Queen had always been different, even when flirting with the popular musical styles of the day, but this was their greatest explosion of creativity yet. Arguably, 'Bohemian Rhapsody' was as much a watershed in the music scene as the Beatles' *Sgt. Pepper's Lonely Hearts Club Band* album had been eight years before. And, despite Queen's phenomenal long-term success, their future compositions never matched it.

From the outset, the song had been Mercury's baby. He had it all figured out before he even arrived at the studio, to the extent that he had had all the harmonies written out so that the others just had to sing them. John Deacon later recalled, 'Freddie played it for us in the studio and Roger, Brian and I played along with it and just came up with that feel. It was very easy to do.' However, the song took nearly three weeks to record; the vocals, with double and sometimes treble tracking of a single line, taking one week alone.

'Bohemian Rhapsody' was technically clever and reeked of confidence. Its meaning would be endlessly analysed, but in essence it's not actually about anything; the lyrics tell an indecipherable story. Mercury, the master of grandiose pomp, refused to be nailed down as to the inspiration behind it, sometimes being flippant, at times scoffing at how seriously it was all being taken. But he would also flare up at the first criticism and irritably demand, 'Who can you compare it to? Name one group.'

Some wondered whether there was another factor in Mercury's penning of this number. His total avoidance of drugs in the late sixties had changed over the years as, with his broadening horizons, his exposure to drugs and drug-taking had increased. Before long, he was known to be using cocaine, which had to have started sometime around the mid-seventies. Could Freddie's early experiments with cocaine have coincided with his writing of 'Bohemian Rhapsody'? Various performers before and since Mercury have been convinced that drugs can release the mind and help them produce their best work.

Whatever its origins, 'Bo Rhap', as it became known, certainly posed a challenge for rock critics who were split down the middle about it. The only thing they could agree on was that it would be unlikely to receive radio airplay in its entirety. But it did and its effect on the public was dramatic – you either loved it or loathed it. This polarised response was best illustrated when, over ten years later, one Midlands radio station poll resulted in 'Bohemian Rhapsody' being voted both the Best Ever Record and the Worst Ever Record.

In 1975 the song's supporters far outweighed its detractors. It captivated a huge chunk of the record-buying public, and, from its starting point of number forty-seven, it winged its way to the top of the UK singles chart. The following year it won the Ivor Novello Award for the Best-Selling British Record, in addition to attracting a

1976 Grammy nomination in the Best Pop Vocal Performance by a Group category.

It made its mark too among Queen's peers, as Abba stars Benny Andersson and Bjorn Ulvaeus both recall. Says Benny, 'Bohemian Rhapsody' took rock and pop away from the normal path. Its sheer originality completely matched Queen's originality.' Whilst Bjorn recalls, 'I was very green with envy when I heard "Bohemian Rhapsody" for the first time. Queen were very inspirational to both Benny and myself. I remember feeling, in a strange way right even from the very start, that Queen were different from anyone else. With "Bohemian Rhapsody", we felt they were going in the same direction as us – towards a more theatrical, dramatic sound. And, of course, "Bohemian Rhapsody" to Benny and I, was another spur on the road that would eventually lead us into musicals.'

Abba and Queen would often be considered the two best bands to emerge from the seventies and definite parallels can be drawn. Both bands became renowned for their studio craftsmanship, for producing intelligent music and for writing strong songs of which one of the hallmarks was the effective use of harmonies. Ulvaeus reveals, 'People can't normally hear the complexity of the harmonies in a song. Certainly in the case of some Abba songs, they sounded simple when they were actually quite complex. With "Bohemian Rhapsody" you could not mistake the brilliant harmonies.'

The stir 'Bohemian Rhapsody' made on its release again ensured heightened media interest in Queen and Freddie Mercury, as its writer, in particular. Says Tony Brainsby, 'Over the years a myth has grown around Freddie, that from the start of Queen's career he rarely gave interviews, but that's not true. Of course he did them. Any aspiring pop star has to, to get their name known. Freddie did tons of stuff for teenybop magazines when he'd throw around a few "my dears" and give out his great fruity laugh. There were no preconditions but whenever he was asked about his background he'd toss back an answer, without really answering. For a long time no one in the press had a clue even as to what his real name was. Freddie avoided at all costs mentioning Zanzibar. He just didn't think it fitted his image and he desperately didn't want to be thought of as an unlikely rock star.'

But Mercury's resistance to talking to the media had since set in, and now, faced with the most frenzied attention Queen had yet received, Brainsby came up with a new strategy to get around this reluctance. He says, 'In this business you must create a mystique, which you won't do by trotting someone out at the drop of a hat. So Freddie became a commodity only to be brought out for the major interviews, like national newspapers, *NME* front covers, etc. The fact that this was right up Freddie's street, was a bonus, I guess. When Fred did do an interview, people never got close to him because he treated these sessions exactly like a performance. He'd put on a big show for the journalists and photographers and be wonderfully camp and outrageous.' John Deacon's quiet reserve did not make him a natural candidate for the interview circuit, and so over the years it mainly fell to Roger Taylor and Brian May to handle the press.

Of course, the biggest plug Queen could get for their latest single was to appear on *Top of the Pops* but that would be difficult because of the highly technical nature of the number. Queen did perform it live on stage – latterly, in the days of stadium giant video screens, they would leave the stage during the middle section. But right then for TV they had to come up with a solution – and fast, as they were scheduled to start a 24-date UK tour.

Their thoughts therefore turned to making a promotional film and, as they were booked into Elstree Studios for tour rehearsals anyway, it made sense to shoot something that same day there, which is what they did on 10 November under the guidance of director Bruce Gowers, who had previously made the Queen film *Live at the Rainbow*. It took a mere four hours to shoot, a single day to edit and cost around £4,500 – yet the result was semi-psychedelic and eerily dramatic and would launch a whole new genre in rock.

Priscilla Presley has maintained that the choreographed performance of the theme song to Elvis's classic 1957 hit film *Jailhouse Rock* – a number which, due to Mercury's love of 'The King', Queen often included in their early repertoire – is 'the music world's first video'.

And throughout the sixties promo clips were steadily developed and it could also be argued that the hugely innovative promotional film produced to accompany the Abba hit 'S.O.S.', released in the summer of 1975, was the forerunner to the 'Bohemian Rhapsody' video. But the modern pop video, as we know it, arrived on 20 November 1975 when Queen's 'Bohemian Rhapsody' premiered on *Top of the Pops*. As a result, the face of pop music marketing changed for ever.

Sales of the single skyrocketed – 'Bohemian Rhapsody' went platinum, swiftly selling in excess of 1.25 million copies in the UK alone. And the following day Queen's new album, called *A Night at the Opera*, was released in Britain. Long before the album's completion Queen had been confident that they had pulled off something different this time, that they had musically surpassed everything they had thus far achieved. Like the single, the album reached platinum status at home; and in America, where it was released on 2 December, it went gold.

Not everyone, however, was blown away by the bombshell single and video. DJ John Peel's initial liking for Queen when they had started out had been eroded by what he felt was the band's conceited style. He says, 'I took the mickey out of them one night on *Top of the Pops* and soon afterwards something appeared in a newspaper, saying that Freddie Mercury and Roger Taylor were going to punch me out if they ever saw me. Thankfully, they never did. But, seriously, most people came to class "Bohemian Rhapsody" as the beginning of Queen. But, for me, it was the end of Queen. After that they became too bombastic in style for my taste.'

The band themselves were already a week into their tour, which had commenced at the Liverpool Empire, and were understandably very much on a euphoric high: 'Bohemian Rhapsody' was just about to hit the top. Perhaps this high-profile success had gone to Mercury's head for he began to display signs of excessive self-importance, as Tony Brainsby discovered. As an independent public relations consultant, Tony handled other artistes and it was because of this that a clash arose between himself and Mercury when Queen hit Manchester to play two shows at the Free Trade Hall on 26 November.

Tony explains, 'At this point I also represented Wings and they were touring Britain at the same time as Queen. Normally I didn't go on the road with any band, but this was, after all, Paul McCartney, and on something like only his second tour of Britain in a long time. The media went mad, giving Wings daily coverage. But, although I went on that tour, I was still dealing with all my other business by phone. I neglected no one. Freddie, however, got jealous that McCartney was getting this massive attention.'

He goes on, 'Queen were basking in all their "Bohemian Rhapsody" glory but they weren't yet superstars. Anyway, I got this imperious summons from Freddie to come to Manchester to see him and that's the only time we had – I hesitate to call it a falling out, but he tried to give me a right bollocking as he paced angrily about the hotel room. He kept demanding, "What's going on? Why are you not on the road with us? And *why* is McCartney getting all this coverage?" Well! I told Freddie I was getting Queen as much attention as was possible and that there was nothing more to do. In the end I had to tell him straight that, although I was talking incessantly to people about Queen, they were queuing round the block instead to speak to Paul McCartney and that was that. Freddie, though, refused to accept it.'

As their PR consultant rejoined the ex-Beatle, Queen carried on with four gigs at London's Hammersmith Odeon, eventually heading north and crossing the border into Scotland after their 11 December gig at Newcastle City Hall for their upcoming date two nights later at the Caird Hall in Dundee. It was at this point that they ran into a spot of trouble. Personal manager Pete Brown recalls, 'Our coach was stopped on the motorway by police waiting for us. An ex-crew member had been sacked by the PA company – not Queen – but he had apparently told the cops, wrongly, that Queen were all high on drugs. Well, roadblocks had been set up, sealing off every exit route. Nobody had anything, but I remember the sinking anxiety that some silly sod in the entourage might have something, however small, on him. But no one had. It didn't stop us all being dragged to the cop shop as the police obviously thought they had the scoop of the year and were rifling through the bus, sticking their noses into the ashtrays – the lot. When they failed to come up with so much as a joint, their disappointment was almost laughable.'

The tour resumed, taking them right up to the Capitol in Aberdeen on 14 December before winding their way back down the length of the country. By now it was a safe bet that 'Bohemian Rhapsody' would hold on to the top slot long enough to be that year's Christmas number one. It was a coveted distinction but, as the tour came to a close and Queen took time off to go and see other bands playing, they discovered that not everyone was overjoyed at the prospect.

One night they visited the Brighton Dome to see a performance by Hot Chocolate, fronted by singer Errol Brown. Pete Brown recalls, 'They were a great band and their number "You Sexy Thing" was sitting at number two. Afterwards we were all in the restaurant of the hotel we were staying at and suddenly Errol burst in. He headed straight for Queen and roared at the top of his lungs, "You bastards! My main shot at a Christmas number one! You bastards!" It was so damned funny!'

A return visit to the Hammersmith Odeon on Christmas Eve rounded off Queen's tour with a performance that was televised live by *The Old Grey Whistle Test* and picked up for simultaneous broadcast on BBC Radio 1. Just after Boxing Day *A Night at the Opera* too hit the number one spot in Britain's album charts, after reaching sales of over 250,000, thereby putting the final punctuation mark to Queen's most successful year yet. They had come a long way in twelve months. And they were sure that this was only the beginning.

# AMERICAN DREAM

QUEEN FACED THE new year brimming over with enthusiasm. Their first number one album *A Night at the Opera* would enjoy a UK chart run of nearly a year. And 'Bohemian Rhapsody' maintained its top slot for the ninth consecutive week (thereby equalling a twenty-year-old record held by American star Slim Whitman with 'Rose Marie'), before being toppled by Abba's 'Mamma Mia' at the end of January 1976. Innumerable accolades would also begin to flow in; Queen had already walked off with a clutch of awards at the annual music press polls. To build upon this success, their tour diary was chock-a-block – starting with three major excursions around the globe by the end of spring.

With rehearsals completed, they embarked on the first of these, a 32-date tour of North America and Canada. Fortunately the pressure was slightly eased by arranging to play more gigs at fewer venues. Wishbone Ash lead guitarist Andy Powell explains, 'A successful band need to be like an army unit. There are an awful lot of idiots in rock land, and you have to be able to depend on those around you.'

Queen always tried to ensure that their support unit was up to scratch and for this trip they had acquired a new team member, experienced tour manager Gerry Stickells, who had the added attraction of having once worked for Queen's idol, the late Jimi Hendrix. Stickells would become an essential cog in the moving wheel of the band's life on the road.

For Queen the days of American audiences being unfamiliar with their work were over. 'Bohemian Rhapsody' would breach the Top Ten, while *A Night at the Opera* achieved number four in the US singles and albums charts respectively. This hike in their Stateside popularity was reflected by the rousing reception they enjoyed from their opening gig, on 27 January 1976 at the Palace Theater in Waterbury, onwards.

At last, it felt like they had arrived in America. They brought the house down at every gig, and wherever then went off-stage they were mobbed by crazed admirers. All four guys had become the object of unfettered female devotion and it often proved tricky even to negotiate the small distance between a car and a hotel entrance. Security precautions had to be tightened to combat an increasing number of groupies determined not only to discover which rooms the band occupied but, specifically, which room belonged to whom. And that included Freddie Mercury's. In contrast to his strengthening bisexual reputation, he had adopted a much more macho on-stage style, particularly in America, and just as girls feverishly fantasised about the dishy drummer, the bashful bass player and the gentle guitarist, so they easily lusted after the slinky singer with wicked glinting eyes who crooked one long black-painted fingernail alluringly at them.

Their schedule left little room for socialising but when, after gigging through Boston and Philadelphia, Queen arrived in New York in early February for four consecutive nights at the Beacon Theater they eagerly accepted an invitation from their old Mott the Hoople mate, lead singer Ian Hunter, to join him at the famous Electric Ladyland Studios where he was busy laying down a solo album for another Queen friend, producer Roy Thomas Baker.

Taylor, May and Mercury wound up singing backing vocals on the track 'You Nearly Done Me In' on Hunter's album *All American Alien Boy*.

It was this four-night stint in New York that ignited Mercury's passion for the city that never sleeps. After a gig, it became Queen's practice to have a civilised meal together, before going their separate ways. In Freddie's case that meant exploring the seedier side of big city life. Descending on local gay bars (and sometimes those in the most dubious parts of the city), he had a particular penchant for cruising the streets sprawled in the comfort of his darkened limousine, drinking his favourite iced vodka and surveying the nightlife. The opportunity and inclination to indulge his decadent appetite to the full would grow apace with his fame.

Queen's fame and its effects were now also beginning to evolve in different ways. Two weeks later, when they arrived in Chicago they learned that their four albums were currently featured in the UK Top Thirty – *Queen* even making it to number twenty-four – two years on from its release. Mercury promptly publicly congratulated themselves and their loyal British subjects back home, by raising a champagne toast on stage at the Auditorium Theater, nakedly revelling in the audience adulation. But off-stage, the euphoric bubbles quickly fell flat for the band's personal manager Pete Brown.

It was one of his duties to settle hotel bills but when their two-day stay in Chicago ended Brown was advised by the hotel receptionist that the Queen credit card was over-extended. 'Worse still,' says Pete, 'it was a Sunday with no banks open. I was worried because I had such a lot still to organise in getting the band and their luggage to the airport and so I argued with the desk clerk, insisting that he accept the credit card now and promising that it would be sorted out later. But he wasn't having it. I didn't have the time for this hassle and began to turn away when suddenly the guy pulled a gun on me. I told him, "Take it easy mate! I've got all the time in the world!".'

This hair-raising incident was resolved when the local promoter was summoned and settled the account in cash but Pete, already very unnerved, was now panicking about something else. 'We'd missed our flight,' he explains, 'and I was scared stiff that Queen would not make it to their next gig, which was in St Louis, on time.' He knew by now that Queen expected super-efficiency from their staff and that they rarely tolerated being let down. This upset in the schedule was clearly not of Pete Brown's making but that was no comfort to him. He admits, 'My nerves were in shreds. I was sure I'd get the sack but I managed to arrange for a fleet of station wagons to get the band on their way.'

Queen made their St Louis gig on time and the remainder of the tour, which took in five shows at the Santa Monica Civic Auditorium in Los Angeles, ended on 13 March at San Diego's Sports Arena without further mishap. With scarcely time to catch their breath, and still buoyed up by the exhilaration of having completed a breathlessly exciting successful US tour, just nine days later they returned to the scene of their first significant triumph when they began their second tour of Japan.

It was to be a run of eleven shows throughout the country, three of which were at the Budokan Martial Arts Hall, where Queen opened on 22 March and to which they would return for two consecutive nights (the latter of which was on 1 April), before winding up the tour three days later at Tokyo's Nichidai Kodo. In the land where Queenmania was born it was surprising that the band's hottest success, 'Bohemian Rhapsody', only reached number forty-eight in the charts. But its parent album gave Queen a number nine hit in the Far East and the fan reaction proved as satisfyingly wild as ever. No more than a week later, their globe-trotting landed them in the Antipodes.

By now the mood was changing. Queen already knew that they were up to the task facing them on this, their first tour of Australia. But, understandably, their anticipation was laced with a decided wariness, after the bad reception they had received two years earlier, both at the music festival in Melbourne and from the Aussie press. They were also suffering from fatigue and Mercury was particularly stressed out. Precisely because of what happened here in 1974, they were determined not only to shine but also to silence their critics and at each gig, starting with the Entertainments Centre in Perth on 11 April, they pulled out all the stops to ensure success. The tangible tension emanating from the band might have infused their performances with extra razor-like vigour but it had to find an outlet, and unfortunately that outlet became the long-suffering Pete Brown.

Halfway through the tour, Queen were to perform two gigs at Sydney's Horden Pavilion and things turned ugly all because, on arrival, it transpired that the theatre could only be reached via a huge fairground which made driving straight to the door in a fleet of cars a bit difficult. Pete Brown reveals, 'One look was enough to see that there was no way you could drive through the crowds so I asked the band to get out and walk. Freddie flashed, "My dear, I can't possibly walk anywhere!", and he remained stubbornly in the limo. That meant we had to drive through at a snail's pace to avoid hurting anyone and Freddie acted up with the champagne glasses all the way. As you might expect, your average Aussie male felt provoked and suddenly the catcalls started. They shouted things like "Pommie Pussies", and worse, at us through the windscreens, giving us the fingers and then as the mood grew uglier, they started banging on the slow-moving car roofs with clenched fists.'

After what must have seemed like an eternity they arrived at the Pavilion and got safely inside, whereupon Mercury, in a white-hot temper, despite the fact that it had been his own arrogance that had sparked off the trouble, immediately rounded on their personal manager. Brown reveals, 'Freddie was so angry that he smashed a big mirror over my head and then ordered me to get a brush and sweep up the broken glass at once. He could be very tough and he often made me cry during my years with Queen.'

Mercury would explain away such temperamental bouts as an involuntary response to the immense pressure he felt under, and declare that it was not at all typical of him. And certainly Pete Brown's affection for Freddie was solid enough not to be shattered by this spontaneous outburst of violence. On the contrary, Pete was amazingly generous. He defends Freddie by saying, 'It was the

humiliation he had suffered, you see. He had to take it out on someone. I was just nearest. I understood.' This incident was forgotten
long before Queen returned home on 25 April, tired but delighted at
having taken another scalp; by the time the last encore note had rung
out at Brisbane's Festival Hall both their new single and album sat
atop the Australian charts – wiping out, for good, the memory of
their disastrous debut down under.

By this time Queen had already spent a third of the year on the
road, practically non-stop touring. While, professionally, it was essential to capitalise on the explosive success surrounding 'Bohemian
Rhapsody', being away from London so much significantly lessened
the space they could make for their individual personal relationships.

Roger Taylor still very much enjoyed the freedom of bachelor-
hood, but the other three had been in stable relationships for years.
Following John Deacon's example, the month after their return from
Australia, Brian May married his long-time girlfriend Christine
Mullen on 29 May 1976 at St Osmund's Roman Catholic Church in
Barnes. Freddie Mercury's position was more complex. He was
facing some serious inner conflicts that would take him several more
months to resolve and in the meantime he remained extremely close
to Mary Austin.

In tune with this pervading sense of personal contentment,
Queen's new single was a gentle straightforward ballad. 'Bohemian
Rhapsody' was an impossible act to follow and inevitably its succes-
sor would suffer by comparison. But 'You're My Best Friend'/'39'
released on 18 June, became instantly popular. Up till now, all
Queen singles had been penned by either Mercury or May.
However, 'You're My Best Friend' was written by John Deacon and
it gave the band a number seven hit.

Because of the previous management upheavals and the financial
drain of the settlement with Trident, Queen only started to reap the
fruits of their labours with their fourth album *A Night at the Opera*; at
least that was how Mercury viewed it. He was now utilising some of
his share of this money to finance his growing use of cocaine and to

indulge his fancies, whatever they were, in a private world that was changing at an unsettling rate. But for Freddie, as for his three band-mates, Queen itself continued to provide their touchstone.

It was time, anyway, to come down to earth. New material had to be written and, though the opportunities for this grew scarcer, the more successful they became, right then they still could set aside what they termed 'routine time'. It was their practice to individually write material which each would then bring into the studio to be picked over by the others. There was plenty of lively, sometimes heated, but always constructive argument as they separated the wheat from the chaff. They hoped to release their new album by the year's end. But, before that, they were to make a welcome return to live performance.

Queen would make only four more stage appearances that year, all in September. The first two kicked off the month at the Playhouse Theatre during the annual Edinburgh Festival where, supported by the band Supercharge, they set their audiences alight. Then, just over a week later, they swapped Scotland for Wales and an outdoor gig at Cardiff Castle. Billed as 'Queen at the Castle' they were backed by Manfred Mann's Earthband, Frankie Miller's Full House and Andy Fairweather-Low. A long summer drought chose that night to break and torrential rain turned the grounds into a quagmire for the 12,000-strong crowd.

But nothing could dampen Queen's anticipation of their final gig of 1976 – a free concert in London's Hyde Park. The date was 18 September and the original instigator was Richard Branson (later to become the multi-millionaire Virgin Group supremo). Says Branson, 'I had come up with the idea of staging a free open-air concert in Hyde Park, an event that would promote a few bands at the same time. The problem was, at that time I couldn't afford to finance it myself, so I approached Queen, through Roger Taylor whom I already knew, to see if they were interested in this proposi-tion. Having been to the Rolling Stones' Hyde Park concert in 1969, I remembered just what a special feeling a huge free gig like that generates. I also thought that Queen might *really* break in Britain as a result of that sort of exposure.'

Queen were immediately up for it but it was Richard who set about pulling the various strands together by working through all the necessary stipulations laid down by the Metropolitan Police and the London Parks Committee concerning, among other things, the facilities to be provided for such a public gathering, security arrangements for the band, even establishing the exact time the concert could start and had to finish. 'When I had all the necessary clearances,' says Branson, 'and the project was a definite goer, I handed it over to the Queen management to take from there.'

Despite following all the required procedures, confusion still descended upon London's already congested traffic system when around 150,000 people converged on the park. Capital Radio was covering the event live, with commentary from Kenny Everett and Nicky Horne, and with support acts Kiki Dee, Steve Hillage and Supercharge, the compère for the day was BBC's Bob Harris. The professional association between Queen and Harris had turned into a close friendship sustained by mutual respect. Says Bob, 'Queen were very bright and their overview was always keen but they were never exploitative and genuinely cared a lot for their fans.'

Harris recalls of the warm-up acts, 'Supercharge's lead singer was a rather overweight fella and he came storming on stage in a costume similar to Freddie's ballet dancer outfits. Not a pretty sight! And Kiki Dee? She'd recently had a number one hit with Elton John called 'Don't Go Breaking My Heart'. She had been desperately hoping to persuade Elton to perform it with her there but he didn't and that night she ended up singing the song to a cardboard cut-out of him instead.'

As darkness fell, Queen came on. According to Harris, 'The crowd by now literally stretched to the horizon and you could feel the rising anticipation. When the band walked on to the strains of "Bohemian Rhapsody" the audience just erupted.' Poured into a black leotard scooped to the navel and wearing ballet pumps, Mercury greeted the throng with the words, 'Welcome to our picnic by the Serpentine', before Queen launched into a high-voltage rendition of 'Keep Yourself Alive'.

Highly charged for the event anyway, the incredible audience reaction lifted Queen's performance to dizzy heights that night, earning them every ounce of the thunderous applause and the deafening demands for an encore that erupted when the band left the stage. Queen were only too eager to oblige but the police literally pulled the plug on them. The schedule had overrun by thirty minutes and the authorities were determined to adhere to the strict conditions laid down. They even threatened Freddie with summary arrest if he so much as dared place a foot back on stage. Queen bowed to the inevitable – but safe in the certain knowledge that they had achieved much. Richard Branson agrees. 'I believe it was a vitally important night for Queen and a turning point in their career.'

The critics were still not disposed to make an about-turn with regard to Queen, however, and when the new single, 'Somebody to Love'/'White Man', was released on 12 November, despite it charting at number two, they dubbed Mercury's love song as lacking in inspiration. They would level the same accusation against the album *A Day at the Races* which followed on 10 December. For his part, Brian May felt that the new album was more an extension of *A Night at the Opera*, rather than its successor, because the material that went into both had been written around the same time and therefore – he believed – did not properly reflect Queen's true development.

As with *A Night at the Opera*, Queen had taken their new album's name from a Marx Brothers film. As a publicity stunt, they held a pre-launch press reception for *A Day at the Races* in mid-October at Kempton Park racecourse near Sunbury-on-Thames.

Their private lives were also moving up a gear. John Deacon and Veronica, like Brian May and Chrissy, now lived in better-class accommodation – in Putney and Barnes respectively. Roger Taylor went the whole hog and bought a luxurious country house in Surrey, complete with extensive grounds and woodland. He'd lately called time on his footloose and fancy free lifestyle, having met and fallen for (during the many meetings to organise the Hyde Park gig) Richard Branson's personal assistant, Frenchwoman Dominique Beyrand, and she now moved in with him.

Freddie Mercury had been sharing a trendy flat in Kensington with Mary Austin but by the end of 1976 he had at last arrived at the major decision he had been wrestling with concerning his future emotional and sexual fulfilment. It had been a very personal struggle, but he now felt impelled to sacrifice his relationship with Mary for stronger desires. He deeply loved Austin and to his dying day he remained devoted to her, and she to him. Freddie once revealed that he considered Austin to be his common-law wife and certainly after his death, according to the terms of his will, she inherited the bulk of his estate. Mary remained involved with him in other ways throughout his life, but undoubtedly making this break brought Mercury huge relief. He could now pursue the gay life he deeply craved and 1977 marked the start of a period of reckless promiscuity that continued for at least five years.

Mercury was a mass of contradictions – for a man whose artistic sensibilities were so refined, he could go extremely downmarket when it came to his choice of bedmate after a night's partying on the gay scene. 'Dullness is a disease,' he boldly announced. 'I really need danger and excitement.' He claimed to have a phenomenal sex drive and boasted that he had bedded hundreds. Overall his stamina levels needed constant boosting and this phase also coincided with a rise in his use of cocaine. His lifestyle became especially hedonistic when Queen embarked on lengthy US/Canadian tours, the next of which was just about to begin.

Their most extensive tour yet got underway with a gig on 13 January at the Milwaukee Auditorium amid America's coldest winter conditions for a century. They were accompanied by the group Thin Lizzy, which featured lead guitarist Scott Gorham and frontman Phil Lynott. Thin Lizzy's manager Chris O'Donnell recalls landing this support slot.

Says Chris, 'Thin Lizzy had themselves been due to tour America.

Then Brian Robertson tried to stop a bottle being broken over Frankie Miller's head one night at the Speakeasy Club and ended up with a badly gashed hand which left him unable to play the guitar. And it was when I was in the States trying to find a way of keeping Lizzy's new album alive that I got a surprise phone call from Howard Rose, Queen's US agent, asking if Thin Lizzy would support them on their upcoming tour.'

O'Donnell admits to being unable to believe their luck but this was quickly tempered by an experience that left him less than impressed. He explains, 'Back in London I'd gone over to the Reid offices to discuss the tour and at that time Queen were hoping to do *Top of the Pops* for "Somebody to Love". But the thing is, it had quickly slipped back three places from number two. Well there was a girl there screaming down the phone to someone at the BBC that Queen just *had* to get on the show. The whole premise of *TOTP* was that it only featured bands whose records were rising up the charts. But this girl's whole attitude spelt out, "But we're Queen! We're apart from all that!".'

Nevertheless, with Gary Moore substituting for the injured Brian Robertson, Thin Lizzy joined Queen when they were a couple of dates into the US tour. The eventful trip proved a revelation for Chris O'Donnell. He states, 'There were definitely times when Thin Lizzy played Queen off the stage. I felt that, as good as Queen were, they were now so stylised that the slightest thing going wrong threw the whole perfect balance right off, whereas Lizzy were so hungry and raw that they had an unpredictable energy on stage and it showed. The two bands were a great package though.'

That they also got along well is verified by Thin Lizzy's lead guitarist, the irrepressible Californian Scott Gorham. He reveals, 'A lot of bands get paranoid about not letting the support act upstage them and to keep you down they won't give you a sound check etc. But we didn't get any of that from Queen. They said right away, "Here's the PA. Now you'll need sound checks and lights, and what else?" Together we had the attitude that we would set out as a British attack to conquer America.' He goes on, 'Of course we were two very different bands. Lizzy was a sort of punk band with street cred, whereas Queen were very polished and sophisticated – so you see there was no competitiveness on that score.'

The claustrophobic nature of touring together, however, can prove to be a 'warts-and-all' eye-opener and this was the case for Chris O'Donnell who began to feel disillusioned, especially with regard to Mercury. He states, 'To me Queen were one of the greatest rock bands ever, but not all America is New York and LA – you play an awful lot of gigs in between. On arrival at one airport we headed as usual for the cars being laid on to pick us up. This was a Midwest town where the facilities were not that great but we found that three shiny black saloon cars had been hired from the local funeral parlour and were the best cars they had. Well, Freddie threw a major wobbly and went into a huge sulk because there was no limousine and he flatly refused to get into the car. What made it seem more pointless to me was that I know for a fact that he had been pre-warned that in these places he should not expect stretch limos and still he had to make a big issue about it.'

An isolated display of petulance would have been easy to overlook but Chris found Mercury difficult in general on that trip. 'He was in a spiral of the lifestyle he led,' states Chris. 'It can happen and, of course, these tantrums really stemmed from other, deeper problems. But he just wasn't in a real situation. He had this great court around him. Pete Brown was on that trip, as were Freddie's two personal assistants Paul Prenter and Joe Fannelli, among others. He also had an American hairdresser who shadowed him everywhere, a personal masseur, as well as a dresser and it was sycophancy all the way with, "Freddie darling this and Freddie darling that." On stage, Mercury was the consummate professional and very driven by fame. But he had to live the whole thing off stage too. Of course, in one way he ended up paying the price for that.'

About two weeks into the tour Chris had special cause to remember the gig at Chicago's Stadium. 'The weather was atrocious and the equipment trucks had been delayed travelling down from Montreal. At the theatre the fans were queuing round the block, stamping their feet and blowing on their hands to try to keep warm and the promoter began pleading with Freddie to let them open the doors and get the kids inside. He told Freddie that many were literally turning blue outside and his only response was, "Darling, we haven't had a sound check yet. We can't possibly let them hear Queen until then." And what's more, I watched him − deliberately, it seemed to me − set about delaying the whole process, just to make his point. I'd stand in the wings night after night on that tour and be amazed at Queen's performance and, as a showman, Freddie had no equal. But close up? He irked me such a lot. It was a big disappointment.'

O'Donnell continues, 'On that tour, interestingly though, what struck me was how Queen was constructed − how each of the four members had a role to play. Everyone talks about Brian May's distinctive signature guitar sound and Freddie Mercury's histrionics but to me Roger Taylor's powerful drumming and John Deacon's throbbing basswork were like a constant heartbeat within Queen's music. They were the powerhouse rhythm section and, to an extent, I feel that that has never been properly acknowledged. Those two were more equal than they are ever given the credit for and together really underpinned the Queen sound.'

He goes on, 'Roger is the consummate rock drummer and I always felt that there was another Roger Taylor inside desperate to explore beyond the confines of playing only in Queen. I felt that at some point he would have liked to have played with other musicians. I don't mean that he felt constricted in Queen, but you never knew with Roger where he could have gone on to, out of all four members. He was always off clubbing with Thin Lizzy and there too it seemed to me that he had a closeness with other musicians that was separate to his friendships within Queen.'

As for John Deacon? 'Every band needs a linchpin,' continues Chris, 'someone who really holds the band together and in Queen I believe, that was John. He was smart in business matters and really looked after their affairs more than people generally know. He is a very astute guy. He always wanted to know what was going on and kept himself aware of the band finances and the structure of the

band's deals. He was quiet certainly, but he noticed absolutely everything that was going on and made a contribution if and when he felt
there was something to say. Bands don't just happen. They have to
work at pulling together and John Deacon, for me, was the one in
Queen who would ultimately make sure that everyone agreed.'

Chris believes that the very fact that all four members had such
different natures was what made them a great band. Those same
differences were why they would go their separate ways after their
sumptuous backstage after-gig meal was over. 'I'd never seen tour
catering like it,' says O'Donnell. 'They went for the four-course
gourmet routine, complete with candelabra. But then what
happened was that Brian and Roger, who were the real rockers of
the band, would slip away with Phil and Scott to hang out at some
club in town, leaving Freddie and John. John gradually drifted away,
at which point Freddie would go off to prowl the gay clubs and even
there I felt everything had to be rigidly planned.'

But not everything could be scripted and audience reaction can be
notoriously unpredictable, as Scott Gorham can testify. He says, 'One
night, in the heat of it all, as I was playing suddenly this thing
whizzed past, missing my face by a fraction, to thud behind me. I
looked round and saw it was a lemon. I thought, Is there a hidden
message behind this piece of fruit here, or what? I mean, why not an
apple or a lettuce? Why a lemon? We did our set and I went out
front to watch Queen and all of a sudden from the same area in the
audience a hail of about a dozen eggs went up in the air! They're all
skating about, and suddenly Brian lands right on his ass. I started to
laugh real hard, then stopped. I thought, What are you laughing at?
You got lemoned! I couldn't work out which was worse – an egg or
a lemon? Anyway I looked into the audience, thinking, There's a
guy somewhere in there with a whole salad bar just waiting for us.
We may not be getting paid much, but hell we'll sure eat well!'

On 5 February Queen played the highly prestigious Madison
Square Garden in New York to a capacity crowd. To them this was
major league. Scott Gorham understands why. 'The building ain't
much in itself but you know you're there. It's Madison Square

Garden – you've made it!' Pete Brown remembers it as having been a terrific night which left the entire band wired. He says, 'Somebody then piped up that Yes headlined three consecutive nights so Freddie leaped up roaring, "Right! Five nights!" meaning he wouldn't be content until Queen had more than bettered the Yes record at the Garden.'

This element of fierce rivalry was also prevalent within Queen itself. Brown continues, 'They were always extremely tough on each other. No one got away with a thing. For example, John didn't feel comfortable wearing certain outfits, but he had to wear them nonetheless because Queen had a very strong sense of image. In some ways they were all, at one point, pushed by the others into things that individually they didn't feel right about, but they agreed to because it was part of being Queen.' He adds, 'They set themselves such high standards and they encouraged one another all the time, driving themselves relentlessly. If Freddie wanted to be the best frontman in the world, then Brian had to be the greatest guitarist, John and Roger determined to prove they were an unbeatable rhythm section and so on. It was that enormous self-imposed pressure that made them unique.'

They played to sell-out crowds as they travelled the country but American rock critics were still not prepared to give Queen a break, this time praising the support band's performance over the head-liners. Scott Gorham declares, 'Papers all over the place were saying that we were out there killing Queen and it just wasn't true.' It was hard to understand where Queen were falling down in appealing to the critics – their habit of comparing Queen unfavourably to the likes of Led Zeppelin and now Thin Lizzy would suggest that they preferred the hard rock style and sound. But that was exactly what Queen were delivering.

Americans had a reputation for being largely homophobic but Queen's stage style had by now already veered well away from projecting a gay image, as Chris O'Donnell confirms. 'Despite having a name like Queen and Freddie being the way he was, it was very much a boys' band. The gay element on stage just wasn't there now. They played hard rock and Freddie never came away with any of those familiar effeminate gestures.'

That is not to say that Queen did not attract its share of homo-sexual fans. Scott Gorham has vivid memories of their date on 6 March 1977 at the Winterland in San Francisco. He says, 'Frisco is kinda known as having a big gay community. So, okay, we were first up and I'm rushing about the left-hand side of the stage, thinking I'll go and mess with the audience on the right. The spotlight is chasin' me and I get over there and look up and there's like five hundred of the gayest guys I've ever seen, man! They were wearing sequinned hot pants, satin jump suits, huge floppy hats with giant nodding ostrich feathers and they're jumpin' off their seats, chuckin' feather boas in the air. When I arrived at their side they all started lunging over shouting, "Yeah! Shake it boy!" Geez, man! I'm thinkin', Whoa there buddy. I'm not real ready for that kinda contact! And hey, I'm already makin' a beeline to the farthest left I can find.'

According to Gorham, although everyone in Queen worked hard at each performance, it sometimes fell to Mercury to pull that extra something out. 'You should have seen Fred on that tour,' he states. 'He was just kickin', man. When Queen weren't going down partic-ularly well, he worked his ass off to ensure they still ended up with, like, three encores.' It wasn't just adrenalin that enabled Mercury to reach these extra heights, and Lizzy's lead guitarist had witnessed Mercury's cocaine use prior to the tour starting.

He recalls, 'I was recording at Olympic Studios before the tour, at the same time as Queen, and I met Freddie in the lobby and he had had a few hits. He said, "Hey Scott, can you come up and check out what we're doing upstairs. I really want you to listen to Brian's guitar sound. I think it's great, but he doesn't like it. Come and give us your opinion." I said, "Well, I'd rather not. Who needs another critic?" But Freddie had this persuasive way about him so I went and it sounded great. Anyway, by this time Fred had had a few more snorts and was really goin' at it. In fact, that was the first time I saw him take coke. I guess that's what was making him buzz the way he was.' Of the tour, Gorham goes on, 'I never actually saw Freddie doing drugs that trip. He wasn't throwing it about and making it a problem. He was very discreet.'

Just after the San Francisco gig, the hitherto illness-free tour was suddenly stalled by Mercury's recurring throat strain which resulted in two gigs being cancelled to allow him to rest. Queen scattered for brief sightseeing excursions, then regrouped to complete the last half dozen dates. Four of these took them to Canada where the tour ended on 18 March at the Northlands Arena in Edmonton.

It had been an arduous though, once again, exhilarating trip. But when the band arrived home it was to discover that their latest single had failed to fly. 'Tie Your Mother Down'/'You & I' had been released on 4 March but a month later would peak at only number thirty-one. The British singles charts were now dominated by easy listening artistes, with the likes of Abba, David Soul, Brotherhood of Man and Smokie packing the Top Twenty, with which Brian May's hard rocking number clearly, on this occasion, couldn't compete.

But another element – called punk rock – had also burst on to the British music scene. Some music fads came and went, but others changed the face of music forever and had a habit of bringing casualties down with them. No one knew whether or not this new abrasive form of musical expression – the very antithesis of the pomp and grandeur synonymous with Queen – was here to stay.

# EIGHT

# NAUGHTY
# NIGHTS

THE PUNK MOVEMENT was personified by groups like the Jam, the Damned and the Clash but it was the Sex Pistols, handled by former New York Dolls manager Malcolm McLaren, who were considered to have near single-handedly launched New Wave music in Britain. It was a style characterised by behaviour of the most uncouth kind and it brought with it a fashion for spiky hairstyles, slashed leather jackets hung with chains and body piercing. Aggressive in every sense and relying heavily on shock-value, it forced itself on to the music scene with all the finesse of the Doc Marten boots its disciples favoured. But, though its influence would be long-lasting, the movement itself would die out in about eighteen months.

Right then though it was so much in vogue that many music critics announced that bands like Queen, among others, had surely had their day. In conjunction with the disappointing performance of their latest single, these were hardly the best circumstances for Queen to be setting out on the road once more – this time with an eight-date European tour. They were determined, however, to remain unfazed by any perceived pressure from this direction. If anything, they went out of their way to emphasise the very elements they were now most famous for, in defiance of the prevailing trend for scruffy drab clothes. For instance, Freddie almost blinded their Swedish audience at the opening gig on 8 May at the Ice Stadium in Stockholm, when he shimmered on stage for the final encore wearing a dazzling silver leotard – after having played the gig dressed in a replica of a diaphanous costume once worn by the ballet dancer Nijinsky.

Ostentation was Queen's watchword and there was no let-up onstage or off, with their post-gig parties becoming legendary. According to May, these were held partly as an outlet for the overflow of post-gig adrenalin but their shindigs rapidly became *the* bash in town wherever they performed, attracting all sorts of guests and gatecrashers. Their penultimate gig was at Rotterdam's Ahoy Hall and it was during a celebration aboard a yacht there that Queen were presented with a total of 38 gold, silver and platinum awards in recognition of their enormous popularity in the Netherlands. But they could not rest on their laurels for long, as the UK leg soon beckoned.

Before that, on 20 May, Queen released their first EP, 'Good Old-Fashioned Lover Boy'/'Death on Two Legs (Dedicated to)'/ 'Tenement Funster'/'White Queen (As It Began)'. This record reacquainted Queen with the Top Twenty, although the EP stalled at number seventeen. Then, three days later, their two-week British tour began at the Bristol Hippodrome, ending with two gigs on 6/7 June at London's Earls Court, where they had decided to make a splash.

It was the Silver Jubilee year of Britain's monarch Queen Elizabeth II and this was excuse enough for Queen to put on their most majestic display yet. Smoke bombs, fireworks and inventive lighting effects were par for the course. So this time, at a cost of £50,000, they had a lavish crown-shaped lighting rig specially designed. This device, measuring approximately 25 feet tall and 54 feet wide, and weighing two tons, rose spectacularly from the stage at the beginning of each show amid a swirling cascade of dry ice. It thrilled the fans, but it left the band's already vocal critics steaming at the ears at what they considered the sheer pomposity of it all. The accusations that Queen were out of step with the current popular punk movement only got louder, culminating in a music press headline asking – with reference to Freddie Mercury – 'IS THIS MAN A PRAT?'

Not surprisingly, Queen now pulled back from speaking to the media. Roger Taylor acknowledges that Queen is the kind of full-on band that provokes an extreme response; people either love or hate them. But he conceded that the relentless press criticism niggled them. 'We got very insular and self-protective,' he said. Meanwhile, Queen's other spokesman, Brian May, analysed it further. He felt that their decision to largely shun the press was forced upon them: 'We had never really got on with the press and had a lot of enemies there, but by this time just about everyone in the press was blatantly against us.' Queen reasoned then that, as there were few out there willing to write anything constructive about them, it served little purpose to give them access.

Def Leppard frontman Joe Elliott, who would later become friends with Queen, understands this predicament, but states on behalf of rock bands in general, 'If we did what the critics wanted, we'd please them and piss off our audiences. Criticism can hurt when it's personal or spiteful and it often feels as though if you're talented they want to knife you. But really critics' effect is limited in music. A music mag's readership may be just 35,000 once a month and you're selling anything over half a million records. Percentage-wise they don't have a lot of clout, I'm afraid.'

Strange to say, the music press seemed more hostile to Queen on behalf of the punk bands, than the bands were themselves. This was the year that the Sex Pistols had a UK number one hit with 'God Save the Queen'. Malcolm McLaren calls this raucous number, which sparked an uproar and was banned from the airwaves, 'The most English, angst-ridden, toughest, mother-fucking rock song that's ever been written.' But when Queen and the Pistols had come into contact for the first time there was no open animosity.

It happened in August at Wessex Studios in North London, where Queen had lately shifted work on their new album, and Malcolm McLaren recalls, 'Queen were recording in studio one and Chris Thomas, the Sex Pistols' producer, was in studio two. On entering studio one on his way next door, Sid Vicious got down on his hands and knees and crawled through Freddie Mercury's legs. That was the day the Sex Pistols had finished their second and most notorious single, "God Save the Queen".'

Shaping their new material proved to be as intense an operation as usual for Queen. Singer Gary Glitter reflects, as an onlooker, 'They were a creative bunch, and sometimes things would get heated. When that happened, Roger was probably the one to make or break it – to stop the squabbling. But it also seemed to me that Freddie was the one with all the flair.'

There were rumours around now that Mercury was to branch out on his own but, in fact, the first Queen member to get into solo recording was Roger Taylor. On 26 August 1977 he released, in Britain, the single 'I Wanna Testify'/'Turn on the TV'. It did not chart but this was hardly surprising, since it received no radio exposure; although Taylor did give a very rare solo performance of it when he guested on the Marc Bolan TV show.

Queen's tenth single meanwhile exhibited a reassuringly familiar solidity. Called 'We are the Champions', it was a sturdy arm-locking rock anthem, guaranteed to be a crowd-pleaser and destined to become a favourite of sports fans around the world for decades. It was backed by the equally effective thumping simplicity of 'We will Rock You'. The promotional video was this time filmed before a live audience, and the band enlisted hundreds of 'extras' from their ever-burgeoning fan club to make up the crowd. Bruce Gowers, already responsible for four Queen videos, was this time unavailable and they hired Derek Burbridge to direct proceedings on 6 October at the New London Theatre Centre.

The new song was released the following day, where in Britain – despite being panned by the critics – it gave Queen their third number two hit single. Across the Atlantic, Elektra were enthusiastic about this latest offering. In America there had been four Queen single releases since 'Bohemian Rhapsody'; the performance of the last two had been particularly disappointing – the most recent being a number called 'Long Away' which had sunk without trace. But the record company was convinced that 'We are the Champions'/'We will Rock You' would attract huge airplay and released it as a double A-side. This instinct was rewarded when it notched up a number four hit – Queen's highest placing yet on the US singles charts. 'Champions' also proved popular in Europe, particularly France where it occupied the top slot for twelve consecutive weeks. All this success neatly primed the band for the release of *News of the World* on 28 October. Overall, this new album presented a far heavier rock sound and for the first time the US performance of a Queen album beat its UK best, when American fans swept it one place higher to number three and it reached platinum status, rather than gold. It went on to top the album charts in nine other countries.

Of all the accolades Queen's work attracted, there were some that would stand out particularly. This had been the case when, ten days prior to the recent album's release, 'Bohemian Rhapsody' won (jointly with Procol Harum's 1967 hit 'A Whiter Shade of Pale') the British Record Industry Britannia Award for the Best British Pop Single 1952–1977. The band eagerly bounced on stage at the Wembley Conference Centre to receive their awards from presenter Michael Aspel.

In contrast to the high-spirited delight displayed at this televised event, behind the scenes there were more sobering developments concerning Queen's management, past and present. Their recent heightened success meant that Queen were in a financial position to buy themselves out of the clause in their severance agreements with Trident which had given Trident a 1 per cent share of six future albums. However, the edge had been taken off their contentment at having successfully severed their last remaining tie with this company by the fact that things were not working out with John Reid.

Pete Brown declares, 'The problem was that Queen didn't feel

that John Reid was able to give them enough of his time, and that
didn't suit them. It's important to understand that the John Reid
offices were really the Elton John offices. All the staff had previously
worked for a long time for Elton, and their loyalties lay with him. If
Elton had a tour, that took priority. And with the different personalities in Queen, you can imagine how that went down!' Brian May
later explained, 'It wasn't so much a conflict, as a feeling that we
weren't getting any further in the relationship.'

Queen fully acknowledge that they made great headway during
the period they were under John Reid's management, and ending
their partnership with Reid was achieved a lot more easily than
dissolving their ties with Trident had been; after proper negotiation,
severance papers were legally drawn up. Pete Brown reveals, 'Queen
were filming the video for "We will Rock You" in the enormous
back garden at Roger's house in near Arctic conditions. There was
about a foot of snow and everybody who was standing around – as
you do on film shoots – was freezing and becoming a bit tetchy.
Anyway, in the midst of the umpteenth take and when the light was
beginning to get poor, John Reid arrived and he, Brian, Freddie,
John and Roger all piled into the back of Freddie's limo to sign the
severance documents.'

A condition of Queen breaking their contract with Reid before
the agreed expiry date was that the band had to pay a substantial sum
of money to John Reid Enterprises and, in addition, they had to sign
over a hefty percentage of royalties on existing albums. Two years
before, their split from Trident had left them effectively broke; their
severance now from John Reid would not impoverish them but
they had no way of knowing at this stage whether the heights they
had recently reached marked the zenith of a career that could go
downhill from then on. The financial penalties they had had to bear
therefore made it imperative that they make the correct decisions
concerning future management.

Queen had always had most confidence in themselves (as opposed
to anyone else), so it was perhaps natural that, after serious debate,
they decided to go for self-management, with assistance from lawyer

Jim Beach, tour manager Gerry Stickells and personal manager Pete Brown, who opted to stay with Queen, as did Paul Prenter, who, like Brown, had been employed originally through John Reid. Roger Taylor partly explained that their thinking was that it was preferable to be the employer than employee, as it were. He added, 'That doesn't mean we're power mad.' Queen indeed viewed this as a welcome opportunity to experience far greater artistic and financial freedom. With this new set-up in place, the band could concentrate their energies on their upcoming American tour; their second that year.

The tour opened on 11 November at the Cumberland County Civic Center in Portland and would sign off at the Los Angeles Forum three days before Christmas, having notched up two consecutive nights at Madison Square Garden, New York, along the way. That fell short of Mercury's earlier vow to beat Yes's record of three consecutive nights at this venue, but they had no complaints for this was the tour that truly marked Queen's conquest of North America.

Before going on the road, the band had gathered in New Haven, Connecticut, and from the start there were changes afoot. First, when John Deacon arrived he shocked everyone by having swapped his long hair for a near skinhead look. There had been times in the early seventies when John had been uncomfortable with the image imposed upon him, as on them all, for the sake of the band. Now he was asserting his right to choose his own style; the fact that it was so drastically different to that of the other three had nothing to do with a desire to stand out on stage and everything to do with common sense. A deeply practical man, Deacon had decided it would be an easier hairstyle to cope with on yet another arduous tour. But this did not prevent the crew from goodnaturedly ribbing him by calling him 'Birdman', as in *Birdman of Alcatraz*.

Travelling for the first time by private plane, on this trip they were also accompanied by DJ friend Bob Harris who was gathering footage for a Queen retrospective. Says Harris, 'I filmed as we went and for my documentary on them I also had individual lengthy one-on-one interview sessions with Freddie, Roger and Brian, and a shorter one with John. The idea was to knock it all together with the tour film but in the end, on my return to London, I just didn't have the time with all my other commitments and eventually Queen took back the film.'

He has glowing memories of the tour, however, declaring the whole trip an amazing experience. He particularly remembers Queen's visit to Las Vegas in mid-December. He says, 'A few days before, we had been in Chicago in temperatures of minus 15 degrees. Then we arrived in Vegas a few days before Queen were due to play and met just this wall of heat.' He goes on, 'Because we had a bit of a holiday, Roger, his minder and I one day worked our way down two strips, frequenting every hotel, casino, bar and club in our path.'

The Las Vegas venue was the Nevada Aladdin Theater and Bob Harris recalls the sight that met them as they rolled up in four limousines. 'The whole ground floor is covered with slot machines and the theatre entrance is right at the back. For a moment we were all thrown. Then the first limo moved off and the others followed, and they slowly drove all the way through between the rows of slot machines to the theatre door.' The next night, in San Diego to play the Sports Arena, John Deacon accidentally stumbled and put his hand straight through a plate-glass window which resulted in him receiving nineteen stitches. Yet he still managed to play bass for the last few gigs to complete the tour.

Harris says of his four fellow travellers, 'Freddie was so special. He always gave one hundred per cent. Brian is very studious, quiet and gentle, yet at the same time so expressive. Roger is the party animal who is up for anything clubbing-wise. While John is very much a family man. He takes his family on tour with him, or if not he goes straight back to the hotel room after gigs – not going on to a club, etc. Each are individual characters, but together the chemistry in Queen was special. So much so that I always felt that no matter what any one Queen member might go on to do individually, it could never ever be the same.'

Queen had no sooner returned to Britain than they had to face the fact that, as a busy recording and touring band, it was not practical for them to also try to manage themselves. Accordingly, they sought the advice of their new accountant, Peter Chant, in setting up a proper management structure. It eventually worked out that Chant took charge of the business and financial side, while Jim Beach left his partnership in a West London law firm and became Queen's manager and head of the newly set up Queen Productions Ltd. They also formed Queen Music Ltd and Queen Films Ltd; their intention was to finance their own videos and thereby retain control of the rights, whilst licensing them to EMI for promotional use.

By now Queen were such high earners that British income tax regulations would cripple them if they were to spend more than sixty-five days out of 365 in the UK. On their accountant's advice, the solution was to record and perform overseas. The income could then legitimately be channelled through a different company from Queen Productions and would be tax-free. After releasing the single 'Spread Your Wings'/'Sheer Heart Attack', on 10 February 1978, which bottomed out at a disappointing number thirty-four in the charts, Queen launched into a spring tour of Europe.

Between 12 April and 13 May they may have trekked over familiar territory but by the time the tour hit Britain for the final five gigs, the band's image was changing. Mercury had forsaken his trademark flashy leotards for a harsher look — shiny black PVC or leather. It made him look like a biker — not a style that Queen fans were used to and many weren't sure that they approved. Mercury, who once confessed, 'I rather fancy myself as a black panther', saw it as strengthening a manly stage image. But in the late seventies this biker image was also popular in gay nightclubs and maybe this was a way in which he could bring his on- and off-stage lives closer together.

Although Mercury maintained that his macho stage performances were all just an act, there were times when his overpowering adrenalin rush led him to reinforce this pretence by displaying aggression, and on at least one occasion abusing equipment. Queen did not have a reputation for destructively trashing the stage, but Freddie was captured on film toppling gigantic speaker cabinets, then leaping on to them and thrashing wildly into them with his sawn-off microphone stand.

In order to fulfil their songwriting and recording commitments Queen soon convened for the summer months in studios, first in Switzerland, then France. Taylor and Deacon left Britain soon after the European tour ended for Mountain Studios in Montreux where they began work on new material; but it was only when they moved to the Super Bear Studios in Nice that Mercury and May joined them and intensive work could really begin.

The pressure of creating fresh material in the shrinking space of time between touring commitments gave rise to a hothouse atmosphere in which inspiration flowed fast – inspiration that could come from any conceivable source. The first product of these sessions to be released was a controversial number called 'Bicycle Race', a Freddie Mercury song influenced by him having watched the annual Tour de France bicycle race as it passed through Nice and being motivated by the alluring sight of all those athletic guys encased in lycra and bent low over their handlebars. The number was paired with 'Fat Bottomed Girls' and the single's accompanying *risqué* video created quite a stir.

Over the years, Queen grew ever more extravagant with their videos, certainly in terms of the budgets allocated to each one, and also in their artistic depiction of the song. Their videos tended to be opulent, outlandish and outrageous, and this latest one definitely fell into the latter category, cheekily interpreting the song title literally.

The band hired Wimbledon Stadium for the shoot, during which, under director Steve Wood, sixty-five models staged a girls' bicycle race – the rub was, that the models were all naked. It was treated as high-spirited saucy fun by everyone – except the company that supplied the bikes. When they were returned to Halfords, Queen had to pay the cost of putting a new leather saddle on each cycle.

'Bicycle Race'/'Fat Bottomed Girls' was released on 13 October 1978, and the naked bottom pictured on the single's cover immediately caused an outcry and led to accusations of sexism. The uproar was such that on later sleeves the picture of the winning cyclist had a pair of skimpy black knickers superimposed on it. When Queen commenced another US/Canadian tour on 28 October 'Bicycle Race' had entered the UK charts at twenty-seven and would peak a month later at number eleven.

Packing thirty-five dates into seven weeks, this new tour was as hectic as ever, with even more elaborate on-stage visual effects. By now Queen were also renowned for the salacious entertainment provided at their post-gig parties. On this trip, one party in particular was to stand out – their Halloween bash was so outrageous that lurid reports of it made the newspapers across America and beyond; in Queen folklore it ranks as one of their most infamous.

It took place at a New Orleans hotel after a gig at the city's Civic Auditorium. Publicist Tony Brainsby, back working with Queen on the PR for their latest single after a three-year absence, remembers a twelve-hour orgy of excess which served up such exotica as a nude model hidden in a huge tray of slippery raw liver, half-naked girls dancing in bamboo cages that hung from the ceiling, topless waitresses and female mud wrestlers.

Brainsby recalls, 'It was a pretty wild night. I flew with a party of press from London to New Orleans, partied for twelve hours non-stop and staggered back to the airport, still not having been to bed. The huge hotel ballroom had been made up to resemble a jungle swamp. Masses of creepy vines dangled everywhere, dry ice smoke pumped all around, and there were snakes, strippers, dancers, dwarfs – you name it! All in all, it was a first-class party!'

He goes on, 'I don't recall seeing Freddie take coke that night. Mind you, he was discreet that way and, anyway, he would regularly go off to a club to hang out and God knows what he got up to then.' Whilst Mercury was still at the post-gig bash Brainsby saw the singer sign his autograph for one of the strippers in an unusual place. He reveals, 'I've got a photograph of Freddie signing his name on a topless stripper's botty as she slightly bends over a table.'

Queen recovered from the party before picking up the tour once more with a gig on 3 November in Miami; and it was while they were in Detroit a week later that their new album *Jazz* was released in Britain. The unusual spiral design on the album cover had been Roger Taylor's concept, inspired by a piece of thought-provoking graffiti that had caught his eye during their earlier European tour when he had crossed Checkpoint Charlie into East Berlin. Also – despite the uproar it had already caused – tucked inside the album sleeve was a free graphic poster of the Wimbledon Stadium bike race. Deeming the poster pornographic, American stores banned its inclusion.

Queen responded defiantly a week later by arranging for six naked women to ride bikes on stage, ringing their bells during the band's performance of this number at their two sell-out gigs at New York's Madison Square Garden. The controversy was good for business – Queen received the Gold Ticket award for performing to over 100,000 fans at the Garden. *Jazz* notched up a number six hit in the US album charts and in Britain it remained in the charts for twenty-seven weeks, peaking at number two.

Queen's relentless touring meant that they scarcely registered the brief break between completing the US tour on 20 December and commencing yet another European trip on 17 January 1979. The fatigue and stress of such an itinerant life was beginning to tell. They were pleased, if somewhat surprised (considering past critical reaction), that reviews were favourable when the single 'Don't Stop Me Now'/'In Only Seven Days' was released nine days into the tour. But, this bonus aside, the band were becoming increasingly demanding off-stage, at least as far as personal manager Pete Brown was concerned.

He reveals, 'It was part of my job to ensure that the accommodation I arranged for all four of them was of the precise same size, style and standard. Queen genuinely were a democratic band and this policy was to make sure that no one member had anything fancier than the other, which was fine, but putting theory into practice was often near impossible. I tried my best, but that European tour

ABOVE Brian May's first band, 1984, included Tim Staffell (1st left) with whom he would later go on to form the pre-Queen band Smile, with Roger Taylor.

BOVE Often a loner whilst growing up, reddie Mercury's unique style and talent vould always set him apart.

IGHT Queen's early look was mean and noody. Right from the start, they were etermined to reach the top.

Freddie's bare-faced cheek at Queen's infamous 1978 post-gig bash in New Orleans - a 12-hour orgy of excess.

Making a visual, as well as musical, impact was vital. Later, Zandra Rhodes was to design some of Queen's flashy stagewear.

In the beginning the whole band carried out countless promotional duties, but gradually Roger Taylor and Brian May became Queen's main spokesmen.

**RIGHT** Mercury introduced a hard-edged biker machismo to Queen's stage style in the late Seventies, which upset many fans.

**BELOW** Whether performing hard rock numbers or ballads it was most important for Queen to make a connection with the audience.

**BELOW** The eyes have it! Freddie's flamboyance reached impressive heights with this scarlet costume for the 'It's a Hard Life' video.

**ABOVE** Queen stole the show at Live Aid, with Freddie's individual performance universally acknowledged as a crowning achievement.

**BELOW** Throughout the Eighties Queen became one of the prime instigators of stadium rock, playing to record-breaking crowds the world over.

**RIGHT** Freddie adored clowning as the king of Queen, but in reality the band was very much a democracy of four strong-willed personalities.

**BELOW** In 1984 Mercury indulged his taste for ballet a second time. Dancer Derek Deane recalls one moment: 'Freddie had to roll on his stomach on top of a line of rotating bodies. He loved that!'

**ABOVE LEFT** Brian May went through the mill when his marriage to Chrissy Mullen hit the rocks.

**ABOVE RIGHT** Vivacious actress Anita Dobson proved an irresistible attraction to the married May, although at first they denied rumours of an affair.

**ABOVE** Brian with Malcolm Thomas, co-founder of the British Bone Marrow Donor Appeal, of which May became the patron.

**LEFT** Brian's reputation in the music industry as a 'diamond geezer' was matched by his distinctive guitar wizardry.

RIGHT Roger Taylor, ever the looker in Queen, revelled in living the rock dream. But the fun-loving drummer also had a more serious, politically-aware side.

BELOW Taylor replaced May and Dobson as tabloid fodder when in 1988 he married Dominique Beyrand, the mother of his two children, only to set up home with his lover, Debbie Leng.

**ABOVE** Only when bassist John Deacon joined the band in February 1971 did Queen consider themselves complete.

**RIGHT** Categorised for years as Queen's colourless quiet man, Deacon in fact became the band's shrewd business brain, watching the stockmarket and scrutinising the deals.

**ABOVE** Few other non-opera singers in the world could complement diva Montserrat Caballe. However, Freddie's duet with Caballe caused controversy in the rock world.

**LEFT** Rockin' all over the world with support band Status Quo.

**BELOW** In 1987 zany TV comedians The Young Ones became the spoof band Bad News, and recorded 'Bohemian Rhapsody' with Brian May bravely acting as producer.

**ABOVE** Mary Austin and Mercury continued to share a unique bond long after Freddie chose to pursue a homosexual life.

**LEFT** Controversial DJ Kenny Everett was crucial in springboarding 'Bohemian Rhapsody' to success.

**BELOW** May lines up proudly with an earlier guitar hero, Bert Weedon, and ex Beatle George Harrison.

RIGHT All the members of Queen seemed to demonstrate a penchant for extravagant fancy dress - as an almost unrecogniseable Roger Taylor demonstrates here.

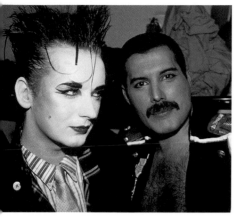

ABOVE Boy George was just one of the many celebrities who regularly flocked to the infamous and outrageous Queen parties.

BELOW No Mercury birthday party was complete without an extravagant cake. On one occasion, a hotel secretary ended up being thrown into one!

ABOVE Freddie became increasingly emaciated towards the end of his life.

ABOVE The tragic news of Mercury's death on 24 November 1991 brought distraught fans in their droves to mourn outside his Kensington mansion. Tributes are still laid each year.

ABOVE Lisa Stansfield and George Michael's emotional duet at the Freddie Mercury tribute concert at Wembley Stadium in 1992.

I couldn't seem to do anything right. In January Brian, I think for the first time ever, was very annoyed at me over the place I'd fixed him up with. Another time it was Roger who had a list of complaints, but when we came to Paris at the end of the tour I managed to upset the four of them. But I couldn't help it. I was supposed to find four houses for them – not apartments – and each one had to be identical in comfort to the other. Try as I did, I never could develop a thick skin and when they blew up at me, it did hurt at times.' He adds, 'I know it was because of the pressures – I guess you would have to have experienced it to understand. But I never regretted a second of my time working for Queen.'

But there was to be no slow-down yet, as Queen next paid their third visit to Japan. Embracing fifteen dates (five of them at Tokyo's Budokan Martial Arts Hall), it was their biggest Far East tour to date. Proof that their popularity had never waned in this region came when, while there, they picked up a slew of awards in the top single, top album and top group categories.

Queen quit Japan in early May, only to swap a tiring life on the road for a two-month packed recording schedule at Mountain Studios once more. Montreux would come to have special significance to all of Queen – although manager Jim Beach later remarked that Freddie initially viewed the coolly beautiful Swiss resort as possibly the most boring place in the world. They were particularly at home in Mountain Studios on the Rue de Theatre, so when they discovered that summer that the complex was on the market Queen decided to buy it.

It was around now that Queen were invited to add a new string to their bow by writing a film score. A movie directed by Mike Hodges called *Flash Gordon*, starring Sam J. Jones and Max von Sydow, was in production. Based on the 1930s comic-strip adventure, the film would be flashy, noisy and lavish, and the producers felt that Queen would be ideally placed to create the big soundtrack needed to match it. Always up for a challenge, the band eagerly accepted. After being shown twenty minutes of the movie, which allowed them to absorb its over-the-top flavour, they were given a free hand to indulge their extravagant musical imaginations accordingly, as long as it was tailored to the film. All four members duly set about writing tracks.

Work on their own material also continued apace throughout the summer of 1979, as did the record releases. On 22 June came the album *Live Killers*, followed a week later by the single 'Love of My Life (live)'/'Now I'm Here (live)'. Since the opening show of Queen's winter 1977 tour of America, 'Love of My Life' had become an audience favourite, with crowds around the world singing the words back to the band. It was strange, therefore, that the same song, now released as a single, should have performed so poorly in the UK single charts. It only scraped to number sixty-three, their poorest ranking since 'Keep Yourself Alive' failed to chart.

This disappointment was easily obliterated by the honour EMI bestowed on Queen when the record company, which that year received the Queen's Award for Industry, decided to launch a 200-copy limited edition of 'Bohemian Rhapsody' pressed on blue vinyl. Each single cost around £4 to produce. Today one of those hand-numbered discs in mint condition can fetch in excess of £1,000.

For Queen the work pressed on at a new location – Musicland Studios in Munich – where they would first meet record producer Reinholdt Mack. Brian May later commented on how difficult it was for anyone to mesh with the band at work, saying, 'It was pretty hard for anyone to sit with us as a producer or whatever, and the ones who managed it, managed it by having very strong personalities.' Mack, as he was known, was unlikely to feel intimidated, having already worked with the likes of ELO and Led Zeppelin, and he would become the first outside producer since Roy Thomas Baker to regularly work on Queen records.

It was in Munich's Hilton Hotel, while relaxing in a bath, that Mercury wrote the song that would give Queen their first American number one single. 'Crazy Little Thing Called Love' was off the beaten track for Queen, and even for Freddie. As he admitted, 'It's not typical of my work'. It was jaunty, an undisguised pastiche of Elvis Presley (whom Mercury imagined he could mimic quite well), and it was knocked together in record time. Roger Taylor said of the song, 'It's not rockabilly exactly, but it did have that early Elvis feel.' Perhaps this was a factor in its enormous appeal in the States.

When it came to laying down the track at Musicland, Mercury – unusually – arrived alone and ahead of the others. It was important to him to have established the exact sound he wanted before Taylor, Deacon and May had the chance to mutate it into a typical Queen record. Although Mercury's skills on guitar were very basic, the record for the first time featured Freddie playing rhythm. When critics mocked this musical debut, Mercury snapped, 'I've made no effort to become a guitar hero, because I can't play the fucking guitar.'

'Crazy Little Thing Called Love'/'We will Rock You (live)' was released in Britain on 5 October 1979, and it hit the number two spot, going gold. It was released as a 12-inch single in Europe for the first time and went to number one in Australia, New Zealand, Canada, Mexico and Holland. Its chart-topping success too in America – besides being a benchmark achievement – reassuringly revived the performance of Queen singles in the States which had hit a largely stony patch over the past two years. It also premiered live on 7 October at a dance gala at London's Coliseum, when Freddie sang and danced on stage alongside members of the London Royal Ballet Company.

This unusual event had come about via the efforts of principal dancer Wayne Eagling. Freddie's long-standing fascination with ballet meant that he had attended many performances around the world but he especially admired the London Royal Ballet. Wayne Eagling recalls, 'I first met Freddie when I was producing a dance gala for mentally handicapped children. Because I wanted to widen its appeal I asked my friend Joseph Lockwood, who was Treasurer of the Royal Ballet as well as being head of EMI, if I could work with Kate Bush. Her manager was not keen on the idea though and Joseph suggested Freddie Mercury.'

They were to work on choreographing two numbers, 'Bohemian Rhapsody' and 'Crazy Little Thing Called Love', and during rehearsals Mercury worked with another principal dancer, Derek Deane. Derek recalls, 'Freddie became a great friend of Wayne's and mine. I saw at once that he liked to think of himself as a good dancer, but he wasn't really. He more than made up for that though by being terribly enthusiastic. In fact, a lot of the time we had to hold him back in case he did himself an injury.'

Of the big night itself, Deane says, 'Ballet audiences can be quite stuffy and never in a million years did they expect a rock star to arrive on stage. But they loved Freddie.' Wayne Eagling recalls, 'Basically we lifted him around all the time, tipping him upside down and throwing him about, but Freddie was a natural showman and he thoroughly enjoyed it.' Mercury later admitted that he'd found it a nerve-racking challenge and clearly felt pride in having pulled it off. He quipped, 'I'd like to see Mick Jagger or Rod Stewart try something like that.' It was during this association with the Royal Ballet Company that Mercury met wardrobe assistant Peter Freestone. 'Phoebe', as Mercury nicknamed him, soon joined the singer's other personal assistants, Paul Prenter and Joe Fannelli.

On 22 November Queen embarked on their last tour of the decade. They dubbed it the 'Crazy Tour' because, in a departure from playing only the big 'barns', they decided to include gigs at smaller venues, places where Queen had hitherto not performed in some cases. The bigger the crowd, the tenser the atmosphere, and they thrived on the volatile emotions that that produced. They had also been missing the intimacy of closer contact with a small audience and it was this that they now sought to recreate.

The tour got underway at the RDS Simmons Court Hall in Dublin on 22 November and ended on Boxing Day with a charity gig at London's Hammersmith Odeon which, in aid of the Kampuchea Appeal Fund, had been organised by Paul McCartney and his company MPL Productions. The actual event involved a series of performances from a number of artistes, including Wings, the Who, the Pretenders, and Ian Dury and the Blockheads, all of which were filmed for television and later an album was produced.

Queen's progress from midway through the decade had brought them a high level of fame and wealth; now, as the seventies ended, they had sold over 45 million albums worldwide. Musical styles had changed and, whilst keeping a finger on the pulse of these shifts, Queen continued to produce their own unique brand of material. Within the group some physical changes were visible on stage. Taylor and May maintained much the same style, whereas to match his sober short haircut Deacon now opted for a smart collar and tie, leaving Mercury, in total contrast, never out of leathers – he had lately taken to topping this ensemble with a leather and chain cap. With a new decade dawning, who knew what changes, personally or professionally, lay ahead?

# LATIN LOVE AFFAIR

R ECORDING COMMITMENTS dominated the first four months of 1980 for Queen, with work on their own new album, as well as on the *Flash Gordon* soundtrack album, taking place at Musicland Studios in Munich. Despite the global success of 'Crazy Little Thing Called Love', much of the British music press remained unmoved and were again disdainful about the new single 'Save Me'/'Let Me Entertain You (live)' on its release on 25 January. But, as reviews were no longer a barometer of the band's popularity, it scarcely mattered to Queen.

The dual workload kept their collective nose to the grindstone, but Mercury snatched a small respite to visit London briefly in March, during which he made a rare television appearance, taking part in a silly sketch on one of his friend Kenny Everett's wacky weekly shows. The friendship between the rock star and the comedian, both of whom would die of AIDS, would stay intact for another few years, only to suddenly founder. Rumour has it that the rift arose after an acrimonious row over drugs but the late Kenny

Everett's agent Jo Gurnett reveals, 'They were very good friends. Their falling out is a grey area, but I know that it was a minor disagreement between them, after which they just drifted apart. Kenny didn't see Freddie latterly. He would've liked to, but it was just one of those things. Then Freddie was too sick, and Kenny himself was too sick. I remember Kenny, when he knew he was dying, saying about Freddie and their lost closeness, "Well, we'll all be up there together, and maybe then we will make it up." '

It was also during this trip that Mercury fell in love with and bought, at a cost of £500,000 (which he paid in cash), the Kensington 28-roomed mansion Garden Lodge at 1 Logan Place. It would be several years, after the property had been extensively renovated, before Mercury moved in but right then the pleasure of owning it was enough and he rejoined the other three to continue recording in Munich.

The first product of these lengthy studio sessions came with the release on 30 May of the single 'Play the Game'/'A Human Body'. It reached a respectable number fourteen in Britain, but when Queen fans glimpsed its accompanying video many were dismayed. They were disorientated by another step in Mercury's altering image. The singer would later defend these changes, stating that it was no more than a natural growth process; that to remain fixed in a time warp style would have made him feel and look quite ridiculous. But, with Freddie now sporting a close-cropped haircut, a bushy moustache and without a streak of black nail polish, it felt to the fans as if he was slipping away from them. The most disgruntled responded by bombarding Mercury, through the Queen office, with gifts of disposable razors and bottles of black nail varnish.

It was a new experience for Queen to realise that some of their fans were discontented and that their discontent would not merely be confined to complaints over their frontman's new dress style. When *The Game* followed, exactly one month later, some supporters were upset all over again. Until this album Queen had proudly boasted that, when creating their music, they never used synthesisers. Now suddenly they had, with the result that many of their long-time followers felt – perhaps disproportionately – let down.

The album also had a distinctly economical feel to it. Never two notes played, if one would do, Queen said. This pared-down approach was completely at odds with the band's usual elaborate way of working, and this doubtless also disorientated the faithful. Queen were not insensitive to fan reaction but they had felt the need to experiment and it paid off, for the first time one of their albums hit the top slot in both Britain and America. *The Game* would also attract a coveted Grammy nomination in the Best Produced Album category.

This was a good launch pad for their first tour of the year – a major incursion into Canada and North America, commencing on 30 June at Vancouver's PNE Coliseum and ending in New York on 1 October at Madison Square Garden, this time after four consecutive nights there. The schedule was arduous, even for a band accustomed to mammoth undertakings. This time around, a distinct sense of claustrophobia would also set in, heightened by the increased security measures needed to protect them.

Speaking of the strict arrangements which ensured that the band were cocooned at every step, Pete Brown recalls, 'It created a rarefied atmosphere that was driving them all mad by now. People imagine that it is a glamorous life, but it's a damned hard slog. Someone would ask me, "How was Boston?" and I'd reply, "Boston had orange curtains and a blue bedspread." They'd look at me strangely, but that was what it was really like.'

The near daily contact with American audiences, however, had a decided upside to it when it helped springboard their latest single release to the top slot – their second number one hit single in the States. On 22 August 1980, when Queen were in Philadelphia performing at the Spectrum, 'Another One Bites the Dust'/'Dragon Attack' was released in Britain, where it peaked at number seven. But when this third single from *The Game* was released in America (with the B-side, 'Don't Try Suicide') it became a colossal hit, selling around 4.5 million copies.

Written by John Deacon, the song had a distinctive throbbing bass line that made it the darling of the discos. Deacon had apparently nursed the idea for the song for some time before doing anything about it. 'Originally, all I had was one line and the bass riff,' he admitted. 'Gradually I filled it in and the others added ideas. But I wanted the heavy bass sound we got.'

Its appeal to US black radio stations was such that it received massive airplay and it also racked up a number two hit in the American Rhythm and Blues charts. It was one of three Queen singles to go platinum in the States and on 30 January 1981 at the Eighth Annual American Music Awards, held at the ABC TV Studios in Burbank, Hollywood, it won the prize as the Favorite Single in the Pop/Rock category.

Over the years, several Queen songs would be adopted by sports fans around the world – 'Another One Bites the Dust' was one of them. But the number was not a hit with everyone, as Kent Falb, then head trainer of the Detroit Lions American football team, can vouch. He says, 'Early in the 1980 season defensive backs Jimmy Allen and James Hunter, along with tight end David Hill, heard "Another One Bites the Dust" on the radio and decided to use the melody. They rewrote the words and made a recording of the song as a novelty tune which was unofficially adopted by the Detroit Lions. However, at this time the team had begun the season with four wins and no losses. As the season went along our fortunes declined and unfortunately this tune ended up being used against us by numerous opponents!'

The tight snap of the number highly dependent on a slick inter-action between Deacon's driving bass and precision drumming from Roger Taylor, meant that it was not the easiest song to perform live – but it was too popular to be left out of their live repertoire. For Mercury, it lent him the opportunity to boost his sex symbol status. Because he never declared his homosexuality, he was always careful not to turn off either female or homophobic fans. But, whilst performing this number, he would produce performances guaranteed to have an ambiguous appeal.

At one such performance mid-tour, at the Forum in Montreal, when he strutted his stuff wearing only a baseball cap, neckerchief and tantalisingly tight-fitting white shorts, he sent the crowd wild – both sexes – by taunting them with the urge, 'Bite it, bite it hard, baby' while rubbing low on his taut stomach in simulated ecstasy. When the press later made suggestive comments about the tightness of his shorts Mercury bragged, 'I don't have a Coke bottle down there. It's all mine.'

When the tour ended, there was little time for relaxation as they had to complete the film soundtrack, this time at London's Anvil Studios, and a European tour loomed. The hectic pace of their professional lives could be tough when it came to finding space for their personal lives, but they made the most of the limited time they had. Brian and John returned to their respective wives, Roger to Dominique, and Freddie to a man called Tony Bastin – his first male live-in lover. Mercury, who liked his men brawny with large hands and preferably with a thick black moustache, had met Bastin, a courier for an express delivery company, at a gay nightclub when Queen had played in Brighton in December 1979. Something had been different about Bastin – he was not just another of the star's numerous and meaningless one-night stands – so they had kept in touch, and just prior to the recent US tour Mercury had moved Bastin into his Kensington flat at 12 Stafford Terrace. But soon Queen were on the move again, this time heading to Switzerland to rehearse for their upcoming tour.

It kicked off at Zurich's Hallenstadion on 23 November; and the following day, back home, 'Flash'/'Football Fight', the first single from the forthcoming soundtrack album, was released. Providing Queen with a Top Ten hit, it helped offset their disappointment that Elektra's choice in America, 'Need Your Loving Tonight' petered out at number forty-four in the Billboard chart. Then, after Queen became the first rock band to perform at the new purpose-built NEC in Birmingham, the soundtrack album *Flash Gordon* was released on 8 December 1980 to astonishingly rave reviews.

Their pleasure at this surprising turnaround in critical reaction to their work was shattered, however, by the numbing news that ricocheted around the world that John Lennon had been cold-bloodedly gunned down outside his New York apartment building by a deranged fan. That night, Queen honoured the second of their three engagements at the Wembley Arena, but found it understandably difficult to control their emotions when, in tribute, they performed Lennon's 1975 hit 'Imagine'.

This shocking, premeditated execution of a rock star brought home to Queen, as it did to most other major performers, just how vulnerable a profession it could be. But life went on. The tour ended on 18 December in Germany and their enormous success was now proved when Queen became the first rock band to enter the category of Britain's highest paid executives in *The Guinness Book of Records*.

Such a healthily competitive-minded group of individuals were only spurred on by this achievement to scale even greater heights in 1981. This was especially true when they decided to make this their tenth anniversary year, in recognition of the fact that they had not considered themselves complete until Deacon became their permanent bass player in February 1971.

Much lay ahead that would be groundbreaking for Queen, but first 1981 got off to a good and familiar start by returning them to Japan for the Japanese movie première of *Flash Gordon*, and a short but profitable five-gig engagement at Tokyo's Budokan Martial Arts Hall commencing on 12 February. The band took the same flight over as the Nottingham Forest football team under manager Brian Clough. The team was heading over to Japan to play a World Club Championship match against the Uruguayan team, Nacional. Former Notts Forest and England international Trevor Francis recalls, 'Queen were up front in first-class, whilst we were all back with the rough. I was absolutely passionate about music, and when we discovered they were on the flight we couldn't wait for a chance to meet them. It was in Anchorage, when the plane was refuelling, that we got chatting.' He adds, 'We invited Queen to come to our game and Roger and John took us up on the offer. Unfortunately we got beat 1–0.'

Queen, by contrast, were winners when the annual *Music Life* magazine polls results were announced in Japan. Mercury and Deacon were voted top of their respective categories, Taylor and May came second in their sections, and Queen itself won the top award for best band. It all went to show that they had lost none of their attraction in the Far East. They hoped that they could carve out similar success in the new territory that they were about to enter.

That new territory was South America (not exactly virgin ground, as other artistes had played in this region before, but none on the scale of Queen, with their extravagant stage sets, gigantic lighting rigs and theatrics). They had just ten days between wrapping up their Japanese tour and tackling the first gig in Argentina on 28 February, but it was long enough for the four to split for a brief break. Brian, Roger and Freddie all opted for separate destinations in America, whilst John flew home to Veronica in London. For Queen's crew there would be no such luxury.

The logistics of transporting by road the 100-plus tons of expensive equipment required to construct the stage and effects used at these outdoor stadium venues meant that Queen tours had to be masterminded and executed with ever-increasing military precision. But, even so, sometimes spanners could end up in the works. This time it happened when the band's production manager spearheaded the crew's arrival in the country and encountered a problem when customs officials checked out Queen's tour security passes. The two topless girls pictured sharing a banana contravened local pornography laws and the man was only released after he had been made to carefully take a black marker pen to the offensive breasts on each pass.

The first gig was to be the giant Velez Sarfield stadium in Buenos Aires, and because football is so revered in this continent, Queen had agreed to protect the turf with expensive artificial grass. But other precautions were more complex. The Argentinian intelligence service, fearful that the unsettled political climate might make Queen a likely terrorist target, liaised with Jim Beach and the local promoters over security measures. But nothing could dampen the band's appetite for the challenge.

No one in Queen assumed that they had a God-given right to a rapturous reception in an alien land but over the course of just seven dates – five in Argentina, two in Brazil – they performed to record-breaking audiences. From their opening night, before 54,000 fans at the Velez Sarfield, they became South America's most popular rock act and the prime instigators of stadium rock.

Fans had queued for twelve hours to get in and the hysteria reached new heights that night. As a result, Queen had to be driven off after the gig in an armour-plated car that screeched away from the stadium, escorted by a squad of motorcycle cops who zigzagged ahead along the route to the band's hotel, clearing crowds and traffic away. Exhilarated by the air of drama, Mercury later crowed, 'My dears, it was fantastic!'

From the start, the entire trip had had a unique feel. Queen were afforded special treatment on their arrival in Buenos Aires when the country's President, General Viola, sent a government delegation to greet the band at the airport. Scenes of delirious fans thronging the airport were televised live on the national news. In addition, parties were laid on in the band's honour. One was at the home of the president of the Velez Sarfield which was also attended by the soccer demi-god Diego Maradonna. They were also invited to dine at General Viola's official residence; Mercury, Deacon and May accepted but Roger Taylor declined, as he strongly disagreed with some of General Viola's policies.

Brian May dubbed Taylor 'The Peter Pan of Rock 'n' Roll', and certainly the drummer with the zany sense of humour loved living the rock dream. 'Being a musician is all I ever wanted,' Roger confirmed. But he was far from only being interested in his own pleasures. He was always socially aware and conscious of the political pressures prevailing in the countries in which Queen performed. Viola's military government imposed a strict regime on Argentinians, and Taylor explained his personal reasons for refusing the General's invitation by stating, 'I didn't want to meet him because that would have been playing into their hands. We didn't go there with the wool pulled over our eyes.' Although the other three did dine with Viola, Queen as a whole did not view themselves as having been political pawns.

The journey from Argentina to Brazil for the remaining two dates at the Morumbi Stadium in Sao Paulo caused another headache for the road crew. They arrived at the Brazilian border to find a zealous customs official who showed an alarming determination to go by the book and literally have each piece of equipment meticulously searched; an operation that would have made the crew about three weeks late for gigs in three days' time. The panic dissolved when customs relented and finally let them through. But, although relieved, the crew were left with a scant thirty-six hours before the next show.

Queen performed the first of the two consecutive dates at the Morumbi Stadium on 20 March before a crowd of 131,000 – the largest paying audience for one band anywhere in the world to date. In total, by the tour's end, their collective audience numbered almost half a million people and the trip grossed around $3.5 million. It made their return visit later in the year an agreeable prospect.

The demanding cycle of touring–recording–touring continued when, after a spell in Britain, Queen soon returned to Mountain Studios where they would work into the summer on their next album. For Roger Taylor it was a particularly busy time. On 30 March, four years after his first solo effort, he released a second single called 'Future Management'/'Laugh or Cry' which peaked in Britain at number forty-nine – perhaps disappointing but better than the performance of his third solo single three months later, 'My Country'/'Fun in Space', which failed to chart at all.

He viewed solo recordings as somehow therapeutic, believing that only after having indulged in them could he feel completely satisfied. On 6 April he also released his first solo album *Fun in Space* – a balanced mix of rock, pop and ballad numbers – which had been recorded over six weeks in Switzerland. This reached a respectable eighteen in the UK album charts, despite attracting a hostile critical reception.

Work on the Queen album had to be suspended when the time approached to commence their second South American tour. They had to rehearse for the tour but not before Mercury threw a spectacular party on 5 September to mark his thirty-fifth birthday. Over the years these birthday bashes became legendary. This one was held in New York where, although he had recently purchased a sumptuous apartment on East 58th Street, he took over an entire floor of the plush Berkshire Hotel. All his closest friends were flown over by Concorde to attend a shindig that continued non-stop for five days!

After rehearsals in New Orleans, Queen set out on what they called their 'Gluttons for Punishment' tour. Commencing on 25 September in Venezuela at the Poliedro de Caracas, the trip threw up a whole new set of problems. The first three gigs in Caracas went well. Then the next day Taylor, May and Deacon agreed to take part in a live TV pop programme which descended into chaos when an overwrought man rushed on camera and prematurely reported the death of the statesman Romulo Ethancourt. He had no sooner declared a two-minute silence than a second equally wired individual rushed on to announce that the statesman had not died at all. All this was on live television, in rapid Spanish, whilst Roger, Brian and John stood there looking totally bewildered and extremely awkward.

It was a great deal worse than awkward when Ethancourt *did* die later that night, because the whole country was automatically plunged into mourning. Queen's gigs were cancelled, the airport was closed, and they were stranded in the middle of a politically unstable situation. The scent of revolution was in the air, and rumours were rife of foreigners mysteriously vanishing off the streets. Queen were widely travelled and had encountered many unusual situations but this definitely felt like one of the dodgiest. They were therefore profoundly relieved when the airport reopened and they could jet out to safety.

This nasty experience rendered them pretty raw for the three Mexican dates which kicked off on 9 October at Monterrey's

Estadion Universitario. That night, to their deep dismay, the crowd began bombarding them with boots, bottles, even batteries. Of all of them, Roger Taylor was at most risk as he had least chance of avoiding the missiles. Their dejection on coming off stage at the end, however, turned out to be astonishingly misplaced for they were congratulated heartily by the local officials; it seems that what they had endured was a traditional show of appreciation. It was hard to feel happy though when, after playing at the Estadion Cuahtermoc in Puebla, they discovered that – because of tax complications – they would not get paid. This was the last straw and it sent them off on a flight to New York, determined never to return to Mexico.

Putting these events out of their minds would be easy in the coming weeks. Back in the summer, whilst recording in Montreux, Queen's friend David Bowie (a resident of the Swiss resort who often socialised with Mercury and Taylor) had occasionally dropped in on the sessions at Mountain Studios. One day an impromptu jam had developed into a tentative songwriting collaboration between them, at the end of which had been a song with possibilities. When Queen escaped from Mexico, they went to New York, where they had a chance to team up with Bowie to put the finishing touches to this song.

The pop duet 'Under Pressure', which Queen backed with 'Soul Brother', was released in Britain on 26 October and hurtled to the top. The ostentatious scale on which Queen did things and their standing in the rock world had camouflaged the surprising fact that it had been six years since they had enjoyed a UK number one hit single. Undoubtedly this disc benefited from Bowie fans also buying it, but it became hugely popular with Queen fans, eliciting one of the best receptions of any at Queen gigs. Roger Taylor hails it as 'one of the very best things Queen have ever done'.

Then, in the last months of the year, Queen launched a series of special releases to celebrate their tenth anniversary; each release featuring a specially commissioned band portrait taken by the Earl of Snowdon. First had been *Greatest Flix*, a compilation of each video for Queen singles since 'Bohemian Rhapsody'. This was followed by *Greatest Pix*, a book of photographs compiled by Jacques Lowe. And thirdly, released on 2 November 1981, the *Greatest Hits* album. It went to number one and remained on the album chart for 312 weeks. Queen, therefore, became the first band to simultaneously top the UK singles, album and video charts. This left only live performance, and to complete the celebrations they played two gigs in Canada at Montreal's Forum in late November. These special concerts were filmed by director Saul Swimmer, with a view to them forming part of a feature film of the band to be released the following summer.

Happy to have reached this milestone anniversary, they were already looking forward to the next ten years. But within a couple of weeks they were off to Munich, where the pressures of their hectic life would all too clearly begin to take their toll.

# TEN

# PRESSURE POT

OSTENSIBLY QUEEN RETURNED to Germany to continue work on their new album at Musicland Studios but Munich itself held an attraction for the band, and for some members the cosmopolitan city became almost a second home. It was hardly surprising. Being a globally successful live act meant constantly jetting about the world. Rooting themselves in Munich for recording purposes gave them the opportunity to get to know some people and places – the Sugar Shack nightclub became one of their favourite haunts.

Mercury, in particular, found Munich a haven of delight. He especially enjoyed wading into the so-called 'Bermuda Triangle – the crowded gay scene which offered a wide range of venues with a very relaxed, 'anything goes' atmosphere. He often favoured clubs that attracted a mix of straight and gay people and, although Tony Bastin was still his live-in lover, Freddie continued to fool around with men and drugs when he was abroad. Yet, while he was guilty of serial infidelity, he could also be very tender and romantic. And when he fancied himself in love his generosity could be boundless, leading him to lavish diamonds and large cash sums on the man of the moment.

Being one of the most famous faces on the gay circuit, Mercury was undoubtedly open to being exploited for his fame. But he knew it. He was no soft target and sometimes chose to turn this to his advantage. There were no shortage of men looking for rich pickings, who would zero in on the superstar in their midst. Playing along, Mercury enjoyed asking those he liked the look of back to his recently acquired apartment (his sex drive still verged on the unquenchable). Once at home, he would invite his hand-picked groupies to strip naked. Wearing nothing but a lady's hat, they would each parade in the hope of being selected as Mercury's bedmate for the night; the rejects were then dismissed.

When it came to gay affairs of the heart, though, Freddie believed he suffered a raw deal. 'No one loves the real me inside. They're all in love with my stardom,' he lamented, ignoring the fact that his own behaviour contributed much to the emotional hollowness of many of his relationships. His hedonistic over-indulgence grew ever more reckless; and his cocaine use increased, along with his relentless all-night partying.

It was also in a Munich disco, however, that Mercury met German actress Barbara Valentin, a cult figure known for her work for film director Rainer Werner Fassbinder. She would become the only other woman, next to Mary Austin, to be special in Freddie's life, as Mercury confirmed when he revealed, 'Barbara and I have formed a bond that is stronger than anything I have had with a lover for the past six years.'

Says Barbara Valentin, 'Freddie and I met at a disco called New York. Nobody introduced us as such. We just sort of came together. I adored him. We fitted together instantly and we never separated for three whole days. He stayed at my house, I went to the studio with him and we went out to the clubs together. We talked all the time and Freddie told me, "Finally, I can talk to someone who understands the real me and what I want to do with my life." That was something he needed badly.'

The vivacious actress's total understanding of Mercury's homosexuality filled an apparent yawning void in him and there quickly developed between Freddie and Barbara a unique and tender relationship that spanned several years and which today she still finds hard to define. She says, 'We had an amazing time together whenever he was in Munich. I loved him, I still love him, and he loved me. It was a once in a lifetime thing between us.'

In early 1982 Queen's pursuit of pleasure was seriously curtailed when they realised that they had to increase their productivity in the recording studio in order to pull their new album into shape. Then, having re-signed with EMI for another six albums, they hit the road again on 9 April for a 30-date European and UK tour. On the other side of the world their number one hit, 'Under Pressure', had just been banned from the airwaves in Argentina (Britain and that country having gone to war over sovereignty of the Falkland Islands). The Argentinian authorities also banned Queen from performing on their soil, at least for the duration of the conflict.

Queen were also facing problems of their own. Wanting to explore new musical avenues, they had again recently departed from their familiar sound, this time moving towards a kind of rhythmic rock, or – as their audiences seemed to see it – the very basic sound of funky disco. This was perhaps partly a result of having recently spent a lot of time on Munich's club scene. The fans gave this new sound a decidedly cool reception at gigs. And when, ten days into the tour, the single 'Body Language' was released it stalled at number twenty-five; although, with Queen's tribute to the murdered ex-Beatle 'Life Is Real (Song for Lennon)' as its B-side, it fared considerably better in America, reaching number eleven.

For the already disaffected fans, though, further upset followed, with the release of *Hot Space* on 21 May, the same day as Queen arrived back in Munich to play the final date of the European leg at the Olympiahalle. The album seemed smothered by a fog of synthesiser mishmash and many were deeply disappointed. Brian May had had doubts about the album and, unusually, admitted to rock journalists that he personally was not that keen on it. Looking back, he also later volunteered that – timing-wise – *Hot Space* missed its mark, as the popularity of disco was decidedly on the wane.

The tour, however, trundled on into Britain with a gig at Elland Road Football Ground in Leeds, two dates at Edinburgh's Ingleston Showground, and finally a performance at the Milton Keynes Bowl on 5 June which was filmed by Channel 4 TV. By this time another single had been released, 'Las Palabras de Amor (The Words of Love)'/'Cool Cat'. Although it went higher than 'Body Language', it peaked at number seventeen and failed to erase the awareness that a section of their fans remained disenchanted.

If their fans were growing restive, Queen themselves were feeling the strain of years of relentless touring and recording. This was not helped by the poor performance of a single which Elektra issued on 19 July in the States, 'Calling All Girls'/'Put Out the Fire'. Having only scraped to number sixty was not a good footing on which to embark, two days later, on another gruelling US/Canadian tour. Still, they pulled out all the stops, whilst gigging nearly every night in practically every state, on a trip punctuated as ever with hugely extravagant parties.

The style of performance was high-energy and demanding and it became an increasingly draining experience, despite intense preparations which placed almost as much emphasis – certainly for Mercury – on physical fitness as on musical tightness. Before its end, Freddie at least was freely confessing that he had begun to hate this endless treadmill.

There was no cheer from home either when the UK single 'Back Chat remix'/'Staying Power', released on 9 August whilst Queen were in Meadowlands, just made the Top Forty. The tour had started at the Forum in Montreal, and ended on 15 September 1982 at the Great Western Forum, Inglewood, in California. This date not only marked the final show; it ended – although they had no way of knowing it then – Queen's last ever American tour.

Returning a month later to Japan they ploughed through six dates, ending on 3 November at Tokyo's Seibu Lions Stadium. After bringing to a close their globe-trotting for the year, they arrived back in Britain to enter into lengthy negotiations with Elektra over renewal of their US contract. In the end the two sides decided to part company and in December, as an interim measure, Queen signed all albums to EMI.

The end of 1982 brought about another crossroads for Queen. Long-since wealthy and successful, they were also now tired and tense. They had dismissed many a rumour of the group imploding, but twelve years of continuously living in each other's pockets, of enduring the stress of major tours and months of stifling studio life, had left their mark. It was never a case of Queen calling it a day but frankly it had been brewing for a while – they were getting on each other's nerves and arguments over material had lately become both more frequent and serious.

With four very different personalities, all songwriters and each with his own influences, likes and dislikes, the process of committing anything to tape always required compromise, which in turn required flexibility and a letting go of the sense of territoriality. All this had been getting harder and harder to achieve. Each band member plainly needed some breathing space from the others and so they decided to take a year off. Roger Taylor admitted, 'We got fed up and were lacking inspiration.'

Faced with the knowledge that their latest album was not what many fans had wanted, some bands might have panicked and been bounced into recording a quick 'safe bet' album, guaranteed to recoup lost favour. They would be unlikely to compound disappointment among their rank and file supporters by going to ground, thereby provoking renewed rumours of a break-up. But Queen announced that they would not be touring for the next twelve months. This brought a predictable reaction from the music press, but the band responded with absolute calm.

Over time, both Mercury and May clarified the way the band viewed their position, with Brian remarking pragmatically that a successful partnership can never be recklessly thrown away, because finding a combination of friendship, talent and personalities that gel might – with luck – happen only once. Meanwhile Freddie baldly made the point that they felt too old to be breaking up. 'Can you imagine forming a new band at forty?' he asked. 'Be a bit silly, wouldn't it?' He added the rider, 'And why kill the goose that lays the golden eggs?'

The sudden freedom opened up all sorts of opportunities for the four, of which the most obvious was the chance to indulge in solo recordings. Roger Taylor, of course, had already been down that road and currently had no plans to try again. With time on his hands, though, his fun-loving nature could lead him into harmless high jinks – as he confessed himself, he might never be a silly teenager again but that didn't stop him from sometimes feeling like one. Especially when he pulled a gentle prank during a short holiday in the ski resort of Aviemore, in the Scottish Highlands. Along with his personal assistant, a guy called Crystal Taylor, Roger went door-to-door along some of the town's streets, wanting to see how long it would take any householder to recognise the star on their doorstep. In the end, though, the joke was on Roger when no one twigged who he was. He soon decamped from Aviemore and went to Switzerland, wishing to lay down some tracks.

John Deacon, by his own admission, had next to no interest in making solo recordings. As the quiet man of Queen, he had already enjoyed many years in the limelight as their highly accomplished bass player. But, due to the fact that he rarely gave interviews and his intense sense of personal privacy, still virtually nothing was known about him; he was a genuine enigma to the public and press alike. Whenever a sufficient break in touring had opened up, being very family-oriented, he had inevitably jetted straight home to snatch whatever time was available. Now he was, therefore, more than delighted to have months on end to blend into a steady life with his wife. He liked occasionally making music with friends and in time he would team up with Roger Taylor at Mountain Studios.

But solo projects *were* to feature for both Brian May and Freddie Mercury. In fact, Mercury quickly booked recording time at

Musicland Studios, intending to start work on his debut solo album, an endeavour he had privately long anticipated and was gingered up about. However, he was soon hijacked off this when the Oscar-winning film producer Giorgio Moroder invited him to collaborate on some music for his remake of the classic silent movie *Metropolis*. On the film's release the following year, Freddie's contribution to its soundtrack joined those of Adam Ant and Billy Squier, among others.

Instead of starting work on his solo album, Mercury then plunged into socialising again. He had long since parted with Tony Bastin and had taken up with another man, a German called Winnie Kirkenberger, but it was not a monogamous relationship and Freddie enjoyed a riotous life in Munich. Perhaps due to his drug intake, his mood swings during this period became more pronounced and he would suddenly erupt into uncontrollable rages, sometimes even demolishing furniture. Afterwards, he couldn't recall his temper fits. However, lurid reports that he once, in the grip of a sexual drug-crazed frenzy, attempted to throttle Barbara Valentin, are apparently unfounded. Barbara declares, 'That just never happened. I don't know where that story came from.'

If he wasn't clubbing, Freddie was jet-setting. He soon left Germany for America, firstly to visit his favoured New York before heading off to California, where he had arranged to meet Michael Jackson, then currently working on his follow-up to *Thriller*. The idea was that they would record together and at Jackson's private studio in Encino they worked on two numbers, 'Victory' and 'State of Shock'. However, whilst Mercury was normally discreet about his cocaine use, it seems he grew tired of endlessly disappearing to the toilet. The American superstar evidently witnessed Mercury snorting coke and that was sufficient to freeze the friendship. The tapes of their two duets would remain unreleased.

Mercury was not usually so sloppy in his behaviour, as Radio 1 DJ Simon Bates can attest. Bates had been granted a rare question-and-answer session with Freddie (after his recording work with Michael Jackson had ended) and they met at Queen's offices. Simon recalls him as a gracious host who plied his guest with Earl Grey tea in delicate bone china cups before the formal ninety-minute interview commenced. Says Simon, 'He was almost Victorian in his manner and quite charming. He showed an interest in what I liked, and was fascinated with art, a subject on which he was clearly knowledgeable. Yes, he was a little insecure and when it came to the actual interview he suddenly didn't want to talk in front of the producer I had with me.'

He goes on, 'Freddie didn't want to discuss his parents, and the gay issue never came up – it had no bearing on his work as a musician. But otherwise, he was happy to talk about himself. He freely confessed to being a party animal who enjoyed life to the full. He believed that there were three of him. One was the hard-working professional, the second was the party animal and the third liked to be alone.'

When Brian May made his first foray into solo recording, he was far from alone. Accompanied by his wife, he had flown to Los Angeles at first to guest on a couple of tracks for his American singer friend Jeffrey Osborne but, whilst in LA, in late April, he roped in a few mates to help him experiment with some of the ideas that were coursing through his head.

He was joined at Record Plant Studios by guitarist Eddie Van Halen, keyboard player Fred Mandell, bass guitarist Philip Chen and drummer Alan Gratzer. Although it started out resembling a rather indulgent twelve-bar blues jam session, May gradually steered the scratch band into working on his own arrangement of the theme tune (originally written by Paul Bliss) for the TV sci-fi serial *Star Fleet*, as well as a number May had written years before called 'Let Me Out', and a more disciplined blues jam.

After adding further work to this base material, May later became the second Queen member to release a solo recording with the single 'Star Fleet'/'Son of Starfleet' on 24 October 1983, followed a week later by the mini-album *Starfleet Project*. Whereas Roger Taylor's 'I Wanna Testify' had failed to chart, May's debut single scraped in at number sixty-five. But his album stalled at thirty-five, nowhere near matching Taylor's *Fun in Space* peak of eighteen.

By the summer of 1983, both Mercury and May had returned to London where Deacon was staying. Taylor, on the other hand, was now at the glitzy Monaco Grand Prix with his personal assistant, Crystal, and also Rick Parfitt of Status Quo. Still unmarried, although committed to Dominique Beyrand, the irrepressible Roger adored the finer things in life – exotic hot climates and refined wines. The zest that characterised his live-wire personality meant that he was also wildly attracted to the clamour, drama and danger of motor racing. Such natural exuberance, particularly in the company of two other fun-lovers, this time became a recipe for trouble and Taylor wound up under arrest in the exclusive principality. His time behind bars was brief, however – only as long as it took Jim Beach to arrive, pay a large sum of money to release the star from jail and helicopter him out, since the authorities requested that Taylor leave Monaco immediately.

Queen were only halfway through their year off when they all got together in July at their manager's prompting. Jim Beach had interests in the film world and, because he was involved in an adaptation of the John Irving novel, *The Hotel New Hampshire*, he asked the band if they would consider recording its soundtrack. After Deacon and Mercury met the movie's director, Tony Richardson, to discuss the prospect, Queen agreed and studio time was booked at Record Plant Studios in Los Angeles for mid-August.

They embarked on the project with great enthusiasm. The break had done wonders and they were also inspired by this being the first time that they had recorded together in America. But unfortunately, although Queen felt rejuvenated, they found they could not tailor their style of music to this particular film and regretfully they ended up having to pull out.

The endeavour had got them firing on all cylinders again, though, and, as they had recently signed to the American giant Capitol Records, Queen set about making a new album, switching the recording to Munich's Musicland Studios. Back on a creative high, they were determined to put everything they had into this album. The first sign that they were succeeding came with their choice of a number written by Roger, called 'Radio Ga Ga', as their next single.

Taylor has described himself as an instinctive musician; a song-writer also proficient in percussion, guitar and, to a lesser extent, keyboards. He had composed 'Radio Ga Ga' using a synthesiser. It was a driving, pounding, very pop-oriented song, the lyrics of which extolled the virtues of sound over the public's increasing fixation with vision. That said, the pioneers of the pop video were deter-mined to outdo their own extravagant tendencies when it came to creating the new single's accompanying promotional film. This time it took on epic proportions.

The director in charge was David Mallett who recruited, at short notice, 500 Queen fan club members to play the extras who were marshalled for the one-day shoot on 23 November at Shepperton Studios. Each extra wore a silver-painted boiler suit; then they were lined up in serried ranks in front of a huge stage. At each chorus they had to clap their hands in sequence above their heads, which they got the hang of quicker than the band themselves did. The shoot finished around midnight, and with it was born the famous hand-clapping sequence that would go on to be adopted by concert crowds around the world. Part of the video also featured excerpts from Fritz Lang's silent movie *Metropolis*.

When 'Radio Ga Ga'/'I Go Crazy' was released on 23 January 1984 – the first single to carry the Queen 1 personal catalogue refer-ence, and the first of their records also to appear on the relatively new cassette single format – it entered the UK charts at number four and swiftly rose two places, but was kept off the top by the Frankie Goes to Hollywood hit 'Relax'. Its American best would be number sixteen. But in a total of nineteen other countries it reigned supreme, in some cases for several consecutive weeks.

And 'Radio Ga Ga' represented another Queen milestone. Because it was written by Roger Taylor, its chart success completed the metaphorical square – all four band members had now individ-ually penned a Top Ten hit. The edge was slightly taken off this, however, a week later when Queen's first live performance in

15 months was briefly marred by a backstage row which almost led to a fight. Although the incident was over in a flash, it seemed to indicate that, even though Queen were 'back together again', there was still a degree of tension among them.

# ELEVEN

# BACK ON TRACK

FREDDIE MERCURY DESCRIBED the incident between Roger Taylor and Brian May which occurred backstage when Queen were preparing to perform at the 1984 annual music festival in Italy's San Remo as a 'very heavy scene' that flared up out of nothing. It was well known that Roger operated on a much shorter fuse than Brian. Some say that the sparks began over material and/or some aspect of the stage but, according to Mercury, 'It was Roger squirting Brian in the face with hairspray or something. They nearly came to blows. It was a very tiny dressing room, very hot, and the whole thing just snowballed.'

The fact that such pent-up emotion still existed so close to the surface took John Deacon and Mercury by surprise but, recognising the potential consequences of the situation, Freddie moved swiftly to save the day – and, some believe, the entire future of Queen. Literally leaping between the rowing pair, Freddie, clowning at his most outrageous, ribbed them relentlessly until he wore the tense two down, breaking through their angry hostility until they dissolved into fits of laughter. His antics could have proved inflammatory but the four were such long-standing friends that Freddie's intuition was seldom wrong. That's not to say that sending his mates up always left him unscathed. If a story Freddie once related is true, Taylor did not always appreciate the finer points of Mercury's sometimes maddening behaviour. 'One night Roger was in a foul mood, and he threw his entire bloody drum set across the stage. The thing only just missed me. I might have been killed!' Freddie exaggerated.

In the event, Queen were a resounding success that night in San Remo. Backed by the strong performance of 'Radio Ga Ga' around the world, the scene was nicely set for them to haul themselves back on track after the disappointment of *Hot Space*, with their latest album *The Works*. This was vintage Queen, bristling with cleverly constructed and executed harmonies, intricate arrangements and precision production. The material, moreover, was much gutsier. Even the reviewers liked it, with May's hard-rocking 'Hammer to Fall' attracting particular praise, something which came as no surprise to many, including one of Queen's friends Joe Elliott, lead singer with the heavy metal band Def Leppard.

Elliott had first met Brian May whilst Queen were recording *Hot Space* in early 1982 when May, taking time out to attend a gig in Munich, had wandered backstage after Def Leppard had supported the headliners, Rainbow. They had become friends and Joe says, 'It's my personal belief that Brian was the big anchor of Queen. I don't mean to take anything away from the other three, but had it not been for Brian then I think they would have become a pop band and probably not so big as they are. Freddie, I feel, would have leaned more towards ballads and Roger to pop. "Radio Ga Ga" is a terrific Queen number, but very pop. The hard stuff is down to Brian. I think he kept a crucial and very unique balance in the band.'

Released on 27 February 1984, *The Works* stormed in at number two and remained in the UK album charts for a total of 93 weeks. When the second single from the album 'I Want to Break Free'/'Machines (or Back to Humans)' followed on 2 April, the critics reverted to slagging Queen but this did not prevent the song from reaching number three at home and, like its predecessor single, it went on to claim the top slot in several countries. 'I Want to Break Free', written by John Deacon, would be adopted as a freedom anthem in some quarters of South America, but there was no such seriousness in the air when Queen came up with their idea for its video.

No two Queen videos were ever quite alike. Each was intended to make an impression of sorts, and the message this time was very much that, despite their continuing success, the same band that was professional to the hilt was also quite capable of larking about. At Roger Taylor's suggestion, they each dressed up as a female character from the top-rated British soap, Granada TV's *Coronation Street*.

Attitudes towards rock stars dressing in drag for a promo had relaxed considerably since the Rolling Stones had done so for their 1966 hit 'Have You Seen Your Mother, Baby, Standing in the Shadow?' Then Mick Jagger had joked that it was just something in an Englishman's blood that meant he needed scant encouragement to slip on a dress for a laugh. Now, eighteen years on, another famous front man cheekily quipped to a television interviewer that it had not been hard for Brian, John and Roger to be persuaded to dress up. 'In fact, they ran into their frocks quicker than anything!' Freddie declared.

The video comprised three sections. The band first shot some scenes of themselves standing amid a crowd of supposedly futuristic brainwashed miners. This had taken place one cold day in a draughty warehouse at Limehouse Studios in London's Docklands. Again, the army of extras were fan club members, this time dressed in black-painted boiler suits.

Then came the drag sequence. It was filmed in a Battersea studio and was a lot of fun. Brian May, his face daubed with beauty cream, had to emerge inelegantly from bed in a pink nylon nightie and, with his hair in curlers, ram his feet into huge fluffy slippers and scramble downstairs to raid the fridge. John Deacon was cleverly aged to become a grey-faced, buttoned-up granny figure who, in hat and coat, hunched on the sofa, flashed frequent disapproving glances from behind a newspaper at Freddie Mercury's character – a sluttish-looking busty dame.

From the moment Mercury's hairy arm, pushing a vacuum cleaner, emerged from the kitchen doorway, a mustachioed Freddie was gloriously over the top in a tarty PVC split-sided mini skirt and tight sleeveless sweater with black bra straps showing. But the instigator of the whole idea was the ultimate scene-stealer, for Roger Taylor had been transformed into an alarmingly convincing sexy fifth-form schoolgirl, the tantalisingly short gymslip revealing his stocking tops with every saucy flick of his hip.

The third sequence involved only Mercury, teaming up again with his dancer friend Wayne Eagling. In preparation he had once more rehearsed with the Royal Ballet and Derek Deane recalls, 'Wayne had recreated the ballet *L'Après midi d'un faune* for Freddie and at one point there was a shot of Freddie rolling on his stomach on top of a line of rotating bodies along the floor. Now he just *loved* doing that bit!' Eagling adds, 'We made Freddie Nijinsky because he had wanted for a long time to appear as a great dancer and this was his chance.'

Choreographing for someone who is not a ballet dancer is difficult, and the scene took an entire day to film, although it features less than a minute in the video. When it was released to accompany the single, the video (which was obviously meant to be funny) provoked accusations of outrageous transvestism and claims that such gay behaviour could corrupt the nation's youth. Shrugging these claims aside, Queen were in Montreux the following month, when they made an appearance at the annual Golden Rose Festival. They would not be touring to promote their latest album until the summer, and this allowed each member time to pursue his own endeavours for a while longer.

Deacon concentrated, as ever, on his family, while May occasionally guested on friends' albums. He was also closely involved with a company called Guild Guitars in New York who were planning to produce a commercial replica version of Brian's world-famous 'Red Special' guitar, the BHM1 (Brian Harold May 1), which would be launched in June. Mercury reverted to his usual hectic social life, which meant haunting the nightclubs in Munich and London.

Peter Stringfellow recalls Freddie around this time. 'Monday night at my Hippodrome club was now gay night and one night I was on the balcony with my girlfriend when suddenly a weird atmosphere came over the place. There was a big buzz of excitement and everyone, about 2,500 people, had stopped whatever they had been doing and looked at something. It was Freddie. He had arrived, dressed all in white, and it was literally as if the Queen of Sheba had walked in. The crowd went completely berserk. It was a strong example of Freddie's personal power. A thunderous applause got up which Freddie took entirely as his due. His attitude was, "Well, of course! *I've* just walked in. What can you expect?" By now Freddie lived in his own world, doing his own thing and very few people got near him.'

In time one of those few would be a stockily built, dark-haired Irishman called Jim Hutton who worked in a barber shop in the prestigious Savoy Hotel. Their first brief encounter in late 1983 in the Cocobana, a gay basement club in South Kensington, had been less than propitious when Hutton, in a relationship, had rebuffed Mercury's offer to buy him a drink. Months later, however, with Hutton and his live-in partner having parted, Mercury was apparently taking a keen interest — albeit still from a distance — in the hairdresser's movements. They would not get together quite yet but Hutton believes that the star was already weighing him up as a prospective future partner.

Jim Hutton would indeed become very important to Mercury but right then Freddie was, if anything, less choosy than ever. Though friends would attest to how refined the star could be, he was also capable of extreme coarseness; he once boasted, 'I'm just an old slag who gets up every morning, scratches his head and wonders who he wants to fuck.'

For Roger Taylor, meanwhile, solo work had been occupying his time at the recording studios in Montreux. The fruits of this came with two single releases that summer, firstly 'Man on Fire'/'Killing Time' which peaked at number sixty-six in June (having been ignored by radio), followed by 'Strange Frontier'/'I Cry For You' which again, starved of airplay, barely scraped into the Top 100 the next month. His second solo album *Strange Frontier*, released on 7 July 1984, however, made it to number thirty.

For Taylor, as for May, it had become clear that – although they enjoyed the release of branching out into solo work – they were indeed stronger within the confines of Queen. And this was borne out when Queen's third single of the year 'It's a Hard Life'/'Is This the World We Created' was released in mid-July and quickly lodged at number six. The title of the A-side was rather apt as Queen, despite having recently been honoured with the Silver Clef Award at the annual Nordoff-Robbins Music Therapy Centre Lunch in London, were currently taking considerable flak from the music press. This was because they had just announced that, after their upcoming European tour, they intended to perform at the Sun City Super Bowl in South Africa.

Several anti-apartheid groups set up an instant chorus of disapproval over this and it also brought Queen into conflict with the Musicians' Union. Queen attempted to quell the rumpus by declaring that they were a very non-political group and had not taken the decision lightly. John Deacon pointed out that the band simply sought to explore new territories and anyway they were not setting any precedent, as artistes including Elton John, Cliff Richard and Rod Stewart had already performed in South Africa. But the controversy would not easily die down.

That this latest to-do came so soon after the contentious 'I Want to Break Free' video in no way deterred Queen from releasing a video to accompany 'It's a Hard Life' that was a study in screen decadence. It had been filmed in Munich, for the first time using director Tim Pope, and the opulent settings were more than matched by the outrageous costumes all four wore. Mercury was hard to miss in a scarlet costume decorated with a startling series of Cyclops eyes; and May looked menacing in a black and gold robe, carrying a specially made guitar in the shape of a skull and bones. Taylor and Deacon, meanwhile, wore outfits of matching splendour: Deacon was in a silver costume, overlaid at the knees, thighs, waist, elbows and neck with a metallic feather effect and carrying a silver unicorn headdress; and Taylor became a decadent Elizabethan courtier in a tunic with diamond-shaped designs, sporting a grand white ruff around his neck. The costumes were all very hot to wear which had made filming uncomfortable.

Leaving the critics to make what they would of their latest offering, Queen went to Munich to spend July in intensive rehearsals for their first tour since November 1982. It might have been a while, but Roger Taylor declared on the band's behalf, 'We still have the rock 'n' roll gypsy mentality,' and so the 'The Works' tour commenced on 24 August at the Forest Nationale in Brussels. With them for the first time on stage, was a new keyboard player who would become a familiar face to Queen fans, Spike Edney.

Edney had lately worked with the Boomtown Rats and his intro-duction to Queen had come via Crystal Taylor. Says Spike, 'Queen invited me to an audition in Munich and I went, thinking there'd be a queue. Only I found that I was the only one. I knew all their material anyway, so that was me in. I was with Queen from that tour right through to Knebworth, two years later.'

From Belgium, the tour touched Eire before arriving in Britain for three dates at the Birmingham NEC, followed by four nights at London's Wembley Arena. And it was just before they headed to Germany for their gig at Dortmund's Westallenhalle that 'Hammer to Fall'/'Tear It Up' was released on 10 September. A powerful and popular stage number, it notched up a number thirteen hit for Queen.

For Freddie, the same date saw the arrival of his debut solo single in his own name ('I Can Hear Music' had been released under Larry Lurex). 'Love Kills', a rock/disco number, co-written with Giorgio Moroder for the film soundtrack of *Metropolis*, and backed by 'Rotwangs Party', would become a massive hit in European gay clubs. And it was no slouch in the British mainstream market either, reaching number ten, thereby beating Queen's latest single and also bettering any chart solo achievement of his fellow band members.

Queen performed the latter gigs of their European tour, which ended on 30 September at Vienna's Stadhalle, with an injured front man; Freddie had tripped on a flight of stage stairs and damaged his knee ligaments. It was regarded as more than a slip-up in judgement, however, when soon afterwards Queen arrived in Bophuthatswana. To the superstitious, the trip might have seemed downright jinxed.

Tickets for all twelve scheduled gigs at the Sun City Super Bowl had sold out in twenty-four hours but, in fact, Queen would perform only half of those dates. The first gig, on 5 October 1984, was only minutes old when Mercury developed voice problems. Instantly recognising Freddie's predicament, the others tried to rally him but it was no use. Spike Edney recalls, 'Fred was in agony and after three songs he had to walk off stage.' Mercury once likened the small painful nodules on his vocal chords to recurring corns, admitting, 'It's misusing the voice that does it.'

Mercury had been known to continue performing against medical advice, but this time he had no option but to obey the doctor's edict that his voice needed a complete rest. Queen therefore scratched the next four gigs; an unpopular decision, as Edney confirms: 'It caused a big scandal because the tickets were sold and there was no time to reschedule dates, but it simply couldn't be helped.'

The six remaining dates would resume on 10 October and end ten days later and, for most of the enforced lay-off, the band stayed within the confines of the luxurious Sun City complex. In October, however, in Soweto on the outskirts of Johannesburg, the annual Black African Awards show is held and – to the nervousness of some Sun City officials – Brian May honoured an invitation extended to him to present some of the prizes. Accompanied by Queen's manager, May went to the south-west township, where the fight for freedom in South Africa had really begun; on a stark stage in an open muddy field, with warm rain falling on his face, he handed out awards. He was deeply moved by the warmth shown him and publicly pledged that Queen would one day perform in Soweto.

The whole band was affected by the plight of many South Africans and they would release a live album there from which all the royalties would go directly to support an ailing Bophuthatswana school for deaf and blind children. Says Spike Edney, 'We'd all been very happy to have the chance to play South Africa. It taught you not to listen to people pontificating about something they really know nothing about. For Queen, it was definitely an enlightening experience.'

Queen were opposed to apartheid but not everyone felt that the rock stars had truly appreciated the serious political implications involved in having performed there. Mandla Langa, cultural attaché with the African National Congress, states, 'Queen came into the country at a time when people didn't need any external influence which could give respectability to the Pretoria regime. Sun City was always regarded as an insult to any right-thinking South African. To perform there, in the midst of poverty and rage, cannot be rationalised as Queen doing their bit through music to break down the barriers. It must also be remembered, that the people who attended those concerts were overwhelmingly white, and that institutions such as the South African Broadcasting Corporation, revelling at their new-found connection with the Western world, would give maximum airplay time to Queen. Their music then, and possibly still now – because people have long memories – has never been embraced by black activists.'

The fall-out from this trip would see Queen being placed on the United Nations blacklist of musicians who played in South Africa, although their name was later removed. And in Britain they fell foul of the Musicians' Union, whose members had been banned from performing in South Africa. The Union's General Committee were not appeased by an impassioned speech Brian May personally made on the band's behalf before them, and fined Queen heavily. They stumped up, on condition that the money be donated to charity.

There were to be more sour notes before the year was out. A week after the release of a four-track video compilation EP called 'The Works', on 26 November came 'Thank God It's Christmas'/'Man on the Prowl'/'Keep Passing the Open Windows'. But Queen's first specifically targeted attempt at a Christmas single failed to make the Top Twenty, and nowhere near threatened that year's dead cert, 'Do They Know It's Christmas' by Band Aid.

The charity single in aid of an Ethiopian famine disaster had been co-written by Boomtown Rats vocalist Bob Geldof and ex-Ultravox singer Midge Ure, and performed by thirty-six invited rock stars, among them Cliff Richard, Paul Young, George Michael, Boy George, Sting, Phil Collins, as well as Status Quo and Duran Duran. Queen had not been invited. The controversy over their South African shows possibly played a part in their not having been asked but, whatever the reason, it pricked the band and Freddie Mercury later lamented, 'I would have *loved* to have been on the Band Aid record.'

While Queen watched 'Do They Know It's Christmas' become the biggest-selling single in Britain for several years, in December they themselves came under attack from the rock critics for releasing a series of singles which, in essence, were all individual tracks from one album. Critics' claims that this was tantamount to fan exploitation – something Queen prided themselves in never being guilty of – was another confidence-shaker as their first year performing as a band again drew to a close.

There was scant time to brood though. They might have been left out of the loop on the Band Aid celebrity charity single but Queen kicked off 1985 by headlining at a star-studded ten-day event near Brazil's Rio de Janeiro which was hailed as the biggest rock festival in the world and was billed as bigger than the fabled 1969 Woodstock. Organised by local businessman Roberto Medina, 'Rock in Rio' was staged at an arena built in the mountains at Barra da Tijuca and the event would feature such acts as Ozzie Osbourne, Yes, AC/DC and Iron Maiden. In front of a record-breaking audience of over a quarter of a million, Queen closed the first show in the early hours of 12 January and Iron Maiden's lead singer, Bruce Dickinson, has vivid memories of the event.

Says Bruce, 'The whole thing was an incredible circus in the sense that it created, locally, hysteria akin to Beatlemania. Everyone was helicoptered in to the site, but because of the opposition from town they weren't allowed to fly at night, so it was, like, five hours in traffic getting back. Once there, though, it was some set-up. There were roving gangs of security guards, all of whom looked in foul moods. Well everything was running behind time and Maiden were already fifteen minutes late in getting on stage. And it was all pretty hairy. This furious row had erupted in the hallway, right outside our dressing room. Two gangs of security guards had gone mental and were waving pistols at each other, on top of their guard dogs all snarling and straining at their leads. We were hiding like cowards. Then suddenly one of our own security guys chanced poking his head round the door and saying, "Hey guys? Would you mind giving it a rest until we can get on stage?" And they did! It all went quiet and we scuttled past. But as soon as our backs were turned, they all started arguing again!'

It was following Iron Maiden's performance that Queen came on stage and things did not entirely go according to plan. Bruce Dickinson reveals, 'Two or three of their numbers didn't go down well with the crowd. Then when they launched into "I Want to Break Free", the audience didn't really take to Freddie having dressed up in women's clothes. But Freddie obviously didn't understand what was wrong.'

A South American audience had once before pounded the stage with missiles, which Queen then discovered had been a traditional show of appreciation and Freddie had later remarked of such exuberant Latin audiences, 'They get over-excited sometimes, but I can bring the whip down and show them who is in control'. But as cans and rubble were hurled at them this time, there was a distinctly menacing feel in the air. Crowds have personalities and Mercury had misjudged this one. Swiftly he dispensed with the drag clothes and Queen soldiered on as if nothing had happened.

They earned their encores and went down a storm, but after they quit the stage on a high Mercury showed the extent of his pent-up emotions. Bruce reveals, 'When Freddie came off stage, he broke down in tears. He just had no idea why the audience had reacted like they did. Someone quickly told Queen that "I Want to Break Free" was regarded as a freedom song there, and that the crowd had resented them sending it up. It explained the situation, but Freddie was very upset by it.'

Queen's minor *faux pas* was easily forgotten at the lavish post-gig party that EMI threw that night for all the festival participants at the plush Copacabana Beach Hotel. The bash was screened live on Brazilian television, including some of the guests' capers, such as diving fully clothed into a swimming pool.

A week would separate Queen's two performances at 'Rock in Rio' – this time they closed the event in the early hours of 19 January. Globo TV had recorded the entire festival and the rights to Queen's performances were brought for a future video release. In between, there was time to relax. Spike Edney recalls, 'The whole thing was treated as a holiday, with loads of stars hangin' out together by the hotel pools and bars. But what "Rock in Rio" did for Queen was reaffirm their standing as South America's top band.'

Once back in Britain, all four involved themselves with their private lives or other professional projects. John Deacon went back to his family, while Roger Taylor produced a single by actor Jimmy Nail, as well as working separately with vocalists Feargal Sharkey and Who frontman Roger Daltrey.

Brian May wrote a chapter for inclusion in an Oxford University Press book by Michael Stimpson called *The Guitar: A Guide for Students and Teachers*, as well as contributing to an accompanying BBC TV short film about the author's work, after which he guested as a disc jockey for a show on London's Capital Radio. And Freddie Mercury returned to London's gay scene to adopt the latest 'high clone' look of tight blue jeans and white vest.

His favourite club around now was Heaven and it was there in late March that he and Jim Hutton would finally click. This time when the singer offered Hutton a drink, Jim instead offered to buy Freddie a vodka. Mercury accepted; then, with crass curiosity, demanded,

'How big's your dick?'. Hutton accompanied Mercury to his Kensington flat later that night where, after petting his two cats, Freddie snorted more cocaine and the pair went to bed. They parted the next morning after promising to keep in touch.

Mercury may not have been in love quite yet but his second solo single, released on 9 April 1985, was the romantic number 'I Was Born to Love You'/'Stop All the Fighting'. Again his solo work fared very well and it reached number eleven; his debut solo album *Mr Bad Guy*, a mix of different musical styles reflecting Mercury's vocal range, did even better, scoring a number six in Britain at the end of the month, despite being savaged by the critics.

April, however, saw Queen busy with a tour of New Zealand and Australia – one that was marked by continual unwelcome reminders of their Sun City trip. When they arrived for their feverishly anticipated New Zealand debut at Auckland's Mount Smart Stadium they were met at the airport, their hotel and the concert venue by groups of chanting anti-apartheid demonstrators.

Three days later, on 16 April, Queen hit Australia for a total of eight gigs, split between Melbourne and Sydney. At the last of the four gigs held at Melbourne's Sports and Entertainments Centre, ex-Genesis drummer, now solo performer Phil Collins, who was himself touring the country, turned up to see Queen. But, as Collins admitted, he annoyed Freddie by going backstage *before* the show, when a tensed-up Mercury was being made ready for the stage whilst downing the vodka.

That night's performance was a disappointment. They had trouble with the lighting effects and the sound quality ended up below their normal high standard. The Sydney dates, by comparison, went smoothly and whilst there they met up with their ex-manager John Reid. Elton John was also on an Australian tour and on a mutual night off they all got together. May and Deacon opted to join Reid for a civilised visit to a performance at the famous Opera House. Mercury, Taylor and Elton John, in contrast, rushed headlong into the colourful Sydney nightclubs.

Hard on the heels of their trip down under, Queen embarked on what would turn out to be their last ever tour of the Far East, which ended on 15 May at the Castle Hall in Osaka. As they returned to London, they were busy mulling over a proposition that had been put to them the previous month whilst they were in New Zealand. Spike Edney explains, 'I had briefly joined the Boomtown Rats between Queen's "Works" tour and them going to Australia, and Bob Geldof rang me up in New Zealand. He told me about an idea he and Midge Ure had to follow up the Band Aid single with a massive rock concert, and he wondered if Queen would appear as one of the acts on the bill.'

Spike maintains that Geldof had approached him first unofficially, in case Queen declined. Edney, as requested, relayed the idea to Queen. He states, 'I know that Brian and Roger had been bitterly disappointed not to have been asked the previous year to be involved in the "Do They Know It's Christmas" single and so I wasn't surprised that at first Queen were piqued by the prospect in theory. But it seemed too ambitious a project to ever really get off the ground. And so they initially said no.'

But when relaying Queen's refusal to Geldof, Spike Edney had impressed on the Boomtown Rats singer that he should not take this as final and should approach the band himself. When Geldof duly managed to track Queen down, their next response was that they would consider appearing *if* he and Midge Ure ever did pull off such a bold undertaking.

By the time Queen were back on British oil, this seemingly problem-laden project was indeed definitely happening. In fact, matters had gathered sufficient pace that the massive concert in aid of Ethiopia was growing in size and shape all the time. It was to be staged at London's Wembley Stadium in the summer and a parallel gig was now planned in Philadelphia. It even had a name – 'Live Aid'. Says Spike Edney, 'By now Bob Geldof had persuaded the BBC to set up a satellite link to the States and Queen absolutely decided that they were in. It was frankly just too good a thing not to be part of.'

From their initial reluctance to be part of the event rapidly dubbed 'A global juke box', Queen were determined to get keyed up for this hot summer's day when they would have a chance to turn on the magic amid a feast of rock giants and before the entire world. They would keep it simple and straight; they would completely steal the show.

# MAGIC
# MOMENTS

O N 10 JULY Queen commenced three days of intensive
rehearsals at the Shaw Theatre in London's Euston Road
for their allocated twenty-minute slot in Live Aid. To the
band the time restriction meant that to produce the best showcase
during their segment, they ought to concentrate on performing a
skilfully edited medley of their most famous hits. Spike Edney
remarks, 'Later, such a fuss was made about how ingenious Queen
had been, but to us it was the most obvious thing to do.'

Live Aid was a truly historic event. The sixteen-hour marathon
gig kicked off at London's Wembley Stadium noon on Saturday,
13 July 1985, and by 6 p.m. British time had hooked up by satellite
to the parallel US gig staged at the JFK Stadium in Philadelphia.
It was the first time that an event involving performances from a
host of rock celebrities had been attempted on this scale. But it
was not the first concert to be simultaneously broadcast live by
satellite to over one billion people worldwide – that distinction went
to Elvis Presley for his legendary 1973 performance, *Elvis: Aloha
From Hawaii*.

Twelve years on, Live Aid's line-up included Status Quo, Paul McCartney, Bob Dylan, Mick Jagger, Tina Turner, Dire Straits, Bryan Adams, Paul Young, David Bowie and many more. Queen followed Bowie on stage around 6.30 p.m. Dressed down, and without their usual extravagant lights and effects, they were nakedly on display as 'men at work' and as such they turned in a truly dynamic performance – practically a lesson in professional excellence. Their music was punchy and tight, and all four played out of their skins. But, even within the band itself, it was acknowledged that the biggest credit for this stunning exhibition performance should go to Freddie Mercury. Modestly, Brian May would later state that the rest of the band perhaps helped but he admitted that it was largely Freddie's triumph.

Looking muscular and fit, Mercury paraded and prowled, taking possession of the stage. He stood with his feet planted wide apart, and controlled and commanded the audience. With his head thrown back, he soaked up their adulation; then, with a flash of his toothy smile, he disarmed that self-same arrogance. But in whatever mode, like a rock pied piper, he would not be denied and within minutes he had the heaving mass of humanity happily eating out of his hand. Roger Taylor once paid tribute to Mercury's ability to communicate with the back row of a giant stadium. This was not a Queen concert crowd. Yet, by the time they performed 'We Are the Champions', the swaying forest of extended arms around the grounds and the sound of the massed voices singing along, provided an unforgettable display of unity. Queen were untouchable that day – a fact that, egos aside, few could dispute.

Fellow performer Paul Young agrees. 'I'd always liked Queen, but that was the night I said to myself, "These boys really are fantastic." The sound they managed to get was absolutely amazing. There was just the four of them on there, with none of their usual trappings, and they *still* blew everyone away. Freddie, too, proved to the whole watching world that evening just what a showman he was.'

While Cliff Richard, who would come to know Freddie and later take his place among guests at exquisite dinner parties held at Garden

Lodge, recognised Mercury's move at once. Says Cliff, 'I myself couldn't take part in Live Aid as I was committed to a gospel charity gig in Birmingham. But I managed to see snatches of the show, and the second I saw Freddie launch into his act it was obvious that he was going to completely steal the show.'

And Thin Lizzy lead guitarist, Scott Gorham, has his own inimitable view of the event. He states, 'Man, there was six hours of Euro wimp! Everybody was thinkin', God, who asked them along? And then Queen came on, and there's Fred stickin' out his chest and daring the world not to like them. It was amazing, like the rebirth of Queen on the spot. When you'd seen those guys, who wanted to see the rest?'

Queen themselves took time to comprehend the full extent of their triumph. John Deacon admitted that, though they were aware that they had done well, it took weeks to sink in just *how* well. Whilst Roger Taylor, recalling the immediate feedback after they had left the stage, told of Elton John barging in on Queen, yelling that they had stolen the show. Even so, the drummer put Elton's enthusiasm down to friendship.

Of course, the *raison d'être* for Live Aid had not been to provide a global platform to boost a rock band's career, but to raise money for, and awareness of, the plight of the starving in Ethiopia and the man originally responsible for it all was the award-winning BBC foreign affairs correspondent Michael Buerk. It had been his special televised report on the crisis in November 1984 that had influenced Bob Geldof to motivate the rock world to help.

Says Michael Buerk, 'When the whole Live Aid thing got going, I must admit, my original feeling was that it was a bandwagon thing which would die out in a week and wouldn't achieve anything in effective terms. I didn't see much connection between the pop world and dying people. Shows you how wrong I was. It certainly increased the level of consciousness about the situation, which in turn placed pressure on governments around the world, and that was a good thing. Two million people were estimated to be due to die in that famine and in the end 800,000 did. So Live Aid was at least, in part, responsible for saving over a million lives.' Giving a rare insight into his personal view of the rock world, John Deacon called Live Aid the one day that he was proud to be involved in the music business.

For Queen there were several spin-off benefits. Extra life was breathed into their record sales, which leapt around the world as a whole new generation got turned on to them. Their triumph at this giant charity gig helped dim down the Sun City débâcle. And it rejuvenated their belief in themselves. Prior to Live Aid, Queen had slightly started to doubt whether the band had anything left to give and they had been considering whether, once again, they wanted to give things a rest for a while. Deacon also reflected that, because they had now achieved such a high level of success around the world, in a sense some of the incentive had been removed. But all that was now forgotten and they were fired up and eager to start planning a major European tour for next year. Before that, however, Queen scattered to have some time off.

It was during this summer of 1985 that Queen, and in particular Freddie Mercury, discovered the delights of Pikes Hotel, a luxurious complex on the Mediterranean island of Ibiza, which had a well-deserved worldwide reputation as an exclusive hideaway of the stars. It is owned by Tony Pike, who recalls, 'I first met Freddie just after Live Aid. I already knew Jim Beach but I hadn't met any of Queen. So this particular day I got word that Freddie and his friends had arrived. I went down to the courtyard to greet Freddie personally and he gave me the campest of handshakes, with an equally camp "Hello" to match, and that was it. He didn't say another word. His entourage included Jim Hutton, Peter Straker and Peter Freestone. They were occupying the whole of the hotel's oldest part for easier security arrangements and without another word Freddie brushed past me and disappeared inside and I thought, Oh ho, this one's going to be difficult.'

As Tony Pike testifies, though, nothing could have been further from the truth. Over the next five years, Mercury often came to

Pikes Hotel and became good friends with Tony who got to know the star well. Says Tony, 'Freddie truly was a wonderful human being, very attentive to others' needs and would always apologise for anything untoward happening. He was unfailingly grateful to the staff for just doing their job, but that was what he was like.'

He goes on, 'It varied, but whilst here Freddie enjoyed dinner parties, playing tennis – often I would partner him – but he was more of a poser than a player really. And he liked to entertain. He'd be lying at the poolside and suddenly say, "Go and get the piano". Well! A piano is a heavy thing but about six men would stagger down with it and Fred would play and sing for everyone, not just his own set. Sometimes he'd then get campy and start horsing around, throwing people into the water and generally having fun, which again inevitably ended up also involving other guests. But he never upset anyone who preferred to keep their distance from this kind of carry-on.'

According to Pike, Mercury was circumspect when it came to his homosexuality. 'In all the years Freddie came here,' states Tony, 'never did he push it onto anyone. Sure he loved camping it up. He was gay, but he was very secure in that fact and unless he was in the mood to caper, you'd never witness his homosexuality. In fact, most women that I saw found him very attractive indeed. He had a good physique and was a very masculine-looking man. He was also not one of those gay men in whose company you feel uneasy. I have experienced that, but never with Freddie.'

Mercury's discretion is borne out by the fact that Jim Hutton had accompanied Freddie to Pikes a few times before Tony learned the nature of their relationship. Pike explains, 'One day I asked Jim where he fitted in because I knew by then that he wasn't involved in music. Jim is very quiet, reserved and very masculine and there had been no demonstrative behaviour between him and Freddie on any occasion, so I wasn't being crass. He looked at me straight and asked, "Don't you know?" I shook my head and he said simply, "I'm Freddie's man." I felt awful for prying when I hadn't meant to.' Tony adds, 'Jim and Freddie never exhibited their love in public. No arms around each other or any other indication that they were lovers. Fred was so publicly the outrageous showman of rock, but in private I think that Jim had a steadying influence on him.'

By late summer Queen would regroup in the recording studio. Only Mercury at this stage was producing any solo material. On 1 July the number 'Made in Heaven'/'She Blows Hot & Cold' had been released, and this was followed on 2 September with 'Living On My Own'/'My Love is Dangerous'. The performance of these solo singles, however, had slipped considerably in comparison to his past form. And his work would take an even worse dip when, two months later, 'Love Me Like There's No Tomorrow'/'Let's Turn It On' languished at number seventy-six. Expectations were, in contrast, very high for Queen's new material.

Just as Live Aid had triggered thoughts of a 1986 tour, now that they were back in the studio, Queen could not wait to knuckle down. This creative energy dovetailed neatly with an approach from director Russell Mulcahy about Queen writing music for what would be his first major feature Hollywood movie – the $20 million *Highlander* starring Christopher Lambert and Sean Connery. With the proviso that one of their numbers be used as the film's theme song, Queen agreed, and by September 1985 they were beavering away on a new album in Musicland, Mountain and Town House Studios.

On 4 November came their only single of the year 'One Vision'/'Blurred Vision'. The A-side would be used on the sound-track for the 1986 action adventure movie *Iron Eagle* and in the UK singles chart it rose to number seven. Their pleasure in this, however, was blunted when 'One Vision' was attacked by reviewers who considered its lyrics to be a blatant Live Aid cash-in (in actual fact, according to Taylor, they had been inspired by the late black American civil rights leader Martin Luther King's famous 'I have a dream' speech). Even though they had become inured to music press criticism, this hurt. Cries also grew that Queen should donate the single's royalties to charity. But the band was already donating money from the number 'Is This the World We Created', performed at Live Aid, to the Save the Children Fund, and supported various charities in other ways.

The embers over Sun City, although cooler, had not altogether died out. To finally extinguish the row, Queen decided in December to issue an unequivocal press statement. It firmly set out the band's anti-apartheid stance and pledged that they would never again visit South Africa (a vow that particularly upset Brian May in the light of his announcement that night in Soweto at the Black African Awards).

On 2 December 1985 Queen released *The Complete Works*, a boxed set of their albums to date (excluding the *Greatest Hits*), digitally remastered, and with a bonus album called *Complete Vision*. This extra album was made up of singles and B-sides that had not featured as tracks on their existing albums. Meanwhile the band concentrated on work for their new album – the *Highlander* soundtrack which took them well into 1986.

On 17 March the first single 'A Kind of Magic'/'A Dozen Red Roses for My Darling' was released in Britain where – accompanied by a stunning video which made startling use of special effects and animated figures that interacted with the band members in performance – it peaked at number three. In a total of thirty-five other countries, however, Roger Taylor's catchy, cleverly composed pop song seized the top slot. When *A Kind of Magic*, which featured Joan Armatrading guesting on the track 'Don't Lose Your Head', emerged on 2 June it entered the UK album charts at number one and would quickly go double-platinum.

But this triumph was not mirrored in the States where the *Highlander* soundtrack album was released the following day, and it was symptomatic of what had been Queen's state of play in America for some time now. This new album, like their last two US releases, failed to make the Top Twenty; and in the singles market their performance was poor. Instead of releasing the title track Capitol Records had opted for the hard-rocking number 'Princes of the Universe' but, despite an impressive video that included an appearance by *Highlander*'s star Christopher Lambert, the single failed to chart.

Iron Maiden's Bruce Dickinson has his own opinion on this dip in Queen's Stateside fortunes. He says, 'There is a white, homophobic – bonehead – bunch of people in the States, and there was a large minority who'd kinda worked out that Freddie wasn't one of us, if you know what I mean. When that minority grew, it put the lights out for Queen in America for a time.'

To others, the reasons were more practical. Queen had not toured the United States since 1982 and this particularly disadvantaged the band, according to Bhaskar Menon, an ex-president of Capitol Records. It seems that Freddie Mercury viewed this as a Catch-22 situation. Personally, he only wanted Queen to return to live performance in America provided it was a cast-iron success. Yet, at the same time, he was apparently disinclined to put in the effort required to ensure such an outcome. Roger Taylor, for his part, later reflected that Queen had 'ignored' America during this period. But he maintained that they had been scarcely aware of their declining popularity there in the mid-eighties, because their focus had lain squarely on other territories. One such territory was Europe where they would commence a major tour in the summer. But, before that, in spring, the four again went their separate ways.

In the past, these breaks had for Mercury marked periods of frantic promiscuity, but this time things were different. Near the end of 1985 AIDS first hit the headlines with the death from the disease of Hollywood screen idol Rock Hudson. While little was as yet known about the fatal illness, its very existence sent terror rippling through the world's gay communities. Of the three known high-risk categories – homosexuals, people who practised unprotected sex with multiple partners, and drug addicts – Freddie fell into two. As for drug addicts? How could he know whether any of his countless one-night stands had used drugs and shared needles.

Secretly Mercury underwent an AIDS test, which proved negative; and in his immense relief he effected a sudden about-turn. Freddie later admitted, 'I lived for sex. I was extremely promiscuous but AIDS changed my life' (meaning the threat of contracting the killer disease). As 1985 ended he shocked his German friends by suddenly abandoning the gay scene that he had adored for so long in Munich, and in London he seriously curtailed his predatory rounds of the gay circuit; although he continued to be unfaithful on occasions to Jim Hutton.

Away from Queen, in April 1986, Freddie involved himself with a London stage musical project at the invitation of one of his closest friends Dave Clark, formerly of the sixties group the Dave Clark Five, whom Mercury had first met ten years earlier at Queen's Hyde Park gig. Called *Time*, the West End musical's central character was a spiritual rock star and was played for its first year's run by Cliff Richard. Mercury contributed three tracks to the musical's soundtrack, including one of the show's best numbers, as Cliff recalls: 'Freddie got to record "In My Defence" for the album, much to my chagrin, because the number was one of my favourites and I'd really wanted to do it myself, but Dave asked Freddie.' On 6 May Mercury released 'Time'/'Time (instrumental version)' as his sixth solo single, but it petered out at a disappointing number thirty-two.

Roger Taylor had, for now, put his solo recording career on hold. He and John Deacon would occasionally guest on friends' albums, and in fact both the drummer and bassist would perform on Elton John's album *Leather Jackets*. But this was the moment when John Deacon chose to make his first – and what would turn out to be his last – foray into solo work. He had been invited to record a number for the soundtrack of a forthcoming film called *Biggles*, a sci-fi adventure based on characters created by Captain W.E. Johns, which was directed by John Hough and starred Neil Dickson, Alex Hyde-White and Peter Cushing. Deacon agreed and, purely for this purpose, along with fellow musicians Robert Ahwai and Lenny Zakatek, he temporarily formed a group he called the Immortals. The *Biggles* soundtrack album was released in June, one month after Deacon's solo single 'No Turning Back'/'No Turning Back (chocs away mix)' which failed to chart.

Brian May, meanwhile, was preoccupied with more personal matters. For a variety of reasons, which he and Chrissy kept private, their ten-year marriage was heading for the rocks. Queen's hectic touring and recording commitments had placed huge restraints on the quality and length of time that they could devote to one another and Brian had been aware for a while that all was not right between them. Because they were both determined not to give up easily on such a long relationship, which had produced two children on whom they both doted, they had been papering over the cracks but their underlying problems continued to multiply.

When rehearsals began for the band's forthcoming European tour, they initially seemed to provide a welcome distraction from May's marital problems. But it was during a break in these that Brian was introduced to actress Anita Dobson when fate brought them together at the London première of the Hollywood movie *Down and Out in Beverly Hills*. The petite dark-haired Dobson was then one of Britain's best-known television actresses (in her role as the volatile landlady Angie Watts in the top-rated BBC soap *EastEnders*) and, although her full-on effervescent energy seemed the exact opposite of May's quiet reserve, some chemistry occurred between the two.

Brian later said that he saw Anita as very much a rock 'n' roll person, in the sense that she had had to fight her way to the limelight. On an impulse he asked if she would attend one of the band's upcoming Wembley Stadium gigs. Whether Brian recognised the significance of his invitation or not, Anita Dobson was destined to become more than just a friend.

Queen would score a number fourteen hit with the single 'Friends Will Be Friends'/'Seven Seas of Rhye' released on 9 June. By this time, they had just embarked on their 'Magic Tour' at Stockholm's Rasunda Fotbollstadion. It was a gig bookended by vastly differing reactions. On their arrival at the venue, the band were dismayed to be met outside yet again by a vociferous crowd of anti-apartheid protestors. However, inside the stadium this first audience on their 1986 summer tour went wild throughout the gig, only to cross over into delirium when, at the end, Mercury pulled off a typical piece of theatre by vanishing off stage and reappearing wearing a glorious red velvet silk-lined robe, trimmed with fake ermine and with a six-foot train. Holding his trademark sawn-off microphone stand as a sceptre, he had a glorious jewel-encrusted Coronation crown on his head. Despite the weight of both crown and cloak, Freddie wore his regalia lightly, as if born to it, and the fans erupted in homage.

Days later they moved on through Holland, arriving in France for their 14 June gig at the Hippodrome de Vincennes in Paris and it was in this city that Marillion joined the tour. Marillion's then frontman Fish recalls, 'We'd gone to support Queen on the open-air gigs, which was to be the last live dates that they'd do. Off-stage, Freddie kept himself very much to himself, but on-stage he was the most outrageous frontman. I watched him a lot during that tour, and I think he made me a little less self-conscious. He was so cocky and totally self-assured, but then anybody who performs in front of crowds of people *has* to have an enormous ego. It's an incredible feeling of power and satisfaction. Some say it's like sex. Others say that it's like standing on top of a tall building and leaning over. You can't equate it with anything else – at least, nothing that I have ex-perienced so far.'

Fish goes on, 'Roger is brilliant. He's the fun one and a great laugh to be with. If I was going to say which member of Queen would you like to party down with for a night, it'd be Roger.' John Deacon kept his customary low profile and the Queen member that Fish spent most time with was Brian May; the Marillion singer remembers finding the guitarist in a state of mental turmoil.

Says Fish, 'Brian gets hurt very easily and he was hurting the night we first got talking. It was in a Paris nightclub and he sat and talked to me about South Africa and apartheid, all the pros and cons of Queen having played Sun City, for which they were still copping a lot of flak. He was deeply hurt by the furore.' He goes on, 'And Brian's marriage was in trouble at this point. He was really going through it. We talked quite a lot about it during that tour. Brian was questioning: Was it right? Was it worth taking all this grief for? He was extremely tortured by it. What you have to understand is that Brian is a painful romantic and quite excruciatingly sensitive. He's the sort of person who churns things over in his head for hours.' When the Magic Tour came to Britain and arrived in London for their two-night engagement on 11 and 12 July at Wembley Stadium – Queen's first proper full-length gig at this famous venue – Anita Dobson was there to watch May perform.

These two sell-out gigs – the second of which was taped for simultaneous broadcast at a later date on independent television and radio – showcased Queen at the peak of their power. Having developed a tremendously tight and powerful playing style, they had never looked or sounded better, and all their experience gelled in two truly magnetic performances from what now seemed the best live rock act in the world. Another special guest at the first of those two gigs, former Formula One motor racing world champion Jackie Stewart, certainly believes so.

Stewart had been invited to Wembley by John Deacon. Says Jackie, 'It's curious, but there always seems to be a link between music and motor racing. George Harrison is a big fan of racing, and Paul McCartney used to come to the Monaco Grand Prix, as did some of the Rolling Stones. Roger Taylor, of course, is mad keen on cars and had been to quite a few races. I'd always enjoyed Queen's music and had been to a few of their concerts. But my first link came through John Deacon. I'd been on radio's *Desert Island Discs* and had requested "Bohemian Rhapsody" and "Killer Queen", as well as the national anthem which Queen play at the end of their concerts. Not long afterwards I got a letter from John inviting me to one of their concerts. What Queen created was extraordinary – there are no copies. And that night at Wembley they were exceptional. You really had to be there to fully appreciate just how exceptional a night it was.'

The spectacle had everything – a massive 160-foot wide layered stage that filled one end of the stadium, a giant video screen fixed overhead, and the largest lighting rig ever. The blinding array of coloured flashing lights was so hot to work under that, by the time Queen roared into 'Hammer to Fall', Roger's hair was plastered in curls to his scalp and Freddie was visibly 'cooking' – steam rose from his head and sweat dripped off his face. The stage set was so huge that special supports had to be embedded into the stadium's concrete foundations to accommodate it. The crowd knew their role well and responded to Queen with tireless enthusiasm, working themselves into a real lather when the crescendo of swirling sound heralded Freddie's final return to the stage, resplendent in his royal regalia.

Queen had always been noted for their extravagant parties. Energised by these Wembley shows, the post-gig rave held afterwards at the Roof Garden restaurant above Kensington High Street would add to this aspect of the band's mythology. There was always a high degree of anticipation among Queen's guests as to the delights in store for them at these lavish bashes, and none of the 500 who arrived for these midnight celebrations were to be disappointed.

Among the many celebrities crowding the restaurant was Gary Glitter who recalls, 'Without any doubt, Queen gave the most outrageous parties I have ever been to, but this one was something else! For a start, every waiter – male or female – had drawn-on suits. I mean body paint. At first you didn't notice that they had actually got nothing on. Then you did a double take and thought, Wow! Only Queen would have thought to do this! A lot of people make a fuss about what goes on at Queen parties. But the bottom line is that they went out of their way to make sure that everyone had as good a time as possible.' The body artistry was the work of German painter Bernd Bauer. And there were other surprises in store – among them, the fact that in the ladies and gents toilets the attendant on duty in each was not only respectively male and female, but they were also rather scantily clad for the job.

That night Anita Dobson was among the guests and Freddie Mercury made a point of being seen with Mary Austin; his lover Jim Hutton was nowhere in sight. That night too was the first time that Cliff Richard and Mercury met. Says Cliff, 'I have to say that previously I had never been a fan of Freddie's, in terms of his kind of vocals. But I certainly admired his ability, including his skill on the piano and, of course, he was such an extrovert showman. I couldn't go to see Queen at Wembley because I was on stage with the musical *Time*, but they invited me to their after-show party.'

He goes on, 'These kinds of parties are always the same. Great crowds of people, most of whom spend hours lining up to meet the star and for usually no more than minutes. So it's not really conducive to getting to know someone. However, subsequently, Freddie invited myself and a group of people to a few of his private parties at his home.'

Queen picked up their tour a few days later and by mid-July had gigged through Germany and Austria, in their free time enjoying such treats as cruising down the famous Danube as guests aboard the Russian President Mikhail Gorbachev's personal hydrofoil. Then, on their arrival in Budapest, the British Embassy held a dinner party in Queen's honour. They were in the Hungarian capital to play the Nepstadion (the People's Stadium) on 27 July – another landmark gig in the band's career.

That night they performed before an 80,000-strong audience made up of fans from all over the Eastern Bloc. The authorities wanted no Western decadence to corrupt their youth and imposed a strict alcohol ban. Another sobering sight was that of patrolling armed guards keeping an eye on those inside the stadium, and the massive crowd of ticketless fans outside. Over the years Queen had built up a unique interaction between themselves and their audiences. Tonight was another example of mutual admiration, which was further strengthened when Queen surprised their Hungarian fans by performing a couple of verses of one of their traditional folk songs, 'Tavaski Szel'.

Queen's Nepstadion gig was the first concert to be filmed in Eastern Europe. And in the coming years there would be claims that the band's performance also made history by being the first rock show behind the Iron Curtain. But, in fact, the Rolling Stones had played at Warsaw's Palace of Culture nineteen years earlier.

Dates in France and Spain wound the 'Magic Tour' down to its last gig, back in England on 9 August 1986 at Knebworth Park in

Stevenage, Hertfordshire. Around 200,000 people gathered in 247 acres of lush parkland, dominated by the magnificent Knebworth House itself with its romantic battlements. Spike Edney recalls, 'The demand to see Queen had been so strong that a third night at Wembley could have been on, but that couldn't be arranged.' This outdoor extra gig had been the brainwave of Gerry Stickells; Queen had only agreed to it on condition that their tour manager could guarantee it would be a sell-out.

The logistics of this gig were daunting. It was to be a huge, almost carnival-like event, with funfairs and beer tents. Queen's reputation for providing quality sound would be maintained this time with a gigantic sound system powered by half a million watts, and several delay towers were erected strategically around the field to carry the massive amplification. They would be performing through 180 speakers on a giant stage above which hung a 20-foot by 30-foot video screen; this visual aid was so top-heavy that it had to be counterbalanced by a large water tank behind the set.

So many fans converging on this famous venue brought traffic problems from early morning, despite all the careful planning that goes into staging these events. Past performers at Knebworth had included the Rolling Stones and Led Zeppelin; Lady Chryssie Cobbold, whose family owns the Knebworth estate, recalls Queen as being, in one respect, unlike the others. She says, 'We usually entertained the groups before, during or after their concerts. But, in the case of Queen, they were not interested in coming up to the house.'

Queen made a showy entrance, arriving by helicopter, one of which had been resprayed with the distinctive *A Kind of Magic* images from the album cover. As the choppers circled in to land, the fans cheered and waved their heroes down to earth. Spike Edney remembers, 'The gig was spectacular and it was just an amazing day. We'd never played to such a large audience in the UK before. It was incredible.' He adds, 'And of course, the party afterwards was the usual Queen extravaganza – with everything, including female mud wrestlers.'

Mercury closed the show with the words, 'Thank you, you

beautiful people. Goodnight, sweet dreams. We love you.' And then, having been particularly tense before the gig, he made an unusually abrupt exit. Lady Cobbold confirms, 'Freddie ignored the backstage party and left immediately after finishing the performance.' He seemed preoccupied.

As the fun and frolics got underway in the singer's absence, none of the other three had any way of knowing that they had reached a momentous point in their career. After twenty-six gigs in eleven countries at twenty venues the 'Magic Tour' was over. But the Knebworth gig – which was Queen's 658th concert – was no ordinary end-of-tour show; it was to be Queen's last ever live performance.

# THIRTEEN

# CREATIVE CLASHES

F IVE WEEKS AFTER Knebworth, on 15 September 1986, Queen released their thirty-second single 'Who Wants to Live Forever'/'Killer Queen'. Its UK peak of twenty-four, though, according to Def Leppard frontman Joe Elliott, did not properly reflect the haunting ballad's true appeal. Says Joe, 'I remember when Brian wrote "Who Wants to Live Forever". He presented it to Freddie as a demo and Freddie said, "Hey, that's good! I'll just come in second," meaning that he thought Brian should take first lead vocal on it and that he would come in on the second verse. I predict it'll become like the Moody Blues' "Nights in White Satin" – a classic. It's got that feel.'

Despite winning the Best Live Performance Video award for *Live in Rio* at the British Video Awards ceremony in October, and their performance album *Live Magic*, released on 1 December, nestling at number three in the charts, the feeling within Queen was that they needed to take another break from recording as a band. A degree of friction had again been brewing and passions had at times run so high that, according to both Freddie Mercury and Brian May, all four had experienced periods when they had thought they hated each other. Roger Taylor nutshelled the root of the strife when he once revealed, 'Our rows are partially a conflict of musical ideas and partially ego problems.'

Fish, who was fresh from Queen's 'Magic Tour', knows just how common such stress can be in major-league rock bands. He states, 'Everyone in a band has to come to terms with ego and understand that every member is important. As a band evolves, there is an incredible amount of friction as the pieces jostle for position. Some bands don't come through that stage. Marillion didn't. Queen did.'

Queen's creative clashes had become confrontational and while they had been recording in Munich tempers had run too high too often not to be a significant sign. At some point every band member, deeply irritated about something major or minor, had threatened to walk out, as Brian May confirmed when he revealed, 'We got very angry with each other. I left the group a couple of times, just for the day. We'd all done that. You end up quibbling over one note, and we always raved about money. A lot of terrible injustices take place over songwriting. The major one is B-sides. "Bohemian Rhapsody" sells a million, and Roger gets the same writing royalty as Freddie because he did "I'm in Love with My Car". There was contention about this for years.'

Abba's songwriting team can sympathise with the level of pressure felt over penning material and the claustrophia redolent in spending endless months in a recording studio. Benny Andersson says, 'Abba rarely toured because to us the essence of the whole thing was the songwriting and if you are out on the road, how can you have time to write? We had eight albums in eleven years, so you can see how much emphasis we put on writing. It takes a year to write ten songs and then when you stand back and look really hard at them, maybe two or three in the end of the day are right.' Bjorn Ulvaeus adds, 'Concentrated studio work can be very fulfilling ultimately when you play back a number and it's just right. But it can also be extremely frustrating because everything takes such a long time.' Benny also points out that when it came to songwriting, 'There was one thing Bjorn and I always stuck to. We would not put out a song that we did not both agree on. There would be material I liked or Bjorn liked, but if we did not both like it, then it was not used.'

Queen's arrangement was different. For most of their career all four wrote songs, then fought their respective corners to get as many of their own compositions as possible on to an album. This created a long-running tension that Mercury once described as an 'inward jealousy', but it was more a robust competitiveness and the tension generated at such times had mostly had a positive effect. Freddie maintained, 'I think because we all fight you get the *crème de la crème*.' And all of them, even at their most fraught, knew that together they shared a rare symbiosis that was ultimately worth preserving. As an act of self-preservation, therefore, Queen decided to take 1987 off and focus on personal matters. In this respect, however, the coming months proved to be no picnic.

By now Brian May was feeling under serious pressure. Chrissy was expecting their third child but their problems had worsened. The situation was becoming complicated because, having agreed to produce some recordings for Anita Dobson, as the chasm yawned between himself and his wife, May found himself gravitating more and more towards the warm-hearted soap star. He resisted it as best he could but, as time would tell, he found it an unequal struggle.

With his fame and Dobson starring in a hot TV show, it was inevitable that, even before the affair actually began, newshounds would be quick to smell a potential scandal. Comments about the pair began appearing in gossip columns and continued to multiply even after both Brian and Anita issued emphatic denials. Brian was in turmoil. His dependable nature was such that he could never have envisaged himself having an affair and that, despite being exposed to the perfumed predators ever-present in the social sphere around successful rock bands. It shook him and, with all the worry about what the publicity would do to his family, his entire world felt up-ended. As the birth of the baby approached in mid-February 1987, he remained at home, struggling with his demons. But, deep down, he probably already knew that cutting Anita out of his life was not an option.

Whilst May had remained in Britain over the winter, Roger Taylor and John Deacon had headed for warmer weather in Los Angeles where they each had homes. For his part, Freddie Mercury had – back in autumn 1986 – finally moved into his luxurious Kensington mansion, although he retained his Stafford Terrace flat. In the early eighties Freddie had stated, 'Sometimes I imagine that when I'm fifty I'll creep into that house as my refuge and then I'll start making it a home.' The brutal reality was that by the time Mercury would have celebrated his half-century, he had already been five years dead.

Among those who had moved in with him to Garden Lodge were personal assistants Joe Fannelli and Phoebe, and Freddie's lover Jim Hutton. The couple promptly entered into an unusual arrangement whereby the barber paid the superstar weekly rent. In time this stopped, but initially Mercury took half Hutton's wages. Jim was entirely happy with this arrangement; a quietly dignified man, it was always important to Hutton to preserve his independence.

With Queen work suspended, Mercury filled his time in various ways, including a one-off special appearance in the stage musical *Time* which was still drawing crowds at London's Dominion Theatre. Cliff Richard explains, 'It was a midnight charity performance and Freddie joined me on stage to sing a couple of numbers – "Born to Rock 'n' Roll" and the final song "Each and Every One of Us". It maybe didn't last long, but at least I can say I've performed on stage with Freddie Mercury.' He goes on, 'Freddie had an amazing grasp of vocal harmonies and to me *that* was absolutely the core of the Queen sound. I think he could very well have been drawn in time to stage musicals. Perhaps he wouldn't have encountered anywhere near the same success. But a performer of his calibre would always bring a certain audience with him to start with, and would've reached out to a new one after that. He was certainly capable of doing it.'

Mercury also indulged his passion for shopping, spending a king's ransom on antiques and works of art for Garden Lodge. He filled specially built pools in his garden with exotic koi carp and acquired another six cats on which to dote. Socially, Freddie had retrenched considerably but he still occasionally went clubbing, at times taking his pick-up to bed at his flat, while Jim Hutton waited for his return to Garden Lodge. Understandably, this behaviour caused some terrible rows between Freddie and his live-in lover. Mercury would not tolerate even the thought of being paid back in his own coin and on at least one occasion Freddie ejected Jim from his house in a white-hot jealous rage; when he had calmed down he inevitably pleaded with Hutton to return, which he did.

Freddie's fear of the AIDS spectre had been allayed to a great extent when he had tested negative at the end of 1985 but then various tabloids picked up on the fact that the Queen singer had undergone a secret test for this disease when the *News of the World* blew his cover on 13 October 1986. Furious at the exposure, Freddie had worse worries when within weeks he then learned that both John Murphy (a handsome airline steward with whom he had remained friends after they had had a one-night stand six years earlier), and separately Tony Bastin (his former lover of two years' standing) had recently died of AIDS. In panic he responded by hardly leaving his house.

By January 1987 Mercury had realised that hibernating was not the answer. To distract himself, he began work on his second solo album at London's Town House Studios where he recorded with song-writer/producer Mike Moran, who became one of Freddie's closest friends. Says Mike, ' "The Great Pretender" was the first cover version that Freddie had done in his own name. He had been attracted to the number because it was very him. He was a terrible show-off anyway. After we put down the track, I said to him, "We really ought to think of a B-side," and Fred replied, "Oh bloody hell! I'd forgotten about that." Well, it was very late one night, and we were the best part of a bottle of vodka down, when Freddie started playing flashy piano and he suddenly said to me, "Wouldn't it be fun to do something classical?" "Exercises in Free Love" was the product of this. There aren't any lyrics. It's more like Freddie flexing his scales.'

Mercury's cover of the Platters' 1956 ballad 'The Great Pretender', backed by 'Exercises in Free Love', was released as his seventh solo single on 23 February. He gave it the old crooner treatment. And, in addition to it scoring his personal solo best with a UK number four hit, it would prove to be the highest-charting solo single to date of any individual Queen member. The song's accompanying fun video was typically extravagant and included scenes of Freddie, Roger Taylor and Mercury's friend Peter Straker once again dressing in drag. Boosted by the single's performance, Mercury booked a block of studio time and set to work with Mike Moran on various ideas. But this was soon hijacked by a development – which had been in the works for some time – just now coming to fruition.

Top Madrid-based concert promoter Pino Sagliocco had handled the Spanish leg of the 'Magic Tour' and he was also producer of Ibiza '92, the celebrations that would culminate in Spain hosting the 1992 Olympic Games. It was Sagliocco who was responsible for bringing the two diverse talents of Freddie Mercury and Spanish soprano Montserrat Caballe together. When Queen were in Spain in August 1986 Pino had successfully cajoled a reluctant Mercury into record-ing an interview for a popular Spanish TV show called *Sixty Minutes of Spain* to be screened in October.

Initially Sagliocco believed that it would make for good exposure. However, something else took hold when he watched the aired result. Says Pino, 'When I watched this programme I was thinking of my main opening for a TV special to be held at the Ku Club in 1987. During the show Freddie was asked which Spanish singer he admired most and he replied, "Montserrat Caballe". At that moment the idea came into my head, why not get Mercury and Caballe to perform together for the Olympic celebrations?'

It would prove an uphill struggle but Sagliocco was determined, and by late February 1987 he had brought the two stars to the point where they had agreed to meet. Mike Moran vividly recalls Freddie first relaying news of this development to him. Says Mike, 'We'd left the studio late one night and gone home when in the early hours

Freddie rang me, very excited. He told me he'd had a call from Spain that Montserrat Caballe wanted to meet him, and we were going over to Barcelona on Saturday. A little sleepy, I sat up and asked suspiciously, "What do you mean *we're* going to Barcelona?" He replied, "Well, I'm not fucking going myself!".'

Moran continues, 'Freddie promptly got himself worked into a right state. He was rushing about panicking, saying, "I'll have to work out what samples of my work to take along. What can I take?" Eventually I grabbed him and said, "Freddie! You're famous! You don't need samples of your work." But he insisted that he did. Eventually he decided that he would play her the B-side to "The Great Pretender".'

Mercury was still skittish when waiting at the Barcelona Ritz Hotel for the opera star to arrive. Mike remembers, 'Freddie was fussing like a mother hen. Then when Montserrat swept in with a whole retinue behind her and with the hotel staff bowing low and almost walking backwards before her, he became even more nervous. But she was really good fun and everyone, except Freddie, loosened up as the champagne flowed.' – Mercury only relaxed after he had played Caballe his track 'Exercises in Free Love', although some confusion arose when Freddie somehow managed to give Montserrat the mistaken impression that this was a number he had written for her.

Caballe liked the number. Says Mike, 'She's this grand diva, and here she was announcing, "I'm performing at Covent Garden next week. I will perform this number and you" – she pointed at me – "will accompany me." Sure enough, we did. Freddie was more nervous on that occasion that at anything I'd ever seen, and he wasn't even performing. Before a gig you could never talk to Freddie. He would be so uptight and want to be alone and would bawl out anyone who intruded on him. But at Covent Garden he was so nervous for me that he suddenly burst into my dressing room as I was getting ready and began talking ten-to-the-dozen. Eventually I snapped, "For fuck sake, Freddie, go away and leave me alone!" It was nice though that he was thinking of me.'

Later that night when Caballe joined Mike Moran and others back at Garden Lodge, Montserrat asked Mike and Freddie to write her a song about Barcelona. Mercury said, 'Of course,' but promptly forgot about it when he received traumatic news around Eastertime. Hoping to quell his fears over his health, he had again taken a series of medical tests, one of which had been to examine some skin taken from his shoulder. The result, this time, was devastating. He had AIDS.

Freddie found the hideous implications impossible to absorb. Under specialist care, his treatment began immediately, and initially Mercury seemingly confided in only two people – Mary Austin and Jim Hutton. Although Freddie made it plain to Jim that he would fully understand if he left him, Hutton chose to stay; it was only at this point, Jim would later reveal, that they began to practise safe sex.

It took a herculean effort, but Mercury somehow managed to hide this terrible development from everyone else. He secretly submitted to a battery of further tests, all of which must have forced the harsh reality of his plight upon him; but, to conquer the riot of terror and emotional pain, he entered – or tried to – a period of denial. He tried to avoid referring directly to the disease ever again and would instantly turn off or away from any media mention of AIDS. He wanted to throw himself instead into work; and in this respect it became a welcome thing that Montserrat Caballe, oblivious of his problems, had been pressurising him over his earlier promise.

Mike Moran confirms, 'She had been calling Freddie from all over the world asking how he was getting on with the song he had promised her. Freddie eventually came to me and said, "Fuck sake! We'll have to write this bloody song!" So we sat down and in pretty short order co-wrote "Barcelona". To let her hear it, Freddie recorded both parts, and we sent her a rough tape of it. She loved it. She whizzed over and it was all recorded in London, except for when I went to Spain to get her vocals on the B-side, "Exercises in Free Love".

Caballe then proposed taking their collaboration further by recording an album together. Moran says, 'Freddie and I both thought, Oh, my God! I just knew it wouldn't be easy to combine these two. We had originally been going to work on a Freddie Mercury solo album, but this took up so much time. And then there were two Queen albums in the offing, *Innuendo* being the last one, by which time Freddie was very poorly. So we never got to do his intended solo album.'

Work on material for the Mercury/Caballé album commenced in mid-April 1987, just as Queen received the Outstanding Contribution to British Music Award at the thirty-second annual Ivor Novello Awards. Mercury's alliance with the opera star, meanwhile, was much talked-about in music circles and became even more so when, in late May, it emerged that the two were to headline at the TV special Pino Sagliocco had organised as part of the Ibiza '92 festival.

In the circumstances it took guts for Mercury to face the prospect of this public appearance anyway, without the further bombshell that hit him in early May when one of his former personal assistants, Paul Prenter, sold his story to the *Sun* newspaper. Prenter's lurid revelations spotlighted the singer's wild days of drinking two bottles of vodka a night and sharing lines of cocaine with a couple of other superstars. Prenter had also provided private photographs of Freddie entwined with a selection of his past male lovers. The three-day exposé dished enough dirt on the Queen star to sink a battleship, without Prenter also claiming that his former employer had recently telephoned him in a panic that he might have contracted AIDS.

Mercury was gutted by the tabloid exposure, which destroyed his stringent efforts to deny the truth of his condition. The betrayal cut particularly deep because of Prenter's ingratitude. In 1986 he had been made redundant and had soon fallen on hard times. Because he had clocked up eight years in Freddie's employ, Mercury had let Prenter stay rent-free at his Kensington flat. Perhaps Prenter – who would himself die of AIDS just months before Mercury in 1991 – regretted his actions, because several times during the course of the serialisation he attempted to contact his ex-boss, who was known among his friends for having a very forgiving nature. But Freddie refused his calls. Instead, in a fragile and troubled state of mind, Mercury quit London for Ibiza: first Pikes Hotel; then two weeks later he arrived at the Ku Club to honour his commitment to close the TV special to be held there.

That TV special would also include performances from bands Spandau Ballet, Duran Duran and Marillion, and Fish starkly recalls his shock when he and Freddie met again. He states, 'I thought I'd go see him, say, "How ya doin'?" you know, and he was, like, really drawn. There were about four close friends in the dressing room with him and it was like someone had fuckin' died! I thought, Something really heavy is going down here, and I'm not part of it. So I got out of there fast. At the time those around him were saying things like, he's got a kidney complaint or a liver problem – stuff like that. But, having glimpsed some of Freddie's excesses, it wasn't too hard to put two and two together.'

For anyone close to Mercury the signs were becoming tragically clear. And for Barbara Valentin, who met up with him at the Ku Club, the instant giveaway was the appearance of large dark red marks on Freddie's face and hands. These were the outward signs of the illness's usual development of Kaposi's Sarcoma – or KS – an otherwise rare cancer. Says Barbara, 'Freddie and I never spoke about his HIV and AIDS, but he knew that I knew. It was in our eyes whenever we looked at each other and was a silent understanding between us. When I joined him in Ibiza for the TV special, I saw immediately that he had not been able to hide the marks on his face properly. And so, before he and Montserrat performed I said nothing, but took Freddie away with me to another room and used my heavy professional make-up on him to make him look better.'

The camouflage did not fool everyone, however. Pino Sagliocco recalls, 'As soon as Freddie arrived we saw that he had begun to get these strange blemishes on his face. We were told it was his liver, and, of course, he *did* drink too much. But I think we already knew then that he was sick.' And Freddie's friend hotelier Tony Pike adds, 'By this time rumours had begun circulating that Freddie had AIDS. But you don't ask a friend if he is terminally ill. No one ever spoke about it. Those around him would have categorically denied it anyway.' After the TV special Mercury returned to London to immerse himself in his recording commitments as part of his drive to keep going, but in the months ahead he would become increasingly withdrawn.

In different ways summer 1987 was a testing time too for Brian May and Roger Taylor. John Deacon, ever averse to the trappings of stardom, contented himself with indulging one of his off-stage hobbies, photography, as well as slipping off to travel the world again, only this time strictly as a tourist. With Queen recordings still suspended, Brian found himself during the month of May working with the members of a spoof heavy metal band called Bad News. This band boasted the combined comic talents of actors Nigel Planer, Rik Mayall, Adrian Edmondson and Christopher Ryan – better known to British television viewers as the stars of the zany comedy series *The Young Ones*. Brian's first connection with them had been when he had taken part in an NSPCC charity gig in November 1986. Now he was to produce their album and work for it began at London's Sarm Studios.

Nigel Planer recalls, 'It all started with Adrian's idea of us recording "Bohemian Rhapsody" and immediately the next thought was, why not ask Brian May to produce it for a laugh? From there, it went on to him producing our whole album. I have to say it was a strange marriage – Brian being a proper musician on the one hand and us a bunch of louts out to have a laugh on the other. During recording we went into character and as Bad News we'd talk, swear and argue, and all the time Brian had the tapes running. We began improvising and, of course, it got way out of hand. But every time I looked up at Brian in the box he was laughing like hell, literally falling about.'

The mirth continued when, later in the year, May accepted an invitation to accompany Bad News to the annual Rock and Jazz Festival at Reading. It was a day to remember, as Nigel Planer explains: 'The audience was just this seething horrible mass of pink. We did our usual act and Brian joined us on stage. We got pelted.

Plastic bottles of urine came flying at us by the dozen, and enough sheep's eyes rained down on top of us to turn the air black! But Brian laughed his head off and dodged away like an old pro.'

But Brian could not laugh at, or dodge, the continuing rumours of an affair with actress Anita Dobson. On 6 July 1987 Anita released a single, 'Talking of Love', which Brian had produced. It peaked at number forty-three but she and Brian nonetheless flew to Vienna to make a video to accompany it. However, it was their possible personal involvement that preoccupied the media. Neither of them were yet ready to reveal their feelings publicly, and, in fact, they went on record on a BBC TV chat show to deny having a relation-ship. But it did little to alleviate a deeply unsatisfactory situation.

Meanwhile what was completely unsatisfactory for Roger Taylor was not being actively involved in a working band. As the months had rolled on, he had not taken well to another Queen year off and was very restless. 'We're always at our most depressed when we're not working,' he stated, adding, 'personally, I've always enjoyed being on the road but sometimes the others go off the idea.' A decade earlier, Thin Lizzy's manager Chris O'Donnell had earmarked Roger Taylor as being the most likely Queen member to some day branch out into forming another band and, sure enough, as a solution to his predicament, Taylor now took this very step. His first priority would always remain Queen. He saw forming a new band simply as an extension to his musical career, but he badly needed this outlet and when he discussed his ideas with the rest of the band, Freddie, John and Brian all gave him their blessing.

Taylor's first move was to advertise in the music papers for mu-sicians to join the drummer of a top rock band wishing to form a new group. He kept his and Queen's name out of it and the notice elicited few replies. The next week he jazzed up the ad by promising that successful applicants could very well be in line to become famous; he was inundated with responses.

Narrowing the applications down to the most promising sixty, Taylor hired a Soho nightclub and spread auditions over four days. To preserve his anonymity, he kept out of sight while the would-be stars were put through their paces. The final decision, though, rested with Roger and he came up with a line-up that included lead guitarist Clayton Moss, drummer Josh Macrae and bassist Peter Noone. He added Spike Edney on keyboards and reserved the post of rhythm guitarist/lead vocalist for himself. This role change was deliberate; in every sense Taylor aimed to make this separate band different from Queen. It was to be called the Cross and, after rehearsals to find their feet, the new unit headed off to Taylor's holiday villa in Ibiza to start recording material for a debut album.

While in Ibiza time was taken out to celebrate Freddie's forty-first birthday on 5 September. Although Mercury knew his future was inescapably grim, he steadfastly refused to crumble and hosting a lavish birthday party was one of his ways of coping. It was to be held at Pikes Hotel and was originally planned as a joint affair with their former manager John Reid, but that fell through.

Tony Pike explains why: 'John Reid and Jim Beach had a massive argument. Beach had been four hours late for their rendezvous, through no fault of his own as he and his family had been caught in a terrible storm at sea. But Reid, unaware of the circumstances, was angry at being delayed so long and promptly cancelled the party. When Freddie discovered this he called me to say he wanted a do regardless, but something for 100 people instead of the previous 250. But then a story of the bash being cancelled somehow got into the English press and Freddie was incensed. He told me that he wanted the biggest party the island had ever seen. I said, "But Freddie, there are only four days to go." He replied, "I know you can do it." '

In the end 700 guests descended on Pikes Hotel to enjoy the exotic delights on offer. Tony Pike continues, 'I had originally arranged for a special cake to be made in the shape of the Gaudi Cathedral, but when the plane it was in landed, the cake collapsed. It was a disaster but we hurriedly made a replacement cake, 2 metres long and decorated with the musical notes to "Barcelona". And when the time came to present it, six men, dressed in white and gold uniforms, carried it in. However, as the high jinks got underway my then secretary, a rather portly English lady in her best silk suit, ended up being thrown into it.'

In less than one hour that night, 350 bottles of Moët & Chandon were opened. The place was hung with black and gold helium-filled balloons which had taken three days to blow up by machine; and these balloons nearly caused a disaster. Pike recalls, 'One guy, out to impress the girl sitting on his knee, put a lighter to a balloon above her head to pop it, and the whole thing went up in a gigantic sheet of flame. The problem was made worse because we had had extra electricity supplied and the massive overhead cables on the roof caught the blast and began to melt. It could have been catastrophic'.

As it was, the night was a blistering success, rounded off with a breathtaking fireworks display. Not for a second did Mercury's mask slip – he remained the perfect genial host throughout; although he had permitted none of the usual photographers any access. As he mingled among his guests none of them could know that that day his white cell count had dropped significantly and that his legs now sported some new and strange marks.

However, Mercury's medical condition did not leave him so withdrawn as to take no interest in Roger Taylor's latest venture with the Cross. On the contrary, to show his support, Freddie sang lead vocal on one of the forthcoming album tracks, 'Heaven for Everyone'. Likewise, Brian May guested on 'Love Lies Bleeding', which became the B-side to the Cross's debut single, 'Cowboys and Indians', released on 21 September 1987. Reaching only number seventy-four, it remained in the UK charts for only a week.

On the same day, 'Barcelona' went on sale in Spain where it instantly became popular. Pino Sagliocco states, 'It's still played at every official event at Barcelona. It's like a national anthem here.' On 26 October 'Barcelona'/'Exercises in Free Love' was released in Britain. It hit number eight, and five years later the BBC would adopt it as the official anthem for their coverage of the Olympic Games.

In 1987 reviews were polarised, as critics were dumbfounded by the single. Some called Mercury a total embarrassment to the rock world, while others applauded his bravery. Cliff Richard declares, 'I thought "Barcelona" was terrific. Again, Freddie dared to do it. It was a most unlikely project for a rock star and was always going to have the stun factor. But our industry is so small-minded at times. It's the tall poppy syndrome – they can't wait to cut someone down who is doing too well.' Benny Andersson believes, 'I think Freddie was amusing himself. I think he thought it would be fun. But it wasn't a musical experience for me.' Bjorn Ulvaeus, on the other hand, declares, 'Oh I enjoyed it very very much. I know people consider it schmaltzy. But its strength, the theatricality and the grand scale of it all appealed to me'.

The Cross had made their live television debut on an ITV show on 24 October but their debut album would not be released until early in the new year. As 1987 drew to a close, on 30 November Queen released a three-volume video set 'The Magic Years'. Each video, which was also available individually, charted the band's career to date and was intended to keep Queen in the public eye.

Privately, for Mercury, the year's end brought further alarming developments. Already depressed by news of yet another former lover having contracted AIDS, his white cell count dropped for a second time, necessitating an intensification of his treatment. Years before, with the exuberance of youth, Mercury had dramatically quoted the familiar rock 'n' roll adage, 'I don't expect to make old bones.' Sadly, in his case, this prediction would prove true. As it was, he adopted a healthier diet which included (after a decade's abuse of cocaine) cutting out drugs altogether, on top of now practising safe sex. But, although he was right to clean up his life, it all seemed like shutting the stable door after the horse had bolted.

By the end of the year Brian too was in further turmoil. The tabloids were still preoccupied with his romance with Anita, and this was fuelled by the fact that he had been spending a lot of time work-ing with her on her album. Journalists were desperate to 'catch them out' and would go to increasingly imaginative lengths to stalk the two. Even in January 1988, when Queen regrouped to get down to some recording, the flames continued to flicker and his dilemma intensified.

Relationship upheavals had by now also hit Roger Taylor. Dominique Beyrand had been his live-in lover for ten years and together they had had two children. But, whilst making a video for the Cross's recent release, Taylor had met and found himself attracted to a model called Deborah Leng, best known then as the star of the TV advert for Cadbury's chocolate flake. Roger admitted that he and Debbie had 'hit it off instantly'. The strength of his feelings for the 22-year-old blonde became clear when he relatively swiftly decided that he wanted to leave Dominique for the younger woman. There evolved a remarkably civilised, and certainly unusual, arrangement.

It was said to be designed to safeguard Roger and Dominique's children's future but on 25 January 1988, at Kensington Registry Office in London's King's Road, the long-standing couple got married, with Freddie Mercury and Mary Austin as witnesses. Yet it was hardly grounds for congratulation, because less than a month later Taylor left his bride and children, and set up home nearby in Kensington with Debbie Leng. Naturally, the tabloids latched on to this story and, giving the May/Dobson saga a respite, they turned the full spotlight of scrutiny on Taylor and his unique handling of this juicy twist in his love life.

The *Sun* headline of 18 February 1988 ran 'Rock Star Leaves Wife for Flake Girl', followed the next day by 'Misery of a Ditched Pop Bride' (in which Dominique was described as a 'jilted bride devastated by his affair'). Said to have been stunned by Taylor's affair with the model, Beyrand was quoted as stating that she hoped that she and Roger would remain good friends, adding, 'We need time to sort out our lives.'

Debbie Leng – when the coverage continued two months later – was quoted in the same newspaper as denying responsibility for the break-up, saying, 'I've been so criticised and it's just not fair. Roger left his wife and family, but it wasn't because of me he left.' Meanwhile, Taylor was reported as stating, 'It's a complicated situation. Without hurting anybody, I can't say much more.' He is said to have called Dominique a terrific woman with whom he would always be friends, and Debbie a wonderful girl whom he adored being with.

The fuss certainly overshadowed the release, on the same day as Taylor's wedding of the Cross's debut album *Shove It!*. It achieved a disappointing number fifty-eight in the charts and the second single from it, that same month, 'Shove It'/'Rough Justice' fared even worse at eighty-two. Then the third single 'Heaven for Everyone'/'Love on a Tightrope', released in March, stalled one place lower still. All in all, Taylor could have safely concluded that, whilst Queen fans were among the most loyal in the world, there was no guarantee that that same support would transfer to a solo venture as distinct as branching out into a separate band.

Still, Taylor's desire to experiment had led to him being the first Queen member to make a solo record and the first to form a band outside Queen. And on 19 February he became the first to take a new band out on the road when the Cross embarked on a mini UK tour – sixteen dates, mainly in colleges and universities – which kicked off at Leeds University and ended on 10 March with a gig at the Town and Country Club in Kentish Town, North London. If, by not flocking out to buy the Cross releases, Queen fans had been sending Roger a message that they preferred to see him stay within the confines of Queen, it did not stop them from turning out to see him perform live, and – by and large – the mini tour was a success.

Taylor's game plan for the Cross was to knock audiences out with the intensity of their live performances, thus establishing a solid bedrock upon which to build the band's reputation. But now it was time to concentrate on Queen recordings. The band, back in harness at the Town House Studios, got to work on a new album. Their year apart, which had been intended to recharge their batteries, had been fraught with personal difficulties but Queen remained the one constant in all four mens' lives and they were eager to collaborate once more.

# FOURTEEN

# PRIVATE PAIN

**PERSONAL PROBLEMS CONTINUED** to blight 1988. Brian May was already in very low spirits through spring and into early summer, when his desperate unhappiness was dramatically deepened by the death of his father, to whom he had always been extremely close. The further trauma brought on by this bereavement dealt a debilitating blow not only to Brian personally but also to his fractured marriage. The rift between himself and Chrissy now split into a chasm.

By this time too his affair with Anita Dobson was such common knowledge that further denials would have been not so much futile, as foolish. Brian's physical and mental health had been under strain for some time and he now plummeted into bouts of dark depression as he wrestled with his conscience and the feelings of all those involved in this unhappy situation. It caused him almost unbearable anguish. He revealed, 'I thought I was a very stable person and not open to anything like that. It actually screwed me up completely.' In the end, although it was a tough and painful decision, he left his wife to start a new life with Anita.

He had hoped that a clean break might alleviate some of the intense pressure but the newshounds, who had been on the scent for months, now felt entitled to go to town and they did – splashing May's private life all over the front pages. Already acutely sensitive as to how his children would be affected by the disintegration of their parents' marriage, this glare of publicity only sent Brian into more turmoil. Set against all this, not unexpectedly his new life with Anita was not at first altogether plain sailing. Apparently the unavoidable tensions created by the reshuffle in his love life and the attendant press attention led to arguments, some of which were also reported in the papers. The new couple's feelings for one another, however, were very strong and they would remain together for several years to come.

For Roger Taylor, July saw the release of another Cross single 'Manipulator'/'Stand Up for Love' which failed to chart. He was therefore more than happy to put his Cross activities on hold and resume work with Queen – although the new Queen album would ultimately take almost a year to complete. The reason for this was that Freddie Mercury was noticeably slowing down.

His work with Mike Moran on the Caballe album would likewise take as long. But his determination to give his best to both recordings never wavered. Mike confirms, 'Freddie worked amazingly hard in the studio. His attitude was always, "I *will* do this!" and that didn't change when he became ill. He was a perfectionist to the last and would not leave anything to anyone else, even when he was latterly very sick. He kind of made it clear, without explaining why, that he would come in when he could, and if he did, he was the same old Freddie. Although he'd get tired and would suddenly just call a halt, saying, "Right, that's it. Got to go." '

By spring 1988 Mercury and Moran were receiving assistance on a couple of the album tracks needed for the *Barcelona* album from the renowned lyricist Sir Tim Rice who, with several of the world's most famous stage musicals to his credit, would go on to win an Oscar for Best Original Song for *The Lion King*. For his collaboration with Mercury he co-wrote 'The Fallen Priest' and 'The Golden Boy'.

Sir Tim recalls, 'Freddie asked if I would put lyrics to a couple of tracks that he and Mike Moran had in mind. He gave me tapes to work with and I wrote some lyrics which Freddie liked, so they went ahead and recorded them.' Rice already rated the single 'Barcelona'. 'I thought it was absolutely wonderful,' he states. 'I don't think Freddie had an operatic voice. Obviously his was more a rock voice, but then most opera stars couldn't get near a rock song. However, if Freddie had trained from childhood, he could very well have sung opera. He wasn't that far off it.'

That October would see the culmination of Freddie's recent collaborations. The single 'The Golden Boy'/'The Fallen Priest' was released mid-month but – at over six minutes long – it was ignored by radio and paid the price by stalling at number eighty. Meanwhile, the Mercury/Caballe album *Barcelona* managed to get as far as twenty-four. Prior to these, on 8 October, Freddie gave what became his last live performance when, with Montserrat, he took part in La Nit, a massive open-air festival staged on the Avinguda de Maria Cristina in Barcelona. This event officially launched the four-year run-up to the 1992 Olympic Games. Performers included Spandau Ballet, José Carreras and Rudolph Nureyev; Mercury and Caballe were due to sing with the Barcelona Opera House Orchestra and Choir on a stage set in front of the spectacular fountains in Castle Square.

Festival organiser Pino Sagliocco recalls the night. He says, 'Everyone had thought I was a lunatic matching these two, but there was nothing wrong with cross-culture and it worked. Montserrat is recognised as a diva, but Freddie was also a diva. He was unique and it was a privilege and a pleasure to work with him. Having built this Ibiza '92 show, it was great to have Montserrat and Freddie open it – all that power of music. It was a piece of art.' He concedes, however, that 'Freddie was anxious about the whole thing', an observation that Tony Pike, who was also there, would agree with.

Says Tony, 'Freddie had been extremely nervous earlier when he was introduced to Spain's King Juan Carlos and Queen Sofia. As time marched on, Phoebe was the only person he allowed near him for about the last half an hour. We kept out of his way, but I caught sight of him and he was pacing about, dressed in his suit, deep in thought and lipping various phrases from the songs.'

These nerves may well have been one of the main reasons why, shortly before joining Caballe on stage, Mercury decided to mime the performance instead, though he put it down to having developed a sore throat. A part of him would have been disappointed not to be singing live, as expected, but this was unfortunately overtaken by embarrassment when, with the last-minute change of plan, a technical hitch made the tape play too slow and the lip-sync was therefore way out. Sagliocco defends, 'No one cared because the occasion was so wonderful.'

During Mercury's attendance at this festival Pino was among those to notice a further downturn in his friend's health. Despite applying even heavier make-up, the dark blotches on his face were still discernible. Says Pino, 'Freddie always showed integrity, even when he was dying. But there was a definite feeling about him right then of being totally closed in in his own world. He wanted to write and record and not tell the world his troubles.'

After La Nit Freddie quickly retreated to London where his only social life took place at the select dinner parties he held at Garden Lodge. Mike Moran, with whom Mercury had by now developed a strong friendship, picks up: 'He was an absolute sweetheart – fab, considerate and kind, and a very loyal friend. He was an intensely private man and kept about him only a very small circle of friends. My wife and I were fortunate to have been two of those. We went to all his anniversaries, like birthdays, and never missed his special Boxing Day dinner parties.'

Other guests at these exclusive affairs included the actress Susannah York, whom Mercury met via their mutual friend Peter Straker. Says Susannah, 'Freddie was great fun, very warm and had tremendous spirit. He offered me the use of his New York flat whenever I liked, and I was touched by the spontaneity of such a generous offer

although I didn't take him up on it. I think he could be very manipu-
lative in his relationships, which can be easy when you reach a position of power. But, having said that, he was generous to his friends.'

Sir Tim Rice found much the same. He states, 'Freddie was a very
sophisticated and charming man. Certainly some evenings at his
house were sort of boisterous – he was a great entertainer in private
too – but he was always jolly.' And Sir Cliff Richard comments
perceptively on the Queen singer's private life: 'What I noticed at
these affairs was that Freddie seemed to have to live out the whole
fantasy all the time. He had lots of people looking after him, ready to
do his bidding at all times. He carried the "star thing" into his private
world too. He loved the mystique, I think.'

He goes on, 'Certainly you need your public persona and in many
ways people can feel desperately let down if you don't roll up in a
Rolls Royce or whatever. But it is important to keep in touch with
reality, to surround yourself with people *not* in the business. It can be
a bizarre world otherwise.'

The hard reality within Queen by November was that, while all four
were recording together again when they could, it was not enough.
Just as the lack of live performance had got to Roger Taylor, so it was
now biting at Brian May for whom touring had been one of the most
fulfilling aspects of being a rock star. There was a single-minded
simplicity about gigging in one city after another that allowed him to
temporarily shelve personal problems. Queen had not toured for two
years and, although no one actually said it out loud, Brian, John and
Roger, who all loved playing live, knew that – as Queen – they
never would again. It was hard on all of them.

For Brian it got to the point where he began admitting in interviews that he could hardly stand not touring any more. He talked of
going out on his own in some fashion, envisaging possibly a low-key
sortie with friends first, before attempting a proper solo tour. But any
such venture would be in the future. Right then, to help fill the void,
May threw himself into making a variety of guest appearances either
on stage or in recording studios. One of the first was with Black

Sabbath, whose lead guitarist Tony Iommi is probably Brian's closest friend and the one person he knew he could always turn to, whatever the circumstances.

Says Tony, 'We've been friends for something like twenty years. Brian was the worrier in Queen and he and I could relate really well to that, because we are very much alike in that respect. Over the years we had often popped in on each other's recording sessions and so when Sabbath was working on the *Headless Cross* album I said to Brian, "Bloody hell, come and have a play." He asked, "Do you really want me to?" Because, you see, Brian is the only other guitar player we have ever had play on any of our records. He appears on the track "When Death Calls".'

The next month, from guesting with a seventies hard rock band, May briefly hooked up with the rapidly rising heavy metal band Bon Jovi at London's Wembley Arena when he attended one of their gigs. Bon Jovi's lead guitarist Richie Sambora recalls, 'Brian, Elton John and a whole bunch of guys came that night and so we just called them all up on stage to jam with us. We played a few numbers, including the Beatles' "Get Back". It was great.'

Sambora considered it an honour to meet the Queen guitarist. He explains, 'I had watched and admired him since the three nights out of five I went to see Queen open for Mott the Hoople at the Uris Theater on Broadway back in 1974. I was knocked out then. Queen were absolutely fantastic. I was just a teenager, but I never forgot it.' He goes on, 'At the Wembley Arena it was one helluva jam, but what I thought was really cool was when Brian gave Jon [Jon Bon Jovi] and me some sound advice backstage. This was right when our career was about to take off big-time and his advice to us was never to work our asses off to the point of burning ourselves out – not taking time to smell the roses along the way, kind of thing. That's what he said he felt that he and Queen had often done, and he couldn't get it over strongly enough to us how important it is to try to live the moment and savour it, because all too soon it will be over and you'll have missed clean out on enjoying it.'

Whether or not Taylor and Deacon shared this melancholic view, Mercury's private state of mind was increasingly tragic. He undoubtedly showed enormous courage in facing up to the inevitable, but he was living out a death sentence and would not have been human if he had not slipped into the abyss now and then. Just like the others, he also badly missed the buzz of live performance. After years of soaking up intense adulation, he had been thrown into enforced isolation, forever conscious that his changing physical appearance would betray his secret. His acute distress could spark shattering rows within the walls of Garden Lodge, and the pent-up fear and anxiety injected venom into arguments that often ended in tears.

Near the end of 1988 Mercury, who had steadily severed contact with some of his friends, re-established his bond with Barbara Valentin. It was a harrowingly poignant moment, as Barbara recalls: 'When Freddie had suddenly quit living in Munich I knew he was worried that he had HIV. I knew he went hurrying back to London to hide. But there was nowhere to hide. Soon after the TV special in Ibiza, I began to see less and less of Freddie. I rang his home often, but he would not take my calls. That Christmas I tried again, but this time was told by someone there to stop calling and I thought, Okay. Fuck this. But then, many months later, my door bell rang one day and it was Freddie. He just stood there and said, "I can't stay away from you. I can't live without you in my life. Take me in and take care of me." And I did. He was in a lot of emotional pain and he *had* to work out a way to live with his illness. But it was very hard.'

January 1989 saw Mercury's tenth and final solo single release in his lifetime, a ballad called prophetically 'How Can I Go On'; it was backed with 'Overture Picante'. This month also saw the completion of Queen's latest album. It had been a long drawn-out affair but far more harmonious that previous endeavours, particularly because of a new policy adopted by the band. It was a strategy that meant that no one had been marginalised during the course of any number's development, irrespective of whose basic idea the song had originally been. Def Leppard's Joe Elliot says, 'Songwriting democracy is good, but it can be artistically restricting.' It suited Queen, however, and it also recognised the past umbrage over uneven earnings. All tracks were now credited collectively to the band, which translated into a four-way equal split in royalties.

The key to successful songwriting collaboration, according to Abba's Benny Andersson, is trusting the other guy. 'You have to be free to be one hundred per cent corny and to know that nobody is going to laugh at you,' he says, adding, 'you have to have the confidence that you don't have to hold back on your emotions.' It was certainly an emotive time for Queen.

Although Mercury had not admitted to his three friends that his days were numbered there was an unspoken sense that the clock was ticking and very soon they would start work on another album, this time at Mountain Studios, Montreux. Then, on 2 May, came Queen's new single 'I Want It All'/'Hang On in There'. Any worries that it might be out of step with lighter-weight numbers from prevailing popular artists, such as Kylie Minogue or the Bangles, proved to be unfounded. The uncompromisingly hard-rocking A-side was an instant hit and slammed into the UK charts at number three (Queen's highest entry yet), while its accompanying video, shot at Pinewood Studios without an audience, showed Freddie in much less energetic mode, dressed conventionally in a collar and tie and sporting designer stubble. There was no disguising his weight-loss and gaunt looks – this was the first public display of his ill-health.

Three weeks later *The Miracle* was released, the first studio-recorded Queen album for three years. It hit the top in Britain and went platinum in its first week of sale. The stylish album was complemented by a startlingly ingenious sleeve design; using the most advanced computer graphics, artist Richard Gray had created an image of each of the four individual faces of the band members merging into its neighbour.

While this innovative design created a stir at home, the four individuals themselves were tucked away in Switzerland working on the follow-up album. And it was in Montreux one night that Freddie called his bandmates together for dinner in a restaurant, saying that he had some news to impart. It had always been their policy to keep out of each other's private lives but May later admitted, 'We knew instinctively something was going on, but it was not talked about.' And the silent foreboding that he, Roger, and John had felt convinced them that they were about to have their darkest suspicions confirmed. But, whether Mercury *had* initially intended revealing all, in the end he did no more than openly admit to them for the first time that he was not well.

This admission fell a great deal short of the whole truth, but Mercury was not even prepared to confess to being unwell when, just days later, Queen granted radio DJ Mike Read their first group interview in nearly ten years. During the one-hour question-and-answer session when Read raised the question currently causing much comment – why Queen had stopped touring – Mercury merely maintained that it was to break the monotonous cycle of album–tour–album. Not many were convinced and in the ensuing period Freddie and the others had to fend off queries from persistent journalists. Once, when tackled as to where the flamboyant party animal had gone, Freddie replied, 'It's no way for a grown man to behave.' And, as to whether his health prevented him from living wildly any more, he flatly denied any problems.

Queen retreated back into work, albeit at a slower pace, while over the next six months four more singles from the latest album were released, starting on 19 June with a number seven hit 'Breakthru'/'Stealin'', followed by 'The Invisible Man'/'Hijack My Heart' on 7 August which reached number twelve. 'Scandal'/ 'My Life Has Been Saved' came two months later and stalled at twenty-five, and lastly on 27 November there was 'The Miracle'/'Stone Cold Crazy (live)' which charted slightly higher at twenty-one. The videos to accompany the first and last of these singles were particularly memorable.

According to John Deacon it was the repetitive chugging throughout 'Breakthru' that suggested to himself and Mercury thoughts of an express train. From there it was no great leap to consider filming themselves performing aboard a speeding train, which they would dub for the day 'The Miracle Express'. They made the video aboard a vintage steam train on the Nene Valley Railway near Peterborough, and Brian White, press officer with the Nene Valley, recalls the shoot.

He says, 'The filming itself took place over the full length of the line, which is chiefly set in water meadows. At the start of the video you see the train bursting through an apparently solid bridge arch. In fact, it had been filled with realistic-looking polystyrene bricks. The effect was brilliant and it was done in one take. The video took three days in all, but Queen were there for just one and they seemed to enjoy the whole thing enormously.'

Freddie's appearance in this video once again presented a bearded, straight-dressed performer. The restriction on movement aboard a moving train neatly explained another less than high-energy display. But, still, he looked good and seemed in good spirits as, lying on his back at one point, he held onto a railing above his head and pumped his body to the music.

When it came to 'The Miracle' video, Queen made only the briefest of appearances at the very end. The shoot involved using child actor lookalikes of each member to mime to the song. The four successful applicants (out of many) portrayed them perfectly; in fact, the band was stunned at just how good the kids proved to be.

Looking back, the brevity of the band's appearance in their own video must have been largely due to Mercury's failing condition. He was growing steadily weaker and this was impacting on the amount of time he could spend in the studio. He had finally been forced to give up smoking to help ease his respiratory problems; and these same problems taxed his ability to sing, although he made herculean efforts to disguise the fact.

On 4 December an album, *Queen at the Beeb*, was released. Consisting of early BBC radio Queen sessions, it was one for the purists and peaked at sixty-seven. But a more successful reminder of the recent past resulted in Queen receiving yet another award. During ITV's *Cilla's Goodbye to the 80s*, hosted by sixties singer turned television presenter Cilla Black, Queen were presented by

Jonathan Ross with the award for being voted Top Band of the Eighties by readers of the *TV Times* magazine.

In his introduction Ross reeled off impressive statistics of the band's career. They had now racked up over 80 million album sales and had performed in front of roughly six million people worldwide. In the mid-seventies Queen had bounced on to another stage to receive an award for 'Bohemian Rhapsody', with the boisterous Freddie Mercury slapping Roger Taylor's shoulders from behind and the band generally capering about. Now, as a more mature and sober Queen filed on, they made a very different sight, with Freddie the first to receive a scroll tied with red ribbon. He gave a small salute and immediately stepped to the rear, while there were handshakes and congratulations all round.

Brian May stepped straight up to the mike to accept the honour on the band's behalf and in his short speech declared that Queen hoped to be performing more miracles for the fans in the years ahead. But his little play on words – referring to the title of their latest hit album – masked the fact that, with Freddie's deteriorating health, it would indeed be a miracle if Queen ever performed live again.

# FIFTEEN

# END OF AN ERA

M EDIA SPECULATION surrounding the state of
Mercury's health heightened considerably as 1990
began and brought incredible pressure to bear on the
band. Freddie managed to foil the journalists more easily than
the others because he rarely ventured out in public. But Taylor,
Deacon and May were waylaid by the press practically everywhere
they went and it became a constant strain having to, in effect, lie
and maintain that any talk of their singer being in bad health was not
true. No one liked having to be economical with the truth but
protecting their friend was more important. As Brian May later
pointed out, some sections of the press were heartlessly intrusive
enough as it was in Freddie's latter days; had they had their suspicions
confirmed too far in advance, they would have made his life a living
hell.

Privately, of course, the reality was that Mercury's suffering – as
well as dictating the pace of work on their new album – was felt even
more acutely by those around him because it was *not* discussed. Each
of them strongly suspected how serious it was but, because they had

not 'officially' been told, there was nothing they could openly say or do to offer support. This painful period is remembered vividly by Mercury's close friend, Mike Moran.

Says Mike, 'Freddie showed immense bravery. He let none of us really know just how ill he was. He didn't want to be a burden to people and he certainly didn't want anyone's sympathy. For about three years it was awfully difficult for us, but we coped by going into denial – the way you do when you don't want to face the fact that someone you love is dying. And so there were often times when we'd say to each other, "He's looking a bit better today, don't you think? Maybe…" We'd semi-convince ourselves that he was going to be okay after all. It was all a case of not wanting him to go.' Similarly, in the studio there was an unspoken acceptance that the album they were working on would be their last recorded as a band.

In the coming weeks Queen's long career would be marked in two ways. Finally, the British Phonographic Industry bestowed on them their Outstanding Contribution to British Music Award on 18 February at London's Dominion Theatre. This public appearance was an ordeal for Mercury but he and the band had been placed in a no-win situation. Had Queen gone to the ceremony minus their frontman, it would have fuelled the rampant speculation about his health. But, equally, to appear looking so gaunt only served to confirm suspicions.

It was not surprising that Queen avoided the official BPI dinner that night. But, in fact, they went on to attend their own special party. In 1981 they had celebrated their tenth anniversary, basing this calculation on the fact that they considered Queen only official when John Deacon had joined them in February 1971, and overlooking the fact that Queen initially formed in April 1970. Now, perhaps because no one knew whether it would be possible to celebrate in twelve months' time, they had adapted their thinking to make 1990 their twentieth anniversary. Held at the Groucho Club in Soho, it was attended by 400 guests made up of Queen employees past and present, who mingled with showbiz celebrities including film director Michael Winner, actress/singer Liza Minnelli and superstar George Michael.

Although many at that party were deeply shocked at the drastic change in the Queen star, all had the decency to hide their reaction. But the same sensitivity was not shown by a press photographer who was concealed in the shadows of the narrow street outside, waiting for just such an opportunity as Freddie unwittingly provided when he left the bash early and alone. His weakened state meant that he tired very easily and he opted to slip – unobtrusively he hoped – from the festivities. Preoccupied and fatigued, he stepped out on to the pavement and was immediately snapped. This tell-tale picture was splashed on the front page of a national newspaper the next day and sent an anxious shudder reverberating among his friends and fans.

Freddie tried to control the fall-out by reiterating his earlier state- ment that he was fine and did not have AIDS; but the genie was far enough out of the bottle for his denial to cut little ice, even with fans who desperately wanted to believe him. Despite the evidence of their own eyes that the man was in no condition to undergo the rigours of touring, journalists still relentlessly pressed for the real reason why Queen live performances had stopped. The response that the band had recording commitments did not wash with the media either.

To become the quarry of a certain aggressive section of the tabloid press was traumatic. It was almost impossible for Mercury to have any privacy in Britain, and he quickly headed for the tranquillity of Montreux and his rented lakeside house there. He joined the others at Mountain Studios if he could, but he spent a lot of time harking back to his days as an art student – sitting by the shore drawing waterfowl (increasing skin sores and weeping wounds made walking for any length of time too painful). His damaged immune system meant that he was highly susceptible to infections though and these sessions, from which he derived some solace, often had to be rationed. He then slipped back to Britain and disappeared into Garden Lodge.

Work on Queen's album was naturally the slowest it had ever been and would relocate in July from Mountain to Metropolis Studios in

London. Because of the long periods of inactivity, Brian May and Roger Taylor, under considerable strain and feeling restless, again looked to solo projects.

With the Cross, Taylor had been recording another album – from which a single called 'Power to Love'/'Passion for Trash' was released in April but only scraped to number eighty-five. Then the next month their second and, what would be final, album, *Mad, Bad and Dangerous to Know*, followed, but failed to chart. In the summer of 1987 Taylor had high hopes for the Cross. 'I think it'll be a force to be reckoned with in six months,' he had declared. But sadly this latest lack of performance probably helped to end his interest in maintaining this separate venture for much longer.

May, meanwhile, became involved in writing a score for a theatre production of *Macbeth*. He had been approached by Jane L'Epine Smith, an experienced casting director who had lately set her sights on directing her first theatre production. Says Jane, 'Shakespeare tends to have a very stodgy image and I wanted my production to be attractive to all walks of life. I'd always admired Queen and thought that Brian would be ideal to compose the music for the play.'

Brian agreed almost immediately and over the summer months he worked on this score at his newly installed home studio; this way he could keep the theatre work separate from Queen recordings. *Macbeth* opened in November 1990 at London's Red and Gold Theatre. May had been both excited and apprehensive about his score. Jane recalls, 'The first time Brian brought the music to us, he was extremely nervous in case we didn't like it. When he heard it through, all of us quite individually stood up and applauded. It was absolutely wonderful.'

Apart from his one involvement with recording a track for the film *Biggles*, John Deacon had had no inclinations towards solo work and, although he enjoyed spending the many lulls in Queen production with his family, he also now found the professional inactivity very testing. 'I went spare,' he admitted, 'because we were doing so little.'

Freddie by now had had to cope with yet another blow. Joe Fannelli had been one of Mercury's trusted personal assistants for years and was responsible for administering Freddie his daily medication. Recently he had broken the news to his friend and employer that he had full-blown AIDS. Jim Hutton had also had bad news. He had submitted himself to an AIDS test, the result of which was that he was HIV positive, but did not have AIDS. Selflessly, to spare his lover further trauma, for the time being he kept this devastating development to himself.

Mercury's condition had deteriorated even further and he had had to be fitted with a small catheter on his chest in order to receive his medication intravenously. He and Hutton now had separate bedrooms because of the heightened risk of infection.

Their personal plights put any professional problems in the shade but Queen had nevertheless entered a new period of upheaval with their record labels. Their association with Capitol Records was coming to an end. Intricate negotiations had been on-going for a while, and the upshot was that the US company – for a substantial sum of money – would sell back the rights to the entire Queen back catalogue. This provided a tempting carrot to new labels and the band went shopping for a new record company. In the end Queen signed to Hollywood Records in early November.

Their strong association with EMI continued, but a degree of strain had recently entered the picture there too. Queen's new album – lately named *Innuendo* – had already been almost two years in the making but in autumn it had been promised for a Christmas 1990 release. This, however, had had to be pushed back and EMI was understandably unhappy at missing the massive festive market. But it could not be helped.

November also brought increased public pressure on Taylor, Deacon and May to come clean about the reclusive Mercury and one day, mid-month, Brian conceded to the pack of journalists cornering him that the years of life in the fast lane had caught up with Freddie and as a result the singer was suffering from strain and exhaustion. He emphatically denied, though, that there was any truth in the rampant rumours that Freddie had AIDS. May had been careful with his words but the next day the *Sun* headline still shrieked 'It's Official!

Freddie is Seriously Ill' and the story, which highlighted the AIDS rumours, was supported by a picture of a haggard-looking Mercury.

The stakes shot up now to photograph the ailing Queen star and the newshounds intensified their surveillance, persistently tailing Mercury on the rare occasions he ventured out. Inevitably their stalking paid off when one photographer snapped Freddie leaving the Harley Street premises of a leading AIDS specialist. In December Queen's video of the 1986 Magic Tour Wembley Stadium gig was released but the glorious spectacle of an energetic, magnetic performer fronting an equally vibrant band now seemed to belong to another world.

Of course Queen continued to record and the first fruits of the last two years' work came in early 1991 with the release on 14 January of the single 'Innuendo'/'Bijou'. Queen considered it a bit risky because its Bolero-type rhythm made it unusual and again it was one of those numbers that people would either love or loathe. It rewarded the band by crashing in at the top, thereby giving them their first UK number one hit single for nine years. Lasting for 6 minutes, 32 seconds, it was also the third longest UK number one single of all time, behind the Beatles' 'Hey Jude' and 'Belfast Child' by Simple Minds.

The video accompanying 'Innuendo' was clever, as animator Jerry Hibbert and director Rudi Dolezal, working with a substantial budget, made innovative use of computer graphics to animate existing live footage of Queen. This video would win the Gold Camera Award at the 1991 American Film and Video Festival in Chicago. On 4 February the single's parent album, *Innuendo*, was released and likewise seized the top slot.

But it was hard to savour such success because by now Freddie had at last decided to confide in his bandmates. It had happened in early January when they regrouped in Mountain Studios. Despite the ordeal that recording *Innuendo* had been, Mercury was determined to return to the studio but he also felt it was now time to come clean with his friends.

It was clear that he wanted no pity. He let loose with a barrage of commands, saying, 'You probably realise what my problem is. Well that's it, and I don't want it to make a difference. I don't want it to be known. I don't want to talk about it. I just want to get on and work until I can't work any more.' After Freddie's death, in a radio interview, Brian May spoke on behalf of himself, Deacon and Taylor about that dreadful moment. He said, 'I don't think any of us will ever forget that day. We all went off and got quietly sick somewhere.'

There was no escaping from the grim reality of Mercury's condition when soon afterwards the band assembled to film the video to accompany the second single, released one month after *Innuendo*, called 'I'm Going Slightly Mad'/'The Hitman'. Shot in black and white, under Austrian director-producer duo Rudi Dolezal and Hannes Rossacher, filming took place on 3 February 1991 at London's Limehouse Studios and it was a heartbreaking experience.

In tune with the single's title, the central theme was to depict various forms of madness and they chose to do so in a jokey manner. Roger Taylor rode a tricycle in ever-decreasing circles; John Deacon, in a court jester's three-pronged hat with bells, bobbed his head inanely; and Brian May, wearing a giant beak held apparently engaging conversation with real-life penguins. Freddie, for his part, in a wild wig, white gloves and wearing heavy make-up, stretched out on a bed of daffodils or bounced about on a pantomime gorilla's knee. But the crazy capers were underpinned by an immense sadness.

It was painfully obvious to all at that shoot that Freddie was very ill. His weight loss was so pronounced that, despite an extra layer of clothes under a black suit, he still looked horrendously skeletal. And his fragility meant that a bed had to be set up nearby for him to lie down on between takes that he found exhausting. He was in acute pain but he soldiered on, even being extremely concerned that the penguins were all right under the hot studio lights. If those on set had lumps in their throats, the hacks lurking outside the studio seemed to have utterly hardened their hearts. They did their best to eke out the slightest whiff of drama from anyone leaving the building.

On 13 May another single, 'Headlong'/'All God's People', emerged and reached number fourteen. Then, two weeks later, Mercury, Deacon and Taylor filmed what would be Queen's last ever video for a poignant ballad written by Roger called 'These are the Days of Our Lives'. May was absent from this shoot, being on tour in America to promote *Innuendo*, but he was filmed separately and later edited into the footage. Simon Bates says, 'Brian told me that when Freddie was making their last two videos he was so desperately ill that he could hardly walk, yet his eyes sparkled, and he'd be saying, do it this way or that way.'

Mercury's brave determination made him professional to the last. But again, it was a distressing experience and Roger, in particular, looks choked in the video as, standing left of Freddie, he keeps a watchful eye on the singer. Again, this video was shot in black and white. The use of monochrome can infuse footage with an otherworldly feel, or suggest a mental distance. In this case it was designed to help disguise the full extent of Freddie's frailty. Still, in the close-ups of Mercury's face during the song, his sunken features stand out in stark relief and his dark eyes stare directly out with a haunting mix of dignity and defiance. His very last whispered words on screen were, 'I still love you.' Taylor later reflected that Freddie probably thought that was a nice note to bow out on.

Queen returned to Montreux that summer, aware that Mercury's determination to continue recording was wholly dependent on how much stamina Freddie could dredge up each day out of his weakened body. Taylor, May and Deacon virtually just waited for the phone call that would bring them to Mountain Studios. Mercury had asked the others to write as much material as possible for him to sing, which they did; material they could work on after his death. If it was mainly intended to leave yet more of a legacy behind him, it was also to use what time he had left constructively – which would, in some measure, help blunt the sorrow of facing each day. Each time Freddie, drained and unable to carry on, left for the day, the others never knew if that was the last time they would ever see him. Brian May described him by then as living on borrowed time. The end would come in a matter of months.

It was difficult for anyone to take their mind off the impending tragedy, but May managed some time out to work as musical director for a major event held in Seville in Spain. Called 'Guitar Legends', it was a massive festival showcasing the world's greatest guitarists and Brian would take part on the closing night on 19 October. For this he had formed a backing band made up of some of rock's elite performers.

He was accompanied by two vocalists, ex-Free and Bad Company frontman Paul Rodgers and Extreme's Gary Cherone, bassists Nathan East and Whitesnakes's Neil Murray and drummers Cozy Powell and Steve Ferrone. Mike Moran was also in the line-up, along with keyboard wizard Rick Wakeman. And the guitarists included Joe Walsh, formerly of the Eagles, Nuno Bettencourt, Steve Vai and Joe Satriani who would soon be hailed as 'the greatest guitarist in the world'.

Satriani says, 'The first time I met Brian was at rehearsals in London and I can vividly remember feeling so thrilled that I was standing there with Queen's Brian May. My friend Steve Vai felt the same and, in fact, there was a moment when Steve and I were standing shoulder-to-shoulder watching Brian get all these brilliant Queen sounds out of his guitar right there in front of our eyes and we were speechless with delight.'

One of the night's highlights was the rendition of the 1970 Free classic 'All Right Now' when Paul Rodgers was in magnificent voice. Paul recalls, 'I'm grateful to Brian for having invited me to be part of that Guitar Legends night because in a way it was that night which got me back in the public eye. It was an incredible experience. We were all rehearsing down in the dungeons below the venue and there was a great atmosphere. One minute you were literally practising away, then the next you were thrust up top, out on stage. I think everyone there will remember that event for a long time.'

The bustle of organising that Seville festival had helped distract May during August and September but for Mercury there was no escaping the increasing daily struggle to go on. He was hit during this time too with the news that his lover was HIV positive, as Jim Hutton had decided that it was time to reveal his sad secret; Freddie was devastated.

Speaking of this traumatic time, Mike Moran says, 'A couple of months before Freddie died, I got a phone call from Phoebe asking, "Are you free on 5 September?" I said, "Yes. Why?" Phoebe replied, "Well, it's Freddie's birthday." And of course we had never missed one – but we hadn't thought that he would be celebrating this year. However, a handful of us went to Garden Lodge, and Freddie was still the perfect host. He didn't have long left, and he knew it, but he was very calm about it, very relaxed and very pleased to see his friends. We watched old videos, told old stories and laughed, and Freddie bravely stuck it out to the end, staying until he saw everyone off. He was amazing. After that, though, he didn't want people to see him, because he was so bad. He and I kept in touch by phone, but if I ever suggested coming over, he would say to me, "No, you don't want to see me today, dear. I'm not looking very good." '

On 14 October Queen released 'The Show Must Go On', backed by their first ever single 'Keep Yourself Alive'. It charted at number sixteen. The song's poignant lyrics sounded horribly close to an obituary. And the fans' anxieties were only sharpened when on *Top of the Pops* the single's video was a compilation of Queen in their heyday. A fortnight later the album *Greatest Hits II* followed and hit the top.

As Freddie entered November his illness ravaged him unspeakably, rendering him a spectral figure. The AIDS virus infects brain cells and the central nervous system, which causes neurological disorders beyond the immune deficiency that renders the body effectively helpless against infection. Freddie had earlier calmly come to the decision that he did not want to hang on longer than his body could stand and so by now, against doctors' advice, he had come off most of his medication.

In his last couple of weeks he suffered from blind spells and night sweats, as well as skin and mouth sores, and he would latterly be dependent on a breathing apparatus to the extent that near the very end he was unable to speak. It was a nightmare for him and for those who tended him. In his final week he knew he was fading and, weighing next to nothing, he insisted on being carried tenderly downstairs. It was agonising for him but he wanted one last look around the beautiful home he had cherished. After that he existed only on liquids and never left his bed.

These final days must have been a living hell for Deacon, Taylor and May, and Brian had an extra burden. In the summer he had written a number 'Driven by You' for a Ford car TV advertising campaign, but its popularity became such that it was to be released as a solo single. The release date for 'Driven by You'/'Just One Life' had been set ahead for 25 November and now that looked to be – unwittingly – hideously insensitive timing. It troubled May greatly and he confided as much to Freddie.

Mercury's response was typical. He told Brian to go ahead because, if he did die, just think of the boost to sales. Though May was well-used to Mercury's shocking flippancy, this still did not entirely soothe his worries over the predicament. May's friend Joe Satriani states, 'Brian told me that Freddie was very insistent that he went ahead both with his single and a whole solo career. Freddie supported his friends literally right up to the end.'

Another friend Def Leppard lead singer Joe Elliott rang Brian around this time and he recalls, 'Brian was in a very bad way. I rang him to ask how he was coping, and as usual he tried to hide it. He saw, "Aw, well – OK, I guess." He told me that Freddie did not have very long left. Forty-eight hours later Fred died.'

Visitors to Garden Lodge had now been restricted only to those extremely close to Freddie – like Mary Austin and Freddie's friend Dave Clark. Outside the house, however, there had been gathering a most unwelcome presence in the shape of a burgeoning press corps, sitting like vultures, practically on the star's doorstep, waiting for news and trying to buttonhole anyone coming or going.

The vexing question of whether or not to make a public announcement had preoccupied Freddie, as well as those close to him. Roger Taylor later admitted that the last thing Freddie wanted was to attract any pity but equally, aware that he was dying, Freddie wanted to be in control of breaking the news. 'He didn't want to be usurped,' maintained the drummer. And so, on Saturday 23 November, the contingent staking out the house were suddenly met by Queen's PR officer, Roxy Meade, who read out an official statement which dramatically laid bare what had been long suspected, that Freddie Mercury had been tested positive for HIV and that he had AIDS. This announcement flashed in TV headline news around the world and would dominate newspaper front pages the next day.

Freddie's public statement ended with the words, 'My privacy has always been very special to me and I am famous for my lack of interviews. Please understand, this policy will continue.' Of course, interviews were not in the least bit possible – within twenty-four hours the man would be dead.

That next day, Sunday, was bleak. Freddie slipped in and out of consciousness as his doctors and closest friends came and went from his room. Jim Hutton, Joe Fannelli and Phoebe had been among those keeping a constant vigil, tending to the desperately sick man. An attempt to carefully move his ravaged featherweight body to change the sheets resulted, heartbreakingly, in one of his extremely brittle bones snapping like a dry twig. By now Freddie had almost no control over his muscles and when, during one of his conscious spells, he wanted to comfort his favourite cat, which all day had been closely guarding her loving owner, he needed help to stroke the warm bundle of fur beside him.

Conflicting accounts later emerged as to who exactly was with Freddie when he breathed his last, but certainly those closest to him were there or thereabouts. In the event Freddie Mercury died in his sleep just before seven o'clock on Sunday 24 November 1991.

A gap of five hours elapsed before news of his death was made public, during which time the appropriate people were informed, including

Freddie's family who had not managed to get to Garden Lodge from Feltham in time, the rest of Queen and the band's manager, currently in Los Angeles. Then, just before midnight, a brief statement was issued which read: 'Freddie Mercury died peacefully this evening at his home. His death was the result of broncho-pneumonia, brought on by AIDS.'

Taylor, Deacon and May described Freddie's death as being akin to losing a brother and were naturally too overwhelmed at the loss to face the media. Instead a joint press statement was released on their behalf. In it they referred to Freddie as 'the greatest and most beloved member of our family' and they praised the enormous courage unfailingly shown by their friend.

Joe Elliott says, 'As soon as I heard the news, I rang Brian. He was extremely upset, but he also felt a deep sense of relief. In the last week especially Fred suffered so very much that it took a bigger love to actually wish him gone for his own sake. The industry rumours about Fred having AIDS had been rife, but it wasn't officially announced until the day before and Brian, Roger and John had had to live with it for a long time, having to lie and deny, and that all added enormously to the strain of their personal pain.'

Distraught fans converged in their droves outside Garden Lodge and vast numbers of floral tributes, which would later be distributed around London hospitals, began arriving from all over. In accordance with Freddie's wishes he was cremated three days later at the West London Crematorium in Harrow Road, Kensal Green. It was a private funeral with a small select number of friends joining Mercury's relations on a bitterly cold day. With his elderly parents being devout Parsees, the 25-minute service was conducted according to the ancient rites of the Zoroastrian faith. Gospel music by Aretha Franklin was also played, as was an aria from Verdi by Montserrat Caballe.

The final resting place of Freddie's ashes has remained a closely guarded secret, but in the immediate aftermath the public eulogies began from celebrity friends. Status Quo had played support to Queen on sections of the Magic Tour and singer Francis Rossi declared, 'I'm shattered. Freddie was one of the elite few who could really set a stadium alight.' Seal declared Mercury, 'One of the greatest performers that ever lived.' And Annie Lennox stated, 'For me he represents an era when people were less afraid of living life to the full.'

His personal friends found it harder to put their sorrow into words. Dancer Wayne Eagling says, 'Freddie was always extremely brave in everything he did. He was never afraid to face up to the world and what was perceived as conventional. It was a great shame that he had to go.' And Mike Moran reveals, 'Freddie was such a great loss to me that I still find it very hard to get over. It's almost harder for me to get over Freddie dying than it was to get over losing my father. With parents, they're older and in some ways you expect it. But not with Freddie.'

Freddie's death deprived people like Mike Moran of a very dear friend. But, also, the mosaic of the music world lost a vibrant and vital component. 'Superstar' has become an overworked word and particularly so today, when idols are regularly synthetically fashioned and packaged for the multi-billion pound industry that pop and rock has become. But occasionally, over the years, there have come along individuals whose uniquely charismatic personality, in conjunction with their innovative talent and impact transcends being merely hugely successful – and they are the genuine article. Elvis Presley was the first *real* superstar; and, although Freddie Mercury may not be the last, he was another. From early on Freddie had become a master at creating the illusion that he radiated greatness; an illusion that became reality. Now, one of the most flamboyant figures in entertainment, who had possessed one of the most distinctive singing voices in rock history, had gone forever. Inevitably, his death would also bring about the end of an era for Queen itself.

# SIXTEEN

# THE LEGEND LIVES ON

COMPASSION PROBABLY HELPED to convey the Queen classic 'Bohemian Rhapsody' for a second time to the number one slot over a Christmas period. It had been released on 9 December as a double A-side with 'These are the Days of Our Lives' and all royalties would go to the AIDS charity, the Terrence Higgins Trust. By the end of the year it was the second-bestselling single of 1991, behind the Bryan Adams hit '(Everything I Do) I Do It for You'.

However, these achievements, though welcome, provided little lasting comfort for Taylor, May and Deacon – for them it was still too soon and they felt too raw. In Brian's case that rawness had become acute. In the past five years he had endured the emotional strain of his marriage collapsing and having to combat press rumours of his affair with Anita Dobson; the intense pain of losing the father he had worshipped; followed by, first, the pressure of keeping Freddie's dire secret; and then the trauma of the singer's heartbreaking decline and death. It was all becoming too much to bear.

Brian later confessed to feeling trapped in a strangely unreal existence where outwardly he behaved normally, whilst inwardly he felt that he was falling apart. By the end of the year his ability to hold it together was fragmenting fast and he was haemorrhaging confidence. He felt he didn't exist as a person any more, and, on his own admission, nearly drove off a bridge in a bid to escape his desolation and despair. Ultimately his inner strength pulled him back from the brink and he left Britain to find the solitude necessary to concentrate on regaining control of his emotions. In their own ways, everyone who had been close to Freddie needed space and time to come to terms with his loss.

For Queen, 1992 would see a rash of record re-releases and the band being laden with various accolades. On 12 February at the BPI Awards, held at London's Hammersmith Odeon, not only did 'Bohemian Rhapsody'/'These are the Days of Our Lives' win the category of Best British Single of 1991, but also Freddie Mercury was posthumously honoured with a special award for an Outstanding Contribution to British Music.

The three remaining band members were in attendance to accept these trophies; and, as Roger and Brian had always been Queen's spokesmen, each said their piece. May ended his by declaring, 'We're terribly proud of everything Freddie stood for. We feel his spirit is with us.' Taylor, meanwhile, took this celebrity occasion to announce that he, Brian and John Deacon were to stage a massive concert in Freddie's memory on 20 April 1992 at London's Wembley Stadium. Called 'A Concert for Life', it was to double as an AIDS Awareness Day, with all monies going to charity, thereby trying to turn the tragedy to good purpose.

Taylor later joked that Mercury's flippant response to this would have been to immodestly query if Wembley Stadium would be a big enough venue for such an event? And certainly the stampede for tickets meant that the gig was sold out within six hours of going on sale the next day, provoking predictions that this Easter tribute would be the biggest show since Live Aid. As the task of organising the day got underway, the responsibility of who to invite to take part fell on the three remaining Queen members.

They were bombarded by many top acts with requests to be included. In the end one of the criteria was said to be that those celebrities who were selected had to have had links with Mercury; although, on the day itself, some people were baffled when Montserrat Caballe, for instance, was glaringly absent and, moreover, Freddie had never even met some of the acts who made it into the final line-up. At any rate, the one common denominator was that the guest performers had to be famous, as the show would be beamed around the world.

Joe Elliott vividly remembers his elation at Def Leppard's invitation. He says, 'Brian rang me and said they were organising this gig. They didn't have a British band, you see, and so we were real honoured. It was a very proud moment for us, to be specifically asked by Queen. I couldn't believe that Brian was actually asking *if* we'd appear. Blimey! I'd have swum over for it!' And heart-throb singer Paul Young recalls Roger Taylor's approach to him. Says Paul, 'I knew the guys socially anyway, and one day Roger phoned me at home to say he was putting some names together with a view to staging a tribute concert to Freddie and would I be interested in taking part. I immediately said, yes, and a couple of months later it was confirmed.'

The gig's' schedule was designed so that half a dozen bands would perform for the first two hours; then at 8 p.m. the 'celeb section' would take over. The idea then was that individual singers would each take lead vocal on a Queen hit, backed by Taylor, Deacon and May. Naturally rehearsals were essential for this second section; and after the Queen stars had rehearsed for a fortnight in March at a Shepherd's Bush studio, they moved to Bray Studios in Berkshire to work with the various superstars who were to be involved in this part of the show.

Among those who set about perfecting their version of a Queen song with the band were George Michael, Elton John, David Bowie, Ian Hunter, Gary Cherone, Annie Lennox, Lisa Stansfield, Liza

Minnelli, Robert Plant and Paul Young, and it was a harder task than many had anticipated. Taylor, Deacon and May easily created the Queen sound, but emulating the integral dynamo of Mercury's vocal was a daunting prospect. Led Zeppelin frontman Robert Plant later admitted that a lot of the numbers had had to be changed to a different key as artiste after artiste found it impossible to 'do a Freddie', as he put it. And Seal frankly confessed that when he had first tried to sing 'Who Wants to Live Forever' he was personally appalled. He thought, he said, that to attempt this number would spell the end of his career. The stars did not all congregate at Bray Studios at the same time, as Paul Young explains. 'Obviously, Brian, Roger and John were there all the time, but each of us had our rehearsal times arranged in advance and we just went along and got to work.'

Queen, meanwhile, continued to accumulate honours. In mid-April, at the Grosvenor House Hotel in London's Park Lane, 'Bohemian Rhapsody' won the Ivor Novello Best-Selling British A-Side award and this time Taylor and May were on hand to receive it. In turn, they handed over to the Terrence Higgins Trust a cheque for more than £1 million – the proceeds from sales of the single 'Bohemian Rhapsody'/'These are the Days of Our Lives'.

When Easter Monday, 20 April arrived the event was, in essence, intended to be a look-back at the days of Queen's life – certainly a testimonial to their long and successful career – as well as a very public goodbye to Freddie Mercury. Around 72,000 people packed into Wembley Stadium for the historic occasion, many having camped outside overnight to be sure of securing themselves the best vantage place when the gates opened at 4 p.m. the next afternoon.

Backstage, too, the guest stars began assembling as the day progressed. Joe Elliott recalls the atmosphere as having been quite strange. He said, 'In one sense it was lighthearted and very positive. People popped in and out of each other's dressing rooms all the time. The good thing was that no hangers-on were allowed in this area – which is unusual. Only the necessary people were there, and it was a great feeling. But, on the other hand, there was definitely a real sadness. And it was obviously different in Queen's trailer. Just as it got to be a bit emotional later, on-stage. But that was understandable.'

To Spike Edney this globally transmitted event differed from some of those that had taken place since Live Aid. He explains, 'Live Aid was great, but over the years I'd become very sceptical of events like this. It's purely a personal view, but it just seemed to me that anybody who didn't get on the Live Aid bill made bloody certain that they appeared at any charity gig that came along afterwards, cynically seeing the exposure as a big boost to their careers. But we knew that it wasn't going to be like that this time.'

Taylor, Deacon and May opened the show at 6 p.m. with Brian taking charge of the mike first. He promised the assembled crowd, and the worldwide television audience, that they were going to give Mercury 'the biggest send-off in history'. Roger then moved in to remind everyone of the gig's dual purpose in raising awareness of the AIDS disease. 'You can cry as much as you like,' he declared, before John thanked the participants for their commitment to Freddie's tribute. He couldn't resist ending with the poignant pun, 'First of all, the show must go on.'

Metallica kicked off the show, followed by bands such as Extreme, Guns 'n' Roses and Def Leppard. Joe Elliott recalls, 'The nice thing about that night – although it probably escaped a lot of people's notice – was that there were a lot of internal tie-ins at work. For instance, Liza Minnelli led the finale because Freddie admired her so much. And, of course, Ian Hunter and Mick Ronson were there because Queen had played support to Mott the Hoople just before making it big themselves.'

At 8 p.m. an explosion of smoke bombs heralded the return to the stage of Taylor, May and Deacon to commence the second half of the show, during which a series of performers, one after the other, joined the trio to sing lead on their chosen Queen hit. Black Sabbath lead guitarist Tony Iommi strolled into the spotlight at one point and launched into the distinctive intro to 'Pinball Wizard' which greeted Who vocalist Roger Daltrey on stage, who in turn then rasped his distinctive way through the Queen belter, 'I Want It All'. Says Tony Iommi, 'I was really proud to play that night. It was a very raw experience. It had been building that way for weeks during rehearsals. It was all friends there that night, and I think it showed just what Queen have achieved over the years.'

This 'celeb section' had been a good idea in theory but it was inevitable that it would illuminate the difficulties some singers – talented in their own right – had in resembling Freddie Mercury's unique delivery, particularly in the case of certain numbers. Elton John's rendition, for example, of Queen's signature tune 'Bohemian Rhapsody' was more courageous than successful. In fact, the crowd promptly hijacked the number and took over, and the night's decided highlight came when Freddie's voice boomed out during the video clip middle section. It instantly quickened the pulse, injecting the atmosphere with a sense that Mercury was making a ghostly guest appearance at his own memorial.

A special guest at the event was the legendary Hollywood actress Elizabeth Taylor, at that time National Chairperson for the American Foundation for AIDS Research (AmFAR), who, after handling a few hecklers in an admirably forthright manner, determinedly delivered an impassioned speech about the disease and its frightening spread. According to Slash, lead guitarist with Guns 'n' Roses, the AIDS issue was something that, hitherto, rock fans had chosen to ignore; and combining Freddie's tribute with an awareness of this disease made a huge difference in educating the entire rock 'n' roll audience.

Leaving aside the issue of raising AIDS awareness, as an actual concert – although well-intentioned – for many people the event ended up being something of a let-down. Bob Harris states frankly, 'I thought it showed up terribly how all the acts struggled with Freddie's songs. The only person I enjoyed was Ian Hunter. He got me up in my seat. But the others were clearly in trouble.'

Fellow DJ Simon Bates is equally blunt. 'It was very hard to take,' he says. 'They meant well, but it didn't come off. I was there, and the audience were not at all sympathetic. It probably ended up being more for the benefit of the remaining three band members. Elizabeth

Taylor tried her best, but it was cringing. And Bowie was just awful.'

Marillion frontman Fish echoes Simon Bates' view regarding David Bowie in respect of the moment when Bowie, having declared his intention to say a prayer for a sick friend, knelt down and solemnly recited the Lord's Prayer. 'When Bowie dropped to one knee and began praying it was *really* embarrassing,' says Fish. 'I cringed in my seat and thought, Oh my God! The tribute was very disappointing. Yet it could have been something sparkling. I believe that the initial feeling behind it was genuine, but I think it was corporately hijacked, which was a great pity.'

Nevertheless, it had been a chance to say an emotional goodbye to Freddie Mercury, the friend and the superstar who had ranked among rock's greatest entertainers. Over 500 million viewers in nearly seventy countries had tuned in and the event had had its moments. Singer George Michael credits Mercury with having given him a great deal in terms of creative craft; and, to repay this inspiration, he delivered a spirited rendition of the Queen ballad 'Somebody to Love' that was universally hailed as the best guest performance of the night.

Undoubtedly, the gig's most poignant moment came when Brian May sang a solo composition, 'Too Much Love Will Kill You'. The evocative lyrics could have been written specifically about Freddie, if anyone had a mind to read them that way, and May's emotional performance brought a deafening hush around the stadium. 'It was very charged in many ways,' said Brian afterwards. 'None of us will ever forget it.'

Liza Minnelli led all the performers in the finale with a bluesy rendition of 'We are the Champions', which brought the tribute to a rousing, sentimental end. They had said their goodbyes, but when the public cheering, hugs and tears had subsided, for Brian, John and Roger there was suddenly a sharp, shocking sense of the bottom falling out of their world.

Tony Iommi reveals, 'Immediately after the show was over, backstage it hit them all very hard and it was so, so sad. John was just in bits. It was a case of: right, that's it, over, final. I'd be as well opening up a shop or something. All three had been very brave and it was highly emotional. There was this dreadful feeling of no more, it's finished. I felt it myself, strongly, had seen it lurking and building up all through the preceding weeks. They'd been so close – all there together for Freddie – then suddenly that was it, nothing but a terrible vacuum.' And Spike Edney adds, 'At the meal afterwards a lot of people were going around patting each other on the back, but the four of us just sat at the table staring silently into space, completely drained.'

Their collective sense of bewilderment was wholly understandable. Queen's extraordinary career had spanned two decades and, although far from plain sailing, the four had steadfastly remained together through thick and thin. When commenting on the regular rumours that Queen would split up, Freddie Mercury had once declared, 'Through anything, we will just carry on until one of us drops dead or something.' Now that time had come, and just days after the Easter tribute Roger Taylor, John Deacon and Brian May emerged from their dazed vacuum to announce publicly that Queen was disbanding.

Freddie had said, 'Without the others, I would be nothing.' Without Mercury, the others could not and would not continue. Wild rumours would briefly circulate that, following George Michael's acclaimed performance at the tribute, Queen might revamp itself with Michael as frontman. But John Deacon bluntly set the record straight when he told reporters, 'As far as we are concerned, that is it. There's no point in carrying on. It is impossible to replace Freddie.'

The dismantling of Queen as a working band was further marked, in due course, by the closure of the Queen Productions London office and the selling of Mountain Studios in Switzerland. But it was not – as would be proved – entirely the end of Queen's recording life. Nor was it the end of Roger Taylor's or Brian May's musical career. In Taylor's words, they did not want to become 'old, rich and useless' and so both would go on to launch themselves separately as solo artistes with varying degrees of success. John Deacon, on the other hand, retired to a private life. And Freddie Mercury's memory would be kept alive in several ways.

In the immediate aftermath of the Easter tribute, the Mercury Phoenix Trust was set up to channel the massive proceeds from the event into helping various charitable projects around the world in the fight against AIDS. But the fans wanted something more tangible to relate to. The secrecy surrounding Freddie Mercury's final resting place meant that they had no obvious place — apart from outside Garden Lodge — on which to focus the outward display of their on-going devotion. No shrine had been erected to their hero and many felt that there ought to be. With typical flamboyance, Mercury had once declared a desire to be entombed like an Egyptian pharaoh with all his treasures. 'If I could afford it,' he said, 'I'd have a pyramid built in Kensington.' More modestly, as the first anniversary of his death approached, ideas of having a statue erected in his honour began to take shape, but encountered problems.

In November 1992 two separate applications were submitted to the Kensington and Chelsea Local Authority to have a statute of the Queen star erected near Logan Place. The application which had the backing of the band's official fan club was placed by Dave Clark, on behalf of a group of people, and he enlisted the help of the then local MP, Dudley Fishburn.

Fishburn recalls, 'I immediately thought it was a great idea. To me, Freddie Mercury was plainly as great a figure as those nineteenth-century generals who have statutes erected to them all over the place. Many's the time when I am walking through Kensington that I have been stopped by groups of European or Japanese tourists all wanting to know where they can find Freddie Mercury's house. I was always in favour of a statue of Freddie, even though it all came to nothing.' In fact, a commemorative statute of the Queen star in classic triumphant pose would eventually be erected on the shore of Lake Geneva in Montreux. November 1992 would also see the release of *The Freddie Mercury Album*, a collection of existing solo tracks, which reached number four in Britain.

For Queen recordings, it would prove to be a bumper year. In addition to the success of their re-releases, their music received a gigantic shot in the arm in America – a territory in which they flagged for a long time – when 'Bohemian Rhapsody' featured in the teen comedy movie *Wayne's World*, directed by Penelope Spheeris. This trigged massive interest, not just in one or two Queen albums but in their entire body of work. 'Bohemian Rhapsody would also, in September, win the Best Video from a Film award at the annual MTV Awards held in Los Angeles.

Then, three years after Queen had disbanded, throughout summer 1995, word began to circulate that the three ex-Queenies were working away, mainly in London's Metropolis Studios, adding live contributions to the material that Mercury had managed to tape in Montreux during his last working months. Anticipation swiftly began to build amongst the band's global legions of fans, as well as in the music industry, that there would be a new album.

When the single 'Heaven for Everyone' emerged in late October 1995, however, it initially caused some consternation because this song, with Mercury as guest lead vocalist, had appeared as a track on Roger Taylor's 1988 Cross debut album *Shove It!* Although this version had been re-recorded, to include input from Brian May and John Deacon, it was not the previously unreleased material that had been expected. It nonetheless zoomed to number two in its first week.

On 18 November the long-awaited album *Made in Heaven* followed and bolted straight in at number one in the British charts. It swiftly went double-platinum and, holding off strong competition, survived in the Top Five for weeks into 1996. After the rollercoaster ride frequently given to Queen by the critics, reviewers largely praised this work which was acknowledged as Queen's final, and certainly their most personal, album.

It was an enormously poignant piece of work; the awareness that a seriously ill Freddie Mercury had struggled to record vocal track after track in order to provide a batch of material which could be worked on by the others, and released after his death, made an enormous emotional impact on people. It was also revealed that the album's penultimate track, 'A Winter's Tale', which debuted at its peak of number six just before Christmas, had been penned by the lakeside in Montreux and was the last song that Freddie ever wrote.

The full extent of Mercury's ordeal during these last working months began to unfold publicly: it was heart-rending to learn how he had pushed his tormented body to the limit, how he had sometimes barely been able to stand upright without suffering agonising pain, and how, at his worst, he had had to numb that pain with shots of vodka to be able to sing. Both Roger Taylor and Brian May paid special tribute to Freddie, marvelling at his dogged refusal to buckle under and his incredible ability to deliver all his old vocal range and power. Taylor recalled, 'Freddie knew his time was limited and he really wanted to work. He felt that was the best way to keep his spirits up.' And May added, 'We were very focused as a group. We all realised how precious those moments were going to be.'

In the same month as the release of *Made in Heaven*, Queen also brought out *Ultimate Queen*, a twenty-CD set. Then, two years later, after having recently received the Lifetime Achievement Award for Contribution to Music at the Comets Awards in Cologne, Germany, on 3 November 1997, they released a compilation album called *Queen Rocks*. And the following year – moving with the times – in March 1998 came the first Queen CD-Rom game, when the interactive software company Electronic Arts launched a five-disc set action/adventure game, inspired by Queen music, called "Queen: The Eye".

All these releases kept the band very much in the public eye and fed the fans' unstinting appetite for Queen products as the decade began drawing to an end. The following year, in spring 1999, the first rumblings were heard that Taylor, Deacon and May were toying with the idea of sifting through a clutch of hitherto unreleased Queen tracks or mixes, with a view to compiling a possible further new release.

The prospect of a Queen 'comeback' seemed to be bolstered when newspaper reports emerged at the end of the first week in April in which Roger Taylor was quoted as stating, 'I spoke to Brian last week and he suggested we book a studio, write a song and see what happens. I haven't spoken to John in ages, but Brian and I are hopeful he will do it.' Again, the music industry was said to be instantly awash with rumours that Queen's friend, George Michael, could be in line to stand in for the late Freddie Mercury in any such recordings. But, while Taylor declared generally that many singers were known to be interested in working with them, George Michael's spokesperson would not be drawn on the subject. A further dimension was added to the picture when a record company executive was said to have suggested that any such record would be scheduled for release at the end of 1999. There was an absence of concrete confirmation, but certainly an air of cautious anticipation.

Whether or not there is still unfinished recording business, what is certain is that Queen irrefutably rank as one of the most innovative, outstanding and extraordinary rock bands of all time. In a career spanning three decades they have retained the unswerving loyalty of their original fan base and continue to fascinate and attract new generations of followers to the fold.

Professionally, Queen also command respect in the music world. Just prior to their own beginnings they had greatly admired the sixties band, the Jimi Hendrix Experience. Three decades later, Noel Redding, bass player with that famous group, reciprocates this musical appreciation. Says Noel, 'I think Queen were a very innovative group because of their sound, but mostly because of their songs and of course their excellent musicianship. I would say that Queen were a *very* important part of the great bands of the century.'

Abba's Bjorn Ulvaeus and Benny Andersson echo this praise. Benny ranks Queen, 'Absolutely at the top. No question.' And Bjorn describes Queen as, 'Unique, a one-off because, I suppose, they were very sophisticated and therefore so difficult to imitate. A lot of bands in the seventies got tired and ended up just doing the same thing over and over. But with Queen you could hear great musical ambition in their songs.' And, likewise, Oscar-winning lyricist Sir Tim Rice unequivocally states, 'Queen ranks as one of the best bands of the century. Their principal strength was that all four members were great individual songwriters.'

Four very different individuals but each talented in his own right and a professional perfectionist by nature, Freddie Mercury, John Deacon, Brian May and Roger Taylor collectively, as Queen, created and sustained their own niche in the notoriously ephemeral world of popular music. And, along the way, they established a powerful and distinctive style that remains instantly recognisable all over the world.

Freddie Mercury's death may have brought about Queen's premature disbandment. But, with typical panache, he once said of the group he fronted, 'If we're worth anything, we will live on.' And they do. Throughout the nineties Queen's popularity has grown to the point where they now rank second only to the Beatles in the UK's all-time successful acts, and, in terms of the demand for memorabilia, they come third in the world behind Elvis Presley and the Fab Four.

In the crowded and competitive music industry, the vibrant Queen legend continues to reign strongly into the new millennium. On Monday 19 March 2001, alongside stars Paul Simon and Michael Jackson, and the bands Aerosmith and Steely Dan, Queen was inducted into the Rock and Roll Hall of Fame at a ceremony held in New York City.

Around the same time in Britain, news first broke that there was to be a West End stage musical structured around Queen music. Six months later these sketchy details firmed up when more facts emerged. Called *We Will Rock You* and directed by Chris Renshaw, it was revealed that the musical would open at the Dominion Theatre in London on 14 May 2002, with talk of a possible Broadway production to follow.

Written by the comedian and novelist Ben Elton, the project – it turned out – had been in the secret making for four long years, during which time Elton had closely collaborated with the remaining Queen members.

Brain May told London's Capital Gold radio station, 'We've been through various ideas, some of which were biographical, which in the end we didn't want to do. But now Ben Elton has written us a fantastic script.'

The story is set in the future and depicts a world in which young people are in chains; rock music being their only saviour. None of the remaining band members will appear in the performance and by late 2001, actors Tim Howard and James Gillan were among those being considered as candidates to play Freddie Mercury.

Ten years after the death of the most flamboyantly theatrical Queen member, it seems almost fitting that their music should find a new medium through which to reach out to a new fan base. And if the phenomenal success of Abba's *Mamma Mia* is any yardstick, Queen's entire back catalogue of songs will be thrust back into the spotlight.

In the best tradition, secrecy still surrounded the musical's plot and cast even in early 2002. But with regard to whether audiences can expect to be thoroughly entertained, the musical's writer Ben Elton was far from coy. Talking to British television's stalwart chat show host Michael Parkinson, he proudly promised, '*We Will Rock You* isn't just the name of the music.' He then added emphatically, 'It's a promise!'

# DISCOGRAPHY

## UK Singles

**KEEP YOURSELF ALIVE**
*Released* **6/7/73**
*Highest chart position* **(–)**

**SEVEN SEAS OF RHYE**
*Released* **23/2/74**
*Highest chart position* **10**

**KILLER QUEEN**
*Released* **11/10/74**
*Highest chart position* **2**

**NOW I'M HERE**
*Released* **17/1/75**
*Highest chart position* **11**

**BOHEMIAN RHAPSODY**
*Released* **31/10/75**
*Highest chart position* **1**

**YOU'RE MY BEST FRIEND**
*Released* **18/6/76**
*Highest chart position* **7**

**SOMEBODY TO LOVE**
*Released* **12/11/76**
*Highest chart position* **2**

**TIE YOUR MOTHER DOWN**
*Released* **4/3/77**
*Highest chart position* **31**

**GOOD OLD FASHIONED LOVER BOY**
*Released 20/5/77*
*Highest chart position* **17**

**WE ARE THE CHAMPIONS**
*Released 7/10/77*
*Highest chart position* **2**

**SPREAD YOUR WINGS**
*Released 10/2/78*
*Highest chart position* **34**

**FAT BOTTOMED GIRLS**
*Released 13/10/78*
*Highest chart position* **11**

**DON'T STOP ME NOW**
*Released 26/1/79*
*Highest chart position* **9**

**LOVE OF MY LIFE**
*Released 29/6/79*
*Highest chart position* **63**

**CRAZY LITTLE THING CALLED LOVE**
*Released 5/10/79*
*Highest chart position* **2**

**SAVE ME**
*Released 25/1/80*
*Highest chart position* **11**

**PLAY THE GAME**
*Released 30/5/80*
*Highest chart position* **14**

**ANOTHER ONE BITES THE DUST**
*Released 22/8/80*
*Highest chart position* **7**

**FLASH**
*Released 24/11/80*
*Highest chart position* **10**

**UNDER PRESSURE**
*Released 26/10/81*
*Highest chart position* **1**

**BODY LANGUAGE**
*Released 19/4/82*
*Highest chart position* **25**

**LAS PALABRAS DE AMOR (THE WORDS OF LOVE)**
*Released 1/6/82*
*Highest chart position* **17**

**BACK CHAT**
*Released 9/8/82*
*Highest chart position* **40**

**RADIO GA GA**
*Released 23/1/84*
*Highest chart position* **2**

**I WANT TO BREAK FREE**
*Released 2/4/84*
*Highest chart position* **3**

**IT'S A HARD LIFE**
*Released 16/7/84*
*Highest chart position* **6**

**HAMMER TO FALL**
*Released 10/9/84*
*Highest chart position* **13**

**THANK GOD IT'S CHRISTMAS**
*Released 26/11/84*
*Highest chart position* **21**

**ONE VISION**
*Released 4/11/85*
*Highest chart position* **7**

**A KIND OF MAGIC**
*Released 17/3/86*
*Highest chart position* **3**

**FRIENDS WILL BE FRIENDS**
*Released 9/6/86*
*Highest chart position* **14**

**WHO WANTS TO LIVE FOREVER**
*Released 15/9/86*
*Highest chart position* **24**

**I WANT IT ALL**
*Released 2/5/89*
*Highest chart position* **3**

**BREAKTHRU**
*Released 19/6/89*
*Highest chart position* **7**

**THE INVISIBLE MAN**
*Released 7/8/89*
*Highest chart position* **12**

**SCANDAL**
*Released 9/10/89*
*Highest chart position* **25**

**THE MIRACLE**
*Released 27/11/89*
*Highest chart position* **21**

**INNUENDO**
*Released 14/1/91*
*Highest chart position* **1**

**I'M GOING SLIGHTLY MAD**
*Released 4/3/91*
*Highest chart position* **22**

**HEADLONG**
*Released 13/5/91*
*Highest chart position* **14**

**THE SHOW MUST GO ON**
*Released* **14/10/91**
*Highest chart position* **16**

**BOHEMIAN RHAPSODY (RE-ISSUE)**
*Released* **9/12/91**
*Highest chart position* **1**

**HEAVEN FOR EVERYONE**
*Released* **4/11/95**
*Highest chart position* **2**

**A WINTER'S TALE**
*Released* **23/12/95**
*Highest chart position* **6**

**TOO MUCH LOVE WILL KILL YOU**
*Released* **9/3/96**
*Highest chart position* **15**

**LET ME LIVE**
*Released* **29/6/96**
*Highest chart position* **9**

**YOU DON'T FOOL ME**
*Released* **30/11/96**
*Highest chart position* **17**

## UK and USA Albums

**QUEEN**
*Released in UK* **13/7/73**
*Highest chart position in UK* **24**
*Released in USA* **4/9/73**
*Highest chart position in USA* **83**

**QUEEN II**
*Released in UK* **8/3/74**
*Highest chart position in UK* **5**
*Released in USA* **9/4/74**
*Highest chart position in USA* **49**

**SHEER HEART ATTACK**
*Released in UK* **8/11/74**
*Highest chart position in UK* **2**
*Released in USA* **12/11/74**
*Highest chart position in USA* **12**

**A NIGHT AT THE OPERA**
*Released in UK* **21/11/75**
*Highest chart position in UK* **4**
*Released in USA* **2/12/75**
*Highest chart position in USA* **3**

## A DAY AT THE RACES
*Released in UK* **10/12/76**
*Highest chart position in UK* **1**
*Released in USA* **18/12/76**
*Highest chart position in USA* **5**

## NEWS OF THE WORLD
*Released in UK* **28/10/77**
*Highest chart position in UK* **4**
*Released in USA* **1/11/77**
*Highest chart position in USA* **3**

## JAZZ
*Released in UK* **10/11/78**
*Highest chart position in UK* **2**
*Released in USA* **14/11/78**
*Highest chart position in USA* **6**

## LIVE KILLERS
*Released in UK* **22/6/79**
*Highest chart position in UK* **3**
*Released in USA* **26/6/79**
*Highest chart position in USA* **16**

## THE GAME
*Released in UK* **30/6/80**
*Highest chart position in UK* **1**
*Released in USA* **30/6/80**
*Highest chart position in USA* **1**

## FLASH GORDON
**(original soundtrack)**
*Released in UK* **8/12/80**
*Highest chart position in UK* **10**
*Released in USA* **27/1/81**
*Highest chart position in USA* **23**

## GREATEST HITS
*Released in UK* **2/11/81**
*Highest chart position in UK* **1**
*Released in USA* **3/11/81**
*Highest chart position in USA* **14**

## HOT SPACE
*Released in UK* **21/5/82**
*Highest chart position in UK* **4**
*Released in USA* **25/5/82**
*Highest chart position in USA* **22**

## THE WORKS
*Released in UK* **27/2/84**
*Highest chart position in UK* **2**
*Released in USA* **28/2/84**
*Highest chart position in USA* **23**

## A KIND OF MAGIC
*Released in UK* **2/6/86**
*Highest chart position in UK* **1**
*Released in USA* **3/6/86**
*Highest chart position in USA* **26**

## LIVE MAGIC
*Released in UK* **1/12/86**
*Highest chart position in UK* **3**
*Not released in USA*

## THE MIRACLE
*Released in UK* **22/5/89**
*Highest chart position in UK* **1**
*Released in USA* **6/6/89**
*Highest chart position in USA* **26**

## QUEEN AT THE BEEB
*Released in UK 4/12/89*
*Highest chart position in UK 67*
*Not released in USA*

## CLASSIC QUEEN
*Released in USA 3/3/92*
*Highest chart position in USA 4*
*Not released in UK*

## INNUENDO
*Released in UK 4/2/91*
*Highest chart position in UK 1*
*Released in USA 5/2/91*
*Highest chart position in USA 30*

## LIVE AT WEMBLEY
*Released in UK 26/5/92*
*Highest chart position in UK 2*
*Released in USA 26/5/92*
*Highest chart position in USA 53*

## GREATEST HITS II
*Released in UK 28/10/91*
*Highest chart position in UK 1*
*Not released in USA*

## MADE IN HEAVEN
*Released in UK 18/11/95*
*Highest chart position in UK 1*
*Released in USA 18/11/95*
*Highest chart position in USA 58*

# INDEX